George Orwell Studies

Volume Eight
No. 1

George Orwell Studies

Publishing Office
Abramis Academic
ASK House
Northgate Avenue
Bury St. Edmunds
Suffolk
IP32 6BB
UK

Tel: +44 (0)1284 717884
Fax: +44 (0)1284 717889
Email: info@abramis.co.uk
Web: www.abramis.co.uk

Copyright
All rights reserved. No part of this publication may be reproduced in any material form (including photocopying or storing it in any medium by electronic means, and whether or not transiently or incidentally to some other use of this publication) without the written permission of the copyright owner, except in accordance with the provisions of the Copyright, Designs and Patents Act 1988, or under terms of a licence issued by the Copyright Licensing Agency Ltd, 33-34, Alfred Place, London WC1E 7DP, UK. Applications for the copyright owner's permission to reproduce part of this publication should be addressed to the Publishers.

© 2023 George Orwell Studies & Abramis Academic

ISSN 2399-1267
ISBN 978-1-84549-821-4

Contents

Guest Editorial
Engaging Critically with a Writer who Can Still Surprise Us – by Nathan Waddell — Page 1

Papers
Big Brother, Big Tech: Doctorow's *Little Brother* and Huber's *Orwell's Revenge* — Page 7
– by Jackson Ayres
The Essayist's Velvet Fist – by Mir Ali Hosseini — Page 25
George Orwell's Gandhi – by Douglas Kerr — Page 44
What Was Orwell's Conception of Free Speech? – by Mark Satta — Page 61
The Labyrinths of *Nineteen Eighty-Four* – by Selina-Marie Scholz and Geoff Rodoreda — Page 77
Critically Ill: George Orwell, Tragic Biography and the Crisis of Endings — Page 93
– by Kristin Bluemel

Other Papers
John Bull's Other Airstrip: Orwell's Irish Blindspot – by Martin Tyrrell — Page 110
George Orwell, Ayer and Russell and the Battle for the Soul of Philosophy — Page 129
– by Peter Brian Barry

Articles
Orwell in Cornwall – by Darcy Moore — Page 142
The Achievement of Ian Angus – by John Rodden — Page 159
The BBC'S *Nineteen Eighty-Four* Remastered for a New Generation — Page 169
– by Hassan Akram
Attwood's Imaginary Interview with Orwell – by Richard Lance Keeble — Page 177
Pedagogy of the Distressed?: 'Politics and the English language' in and out of the — Page 181
Classroom – by John Rodden

Two Poems
To George Orwell/Eric Blair – by Paul Abdul Wadud Sutherland — Page 195
A Song for Orwell – by David Punter — Page 196

Tributes to the Founder of The Orwell Society
Dione Venable's Contribution to the Development of Orwell Studies — Page 199
– by Quentin Kopp
Dear Dione – by Darcy Moore — Page 201

Book Reviews
Kristin Bluemel on *George Orwell: The New Life*, by D.J. Taylor; Bryan Yazell on *The Tramp in British Literature, 1850-1950*, by Luke Lewin Davies; Peter Brian Barry on *George Orwell's Perverse Humanity: Socialism and Free Speech*, by Glenn Burgess; Richard Lance Keeble on *In Praise of Failure: Four Lessons in Humility*, by Costica Bradatan — Page 204

And Finally
New Pitcher (appropriately anonymously) launches a new, lively diary item to intrigue — Page 225
and entertain Orwellians

Editors
Richard Lance Keeble — University of Lincoln
Tim Crook — Goldsmiths, University of London

Reviews Editor
Megan Faragher — Wright State University

Production Editor
Paul Anderson — University of Essex

Editorial Board
Kristin Bluemel — Monmouth University, New Jersey
Dorian Lynskey — Author, journalist
Peter Marks — University of Sydney
John Newsinger — Bath Spa University
Marina Remy — Paris Sorbonne
John Rodden — University of Texas at Austin
Jean Seaton — University of Westminster
Peter Stansky — Stanford University, US
D. J. Taylor — Author, journalist, biographer of Orwell
Martin Tyrrell — Queen's University, Belfast
Nathan Waddell — University of Birmingham
Florian Zollmann — Newcastle University

With editorial assistance from Marja Giejgo

Cover image by designer, illustrator, artist and author Trevor Bounford. His design and illustration work has appeared in museums and galleries worldwide and his art has been selected for exhibition in the annual Royal Academy Summer Exhibition and the ING Discerning Eye exhibition at the Mall Galleries, in London. See www.bounford.art

GUEST EDITORIAL

Engaging Critically with a Writer who Can Still Surprise Us

NATHAN WADDELL

It's always a pleasure to read new scholarship on Orwell, and it's an honour to be given the floor as guest editor for this section of the current issue of *George Orwell Studies*. In this capacity I have had the privilege to invite a group of papers for publication from among those delivered at the 2022 *Critical Orwell* conference. Hosted by the University of Birmingham in an online-only format, the conference enabled participation from scholars all over the world and featured exciting new research on Orwell and his legacies. The thought behind the event was that because Orwell's ideas so often inspire how people analyse trends in politics, culture, society, economics and technology, identifying the differences between Orwell the myth and Orwell the man himself has never been more important. Another consideration: given Orwell's omnipresence in contemporary life, those of us who work on him in a scholarly capacity should continually scrutinise how he shapes the ways we think and live now. Among the questions participants in the event were invited to answer were: Is Orwell's prestige a blessing or a curse? Do we need new strategies for assessing his achievements and their politically and morally ambiguous remnants in our time? Is Orwell critical, and how, in all senses of the phrase, should he be criticised?

Presentations relating Orwell to new lines of thematic inquiry and to original contexts for interpretation were particularly encouraged, with suggestions given for papers on Orwell and empire, capitalism, nationalism and surveillance; the prejudices in Orwell's life and work; Orwell and philosophy and Orwell as a philosopher; the role of the public intellectual; Orwell as a cultural critic, literary scholar and media analyst; Orwell's afterlives in scholarly criticism and posthumous reputation; post-colonial and (post-)feminist approaches to Orwell's writing; and the critical importance and relevance of Orwell's work in the twenty-first century. From those papers that were delivered, I've chosen six for expansion and publication here. Each of them considers a fresh topic in Orwell's

NATHAN WADDELL

life or considers a familiar emphasis from an innovative perspective – Jackson Ayres on 'big tech', Mir Ali Hosseini on Orwell's essays, Douglas Kerr on Orwell and Gandhi, Mark Satta on free speech, Selina-Marie Scholz and Geoff Rodoreda on the labyrinthine structures of *Nineteen Eighty-Four* (1949) and Kristin Bluemel on tragic biography. All of them signal how much there's still to learn about even the most well-trodden aspects of Orwell's writing.

This is an intriguing moment for Orwell scholarship. We're at a juncture full of new projects seeking to uncover less well-known sides of his life and career, and to bring new interpretative contexts to bear on what's already familiar about him and his work. Much of the scholarship these projects have produced has been published in this very journal, with the promise of more to follow. Biographical scholarship continues to hold sway – no surprise for a writer who had such an unusually full and intriguing life – and this impulse to dive into the nooks and crannies of Orwell's experiences has led to several fascinating book-length treatments not only of the man himself but also of his first wife, Eileen, whose importance both as his partner and as a woman in her own right has never been more evident – for which see Sylvia Topp's path-breaking *Eileen: The Making of George Orwell* (2020) and Anna Funder's *Wifedom: Mrs Orwell's Invisible Life* (2023). D.J. Taylor's *New Life* (2023), reviewed in this issue of *George Orwell Studies* by Kristin Bluemel, indicates that there's still much to uncover in a life that so many Orwell scholars know inside-out, just as books like Oliver Lewis's *The Orwell Tour* (2023) show some of the cunning narrative possibilities with which we can weave our lives into Orwell's.

Lewis's text considers a certain kind of Orwellian or Orwell-inspired afterlife: one traveller following in another's footsteps. Jackson Ayres by contrast, in his contribution to this issue of the journal, looks at the question of 'afterlives' from a more strictly literary perspective. Ayres focuses on two novels about so-called big tech: Peter Huber's *Orwell's Revenge* (1994) and Cory Doctorow's *Little Brother* (2008). Reading across and between Huber's and Doctorow's fiction, Ayres considers how differently these texts work with Orwell's accounts of the technological and thinks through Orwell's presence in debates about the distortions of big tech in our lives today. Among other things, Ayres's paper invites us to reconsider the familiar idea of Orwell as a technological sceptic. In this same vein, Mir Ali Hosseini's paper on Orwell's essays invites us to think differently about the relationship between anti-totalitarianism and the essay as a genre. Questioning the idea that there is some essential link between the essay form and anti-totalitarian thinking, Hosseini argues not only that the essay is a rhetorical form marked by the urge to persuasion but also that Orwell's essays are marked by complex tensions between authorial 'presence' and the drive to persuade others, one that is such an important, recurring feature of the essay as a mode of political and cultural discourse.

Essays likewise feature prominently in Douglas Kerr's paper on Orwell and Gandhi, in which he traces the reluctant admiration for and guarded hostility towards Gandhi evident in Orwell's writing. Given the extent of their hostility to imperial rule and conquest, it's odd that Orwell felt as he did about Gandhi who, as Kerr notes, was seemingly one of Orwell's natural allies. But as Kerr shows in compelling detail in *Orwell & Empire* (2022), Orwell's relationship with imperialism was full of contradictions: his anti-imperialism, for example, which he expressed in so many places in his writing, rubbed awkwardly against his view that colonised peoples were unable to free themselves from colonial oppression. There is also the question of where and how we can trust Orwell's retrospective accounts of his gradual embitterment with empire, which seems to have inflected his politics to varying extents throughout his career. Like so much else in his life and work, Orwell's thinking about empire was never static and never simple. This forces us, in turn, to be nimble in how we account for it.

It should be evident that these contributions to the current issue of the journal belong to a new and impressive wave of thematic scholarship. It's not that Orwell has never been treated or assessed thematically – far from it – but rather that a fresh commitment to the importance of the thematic in Orwell seems to be emerging in the field. Whereas in past decades this sort of work has tended to focus on Orwell's politics, and on his responses to the politics of his time, the trend now seems to be more open-armed, with a more varied understanding of what matters in Orwell's work and a more resourceful assessment of what is fair game for analysis. A key example is the emerging interest in Orwell and philosophy. Broadly speaking, there are two sides to this coin: first, the idea that Orwell was himself a kind of amateur philosopher; and second, the thought that Orwell's work can and should be analysed philosophically. David Dwan has already made influential inroads into Orwell's work on this front, in *Liberty, Equality, and Humbug: Orwell's Political Ideals* (2019), and Peter Brian Barry's *George Orwell: The Ethics of Equality* (2023), part of the 'Philosophical Outsiders' series published by Oxford University Press, does a great deal to advance our sense of Orwell's philosophical sympathies (not only his interest in philosophy but also his informed understanding of its traditions).

Mark Satta's forensic contribution to this issue of the journal, 'What was Orwell's conception of free speech?', takes Orwell seriously as a subject for philosophical inquiry (as, in fact, does Hosseini's). This is an important move. Satta's analysis of Orwell's

EDITORIAL

NATHAN WADDELL

thinking about free speech, and its interrelations with the concept of liberty, reveals that there are nuances which complicate any simple model of an Orwellian attitude to freedom. Drawing productively on Glenn Burgess's *George Orwell's Perverse Humanity: Socialism and Free Speech* (2023), reviewed below by Barry, Satta's patient investigation of the wrinkles in Orwell's thinking about free speech shows how carefully he resisted the situation diagnosed by *Nineteen Eighty-Four*: the annihilation of free speech. Orwell gave us new ways to think about how the conditions in which free speech thrives can dissolve and, therefore, new ways to think about how to stop the enemies of free speech gaining the upper hand. He had in mind not only dictators and their followers, of any period, but also those with what he called a 'gramophone mind' – those who speak unthinkingly and who regurgitate the trendy moralising of their time.

If the twists and turns in Orwell's thinking on empire and on free speech imply one kind of labyrinth, then the material and ideological structures of the totalitarian society depicted in *Nineteen Eighty-Four* present another. Selina-Marie Scholz and Geoff Rodoreda situate Orwell's most famous novel in the cultural history of the labyrinth in order to draw out two under-appreciated aspects of the book: Ingsoc and Oceania are formulated in accordance with different kinds of labyrinthine political principles; and Winston's journey into the centre of Oceanian power can be understood as a journey into the labyrinth of legend, with the minotauric O'Brien at its heart. This way of reading *Nineteen Eighty-Four* shows that we have barely begun to scratch the surface of the novel's cultural-historical reverberations. *Nineteen Eighty-Four* isn't merely one of the best dissections of totalitarian power available to readers everywhere in the world, but also a work of literary craft whose intertextual resonance remains underestimated.

There is a risk, all the same, in being too fawning about a book its author intended neither to be his last nor to be the cultural monument it has long since become (or, more precisely, been allowed to become). If this is a moment to consider new ideas about Orwell, and to think in new ways about how we consider old ones, then it's also a moment to reflect on how outdated images of the man and his work are no longer easy to sustain. Not that they have been easy to sustain for a long while. Orwell's 'iconic status', in Stefan Collini's words, 'both as the courageous truth-teller and as the champion of the individual in the face of the totalitarian tendencies of modern states' has lost none of its appeal, but it's increasingly true that scholars of Orwell are looking into different and differently problematic sides of his life and career – including the aspects of his thought and character (e.g. his racial insensitivity and racism, his misogyny and homophobia, his antisemitism) that the hagiographers would rather ignore.[1] The result is not a lesser or diminished Orwell *per se*, but an invigorated scholarly response to a writer who remains massively important to many communities across the globe, coupled with a new suspiciousness towards his celebrity.

It should go without saying that it is highly unlikely Orwell will be dislodged from his pedestal in the foreseeable future. All the same, it is nigh-on assured that his most engaged, most attentive critics will not be hoodwinked by the myths and legends that canonicity can generate. Ian Dunt puts it well when he writes that although the view of Orwell as 'a heroic, plain-speaking visionary, with a piercing glare and an unflinching commitment to the truth' is 'true, in its way', it's also crucial to remember that 'life is made of many parts which myths cannot encompass. [Orwell] was also, in many of his personal relationships, shy, awkward and dejected. He was always on the edge of things'.[2] Being on the edge can itself be doubled-edged, of course, and although there are many senses in which Orwell's awkwardness was a virtue, enabling him to bring an outsider's view to so many people, practices, politics and problems, it has also come to be seen as the source of his weirdest character traits. And there is also a sense in which an idea of Orwell on the edge of life itself has skewed how we tend to think about the arc of his life and accomplishments.

This is the subject of Kristin Bluemel's important contribution to this issue, in which she thinks with typically perceptive insistence about how a certain kind of tragic imaginary can give Orwell's biographies a questionable teleological thrust: a sense, among other things, that as his life came to an end, his heroic stature increased. For Bluemel, Orwell's death presents a test for how biographers write about the end of Orwell's life – about the end of all lives, in fact. The difficulty lies in writing our way past a construct for which Orwell scholars themselves are largely responsible, one in which Orwell's end is imagined (and thereby produced) as a tragic end, as a moment full of 'meaning' in large part read into it, rather than innocently discovered in it, by later generations of biographers. Seeing Orwell's end through the language of tragedy makes it harder to see his death in different and arguably more productive terms as *an end*, a moment marked by all the incoherences, incomprehensibilities and incompletions that characterise any death.

The Orwell who emerges from these papers is an Orwell less available to those who prioritise fixity and certainty. Critical fashions ebb and flood as surely as the tide, and the more indeterminate understanding of Orwell collectively identified here is just one step on the long road of Orwell scholarship. There will no doubt be many more Orwells to come in future, and the drive to monumentalise him, which has been so powerful in his posthumous reception, seems unlikely to abate. But what these six papers do very powerfully, I think, is remind us that however we think about Orwell we are always thinking about a writer who exceeds our grasp. And this is all part of the fun in writing about him in the first place: to criticise a man and a man's work which themselves, in a generative loop, raise uncomfortable questions about the critical procedures brought to bear on them. To criticise Orwell is to engage with a writer who can still surprise us. It means engaging with a writer whose work demands better kinds of critical surprise in the very act of criticising it. It's this dynamic that makes the papers gathered here so invigorating and so valuable as prompts for new thinking about Orwell's writing, in all its elusive, unignorable sophistication.

NOTES

[1] Stefan Collini, *Absent Minds: Intellectuals in Britain*, Oxford: Oxford University Press, 2006, p. 350

[2] Ian Dunt, *How to be a Liberal*, Kingston upon Thames: Canbury Press, 2020, p. 244

NOTE ON THE CONTRIBUTOR

Dr Nathan Waddell is an Associate Professor of English at the University of Birmingham. He has edited Orwell's *A Clergyman's Daughter* (Oxford University Press, 2021) and *The Cambridge Companion to Nineteen Eighty-Four* (Cambridge University Press, 2020), and is currently researching connections between Orwell and the modernist painter and writer Wyndham Lewis.

PAPER

Big Brother, Big Tech: Doctorow's *Little Brother* and Huber's *Orwell's Revenge*

JACKSON AYRES

This paper attends to two novels largely overlooked within scholarship on Orwell's literary afterlives: Peter Huber's Orwell's Revenge *(1994) and Cory Doctorow's* Little Brother *(2008). These two appropriations of Orwell and* Nineteen Eighty-Four *invest in their representations of new digital technologies, fitting them into discourses entwining Orwell with Big Tech. Although both novels reject Orwell's alleged technophobia, embracing the digital tools advanced by Big Tech, Huber does so to dispute Orwell's socialist politics whereas Doctorow offers a non-capitalist alternative image of Big Tech.*

Key words: Big Tech, Doctorow, Huber, *Little Brother*; *Orwell's Revenge*

'On 24 January, Apple Computer will introduce Macintosh. And you'll see why 1984 won't be like *1984.*' These words, gravely intoned in voice-over narration, conclude a lavish commercial for Apple Computers. Directed by filmmaker Ridley Scott, the ad was aired once in the US, on 22 January 1984. Visually alluding to George Orwell's *Nineteen Eighty-Four* (1949), the advert depicts an athlete smashing a screen blaring propagandistic paeans to conformity. Apple's landmark commercial symbolically inaugurates a potent discursive relationship between digital technologies industries with Orwell's writing and persona.

This dialogue between Orwell and the powerful digital technologies industry – known by its geographical metonym Silicon Valley or the more loaded term Big Tech – persists today. Often used derisively, Big Tech refers to technology industries generally, but typically connotes their largest, most powerful firms, such as Google, Microsoft, Apple and Meta, as well as influential social media platforms like Facebook, Twitter (now X) and TikTok. If Apple's 1984 advertisement suggests emancipation via technology, more recently journalistic and political commentaries on Big Tech tend to invoke Orwell as a rhetorical cudgel. Rightwing media vociferously enlists Orwell in broadsides against Big Tech, but left criticisms of Big Tech's surveillance and data-mining practices also often conjure Orwell. From left or right, such deployments of Orwell often share phraseology and a core premise. Illustrating this point, a 2021 headline in the conservative tabloid, the *Washington Examiner*, 'Big Tech is behaving more like Big Brother', mirrors the progressive intellectual and activist Rebecca Solnit reprovingly referring to tech giant Google, in a 2014 essay, as 'Big Hipster Brother'.

Accordingly, much Orwell scholarship and commentary attends to the dynamics between Orwell's writing and the social and political worlds that Big Tech constructs. The 2006 collection *On Nineteen Eighty-Four: Orwell and Our Future* (Princeton University Press) includes a section on 'Technology and privacy', featuring essays considering the degree to which the novel provides insight into current questions about technology, surveillance and privacy. Orwell's legacies, in sum, clearly entwine with digital technologies. Dorian Lynskey's 2020 'biography' of *Nineteen Eighty-Four* (Doubleday) surveys competing claims made over what Orwell's work can tell us about digital technologies, and Richard Bradford's *Orwell: A Man of Our Time* (Bloomsbury Caravel) also from 2020, links Orwell's warnings against political distortions of language to social media's effects on public speech.

Not only is *Nineteen Eighty-Four* a key reference for commentaries on Big Tech, but Orwell's shadow also looms over fictional treatments of Big Tech. Tim Maughan's 2019 speculative novel *Infinite Detail* centres on hacker and 'anti-surveillance activist' Rushdi 'Rush' Manaan. The novel features an embedded transcript between Rush and a journalist who asks him 'whether he isn't painting a rather dystopian picture – it's not as though all this monitoring and data collection is being done by one Big Brother-style organization' (2019: 74). As another example, Robert Harris grants that his thriller *The Fear Index* (2012), which draws narrative suspense from global finance's reliance on machine learning and algorithms, takes 'inspiration from George Orwell's *1984*' (NPR 2012). Turning to US fiction, Dave Eggers's *The Circle* (2013) reworks *Nineteen Eighty-Four*'s Party slogans for the 'mantras' of its fictional, malevolent social media company: 'Secrets are lies, sharing is caring, privacy is theft.' Despite examples like Maughan, Harris and Eggers, novelists' uses of Orwell's work and persona for renderings of Big Tech in contemporary fiction appear marginally in Orwell criticism. To be sure, novels that draw on Orwell to depict and contend with information technologies appear in surveys of Orwell's literary afterlives; see, for one, Hollie Johnson's 'Orwell's literary inheritors, 1950-2000 and beyond' (2020). Harder to find, however, is scholarship that attends directly with novels' representations of Big Tech and how Orwell's legacy figures into them.

Filling that gap, this paper juxtaposes two texts: Peter Huber's genre-bending *Orwell's Revenge: The 1984 Palimpsest* and Cory Doctorow's young adult thriller, *Little Brother*. Both novels rely on Orwell to comment on digital information technologies and their political valences. Published, respectively, in 1994 and 2008, *Orwell's Revenge* and *Little Brother* continue to contribute to discourses on Big Tech. In 2015, Mark Zuckerberg – chief executive officer of the giant tech firm Meta – included *Orwell's Revenge* as part of a 'Year of Books' reading list. *Little Brother*'s success spawned a small franchise: a 2012 stage adaptation, two sequels and a reported film version in the works. Both novels thus are touchstones for a small but potent tradition of novels that use Orwell as a resource to comprehend digital technologies. Notably unlike dominant trends in journalism, the novels resist as well as accept Orwell as a political lodestar, expressing doubt toward any 'Orwellian' idea of Big Tech. Unlike mainstream discourse and other literary examples like Eggers's and Harris's novels, which draw on Orwell to render Big Tech in dystopian terms, both Huber and Doctorow tap Orwell to sketch utopian images of Big Tech's potential – but these portraits contrast based on their authors' opposed ideological positions.

PETER HUBER: BIG TECH AS BIG FREEDOM

Peter Huber, a true polymath, wrote several books on issues involving the law and science, technology and telecommunications. *Orwell's Revenge: The 1984 Palimpsest* is a curious entrant into this body of work. Defying genre boundaries, *Orwell's Revenge* alternates from passages of political, technological and literary analysis to a narrative continuation of *Nineteen Eighty-Four* that reverses much of the older book's diegesis and, by extension, its politics. Huber's text incorporates language lifted from Orwell's writings, *Nineteen Eighty-Four* included, which he collated and then rearranged using a computer program. Driving this dual revision – nonfiction critique and literary appropriation – is Huber's belief that *Nineteen Eighty-Four* remains 'the most important book' published since the Second World War (2015: 2). Indeed, much of the novel's ongoing relevance owes to its attunement to advances in 'teletechnology' that were nascent at Orwell's mid-century but, at the time of Huber's writing, were radically 'transforming our lives today' (ibid). Despite venerating Orwell's prescience, Huber argues that Orwell misunderstood the technology and its implications. On matters of modern telecommunications systems – archaically called 'the information superhighway' by Huber – Orwell, he says, was all wrong.

Orwell's Revenge, therefore, reads as both celebration and rejection. On one hand, Huber's book lauds Orwell's insight and accomplishments as a writer, affirming *Nineteen Eighty-Four*'s standing as a cultural milestone, while on the other hand it aims to dismantle and then rebuild what Huber calls the rotten 'architecture' (ibid: 2) constituting *Nineteen Eighty-Four*'s politics – namely, its author's socialism. At issue, Huber alleges, is the faulty foundation caused by Orwell's miscalculation with 'a gadget' (ibid), the telescreen, which Huber takes as a synecdoche for telecommunication technologies. Huber posits the telescreen as the bedrock for Orwell's narrative and political vision. Noting that the word 'telescreen' appears 119 times in *Nineteen Eighty-Four* – more than other key terms like 'doublethink', 'Newspeak' and 'Big Brother', appearing, respectively, 31, 79, and 74 times, by Huber's count – Huber declares: 'The telescreen is the key to everything else in *1984*' (ibid: 23). He adds: 'From a strictly engineering perspective, the telescreen is the scaffold. It is the single, ubiquitous techno-spy that makes possible Big Brother's absolute control' (ibid: 24). Despite its perceptive attunement to developments in telecommunications, Huber argues *Nineteen Eighty-Four* betrays Orwell's ignorance about the workings of such technology as well as what Huber sees as a prejudice against mechanisation found across Orwell's political writing.

Even basic information about the operations of the telescreen, Huber charges, is missing from *Nineteen Eighty-Four*: Orwell 'is in fact remarkably unspecific about the single critical piece of technology on which his book so completely depends' (ibid: 24-25). Extrapolating from the limited details that Orwell provides, Huber compares the telescreen with actual technological advances. For instance, since telescreen's visual and audio transmissions are two-way, Huber makes a fleeting comparison to modern teleconferencing (ibid: 71). Yet, the book's sustained comparison for the telescreen is the internet, a timely similarity since *Orwell's Revenge* arrived in 1994 as the infrastructure of the World Wide Web solidified and internet usage mainstreamed and commercialised. Toward this analogy, first, Huber notes that Inner Party users can turn off their terminals, presumably disconnecting from the network. Picking up this observation, the narrative portions of *Orwell's Revenge* establish a backstory for the construction of telescreens' underground, networked infrastructure. Huber names the engineer responsible for the Party's surveillance system 'Orwell' – one of many insertions of Orwell into the text ('Eric Blair', for instance, is also a character). Early in the narrative, set several years after *Nineteen Eighty-Four*, an aged O'Brien reflects on the efficacy of the telescreens as designed by Orwell the engineer: 'Orwell's design had worked well. ... As promised, the network was now entirely self-powered. ... The system was "robust," Orwell had said, it was "fault tolerant", it operated "peer-to-peer." No single screen, no single cable, could bring down the whole network if it failed' (ibid: 64). The decentralised peer-to-peer network design Huber describes clearly resembles the internet. Crucially, by 'correcting' technical details for the telescreen within his palimpsest, purportedly repairing *Nineteen Eighty-Four*'s technical 'core', Huber constructs a likewise transformed political edifice. This new political structure champions laissez-faire capitalism, individual rights and cultural conservatism – a firm reversal of Orwell's democratic socialism.

The fatal flaw for the Party, in Huber's account, is that their surveillance technology *works*. Replicating Winston Smith's reading of Emmanuel Goldstein's *Theory and Practice of Oligarchical Collectivism*, Huber's elderly O'Brien reads from Winston Smith's journal. In Huber's version, Smith's journal segues from the repeated sentence 'DOWN WITH BIG BROTHER' to its own treatise: *The Theory and Practice of Networked Individualism*. Smith's manifesto lambasts the Party for its arrogance: 'The Party understood that telescreens could connect the Ministries to the people. But it failed to grasp that telescreens could equally well connect people to each other, to form new communities, new alliances, new collaborations of every kind outside the Ministry' (ibid: 151). Once the people experience this truth about the telescreens, the proles' dingy street market transforms from a smattering of meagre stalls to a teeming bazaar. Huber writes: 'Once subdued and secretive, the stallkeepers now openly touted their goods everywhere but in the immediate vicinity of the Ministries. Where there had been only the stamp and shuffle of feet, and surreptitious whispers in between telescreens, the noise of the market now filled the streets. ... Even O'Brien had found himself marveling at the abundance' (ibid: 131). From the technological capacities of networked telescreens follow a thriving and bountiful market, one apparently operating frictionless and with even power relations. Huber's dream for the internet is that it will at last realise a genuinely open and unlimited market, a romanticised view aligning the market with freedom.

The political superstructure Huber erects around telecommunications reflects a right-libertarian ideology endemic to Big Tech. In *The Know-It-Alls* (2017), Noam Cohen documents Big Tech's political culture. Cohen calls the pioneers of Big Tech 'powerful, uber-confident men ... who helped nurture the World Wide Web to prosperity in the 1990s before switching to investing' (ibid: 3). Across his survey of entrepreneurs – Mark Zuckerberg,

Jeff Bezos, Peter Thiel, among others – Cohen detects a 'libertarian blueprint for us all' (ibid: 4). Cohen elaborates:

> Collectively, these Silicon Valley leaders propose a society in which personal freedoms are near absolute and government regulations wither away, where bold entrepreneurs amass billions of dollars from their innovations and the rest of us struggle in a hyper-competitive market without unions, government regulations, or social-welfare programs to protect us (2017: 4).

Huber shares this view, yet he pitches his project as chiefly a technological one, chiding Orwell for his techno-phobia and drawing on his expertise as a mechanical engineer to correct Orwell on the technical details of telecommunications systems. According to Huber's logic, his rebuttals to Orwell's socialism are objective deductions flowing from an accurate understanding of technology. In other words, 'correcting' *Nineteen Eighty-Four* on technical grounds in turn yields a 'correction' to the book's politics.

To Huber's libertarian eyes, any device that expands the reach and size of the market – including his understanding of the internet – by definition expands freedoms. Yet, in an even-handed retrospective commentary on *Orwell's Revenge*, from 2005, Lawrence Lessig explains how hindsight exposes the book's blinkeredness: 'Huber sees the internet producing the functionality the telescreen needs, and he concludes from this that the telescreen must embrace freedom. But there are obvious – and increasingly extant – ways that the internet could be modified to eliminate the freedom Huber celebrates' (2005: 216). Lessig points to data-tracking algorithms and programs like 'cookies', mechanisms of monitoring absent from Huber's portrait of an internet acting only to enhance freedom. In Lessig's analysis, Huber is at best naïve about the internet. Huber, therefore, inflicts 'revenge' on Orwell himself by flipping Orwell's socialism – using his own words – into a simplistic, idealised picture of raw capitalism.

CORY DOCTOROW: BIG TECH AS COUNTERCULTURE

Like Huber, the author of the young adult novel *Little Brother* is a wunderkind. The varied career of Cory Doctorow includes co-founding a software company, non-profit activism on issues related to digital rights and copyright law, fellowships at research centres and, of course, writing fiction. *Little Brother*, published in 2008, is Doctorow's sixth novel. Doctorow's protagonist for this young adult novel is Marcus Yallow, a 17-year-old student and computer hacker living in urban San Francisco. The novel's inciting incident is a terrorist attack on San Francisco's Bay Bridge and its mass transit system. At the time of this event, Marcus and three friends are truant from school, playing a live-action role-playing game in the attack's vicinity, which prompts suspicion from the Department of Homeland Security. DHS agents seize the teenagers for questioning, and their reputations as hackers – as well as Marcus's refusals to cooperate – result in torturous interrogations. After nearly a week, DHS releases all but one of the three young people from detainment. In retaliation, Marcus launches a hacktivist campaign against DHS to free his remaining imprisoned friend and to disrupt the agency's surveillance and security measures in the Bay Area. Capturing a spirit of mid-aught disillusionment with the 'War on Terror', *Little Brother* is equal parts coming-of-age adventure, catalogue of strategies for digital privacy and security, and narrative manifesto for a youth-oriented, technology-driven politics of free speech and civil liberties.

Orwell's presence hangs over Doctorow's *Little Brother*, starting with its allusive title and ending in the Acknowledgements with Doctorow's inclusion of Orwell in a list of 'the heroes'. Within the narrative, 'Little Brother' is one of the names adopted by Marcus's loosely organised and largely anonymous network of subversives; the title thus acts ironically, naming the *resistance* to an oppressive American security state that is itself implicitly aligned with Orwell's authoritarian Big Brother. Furthermore, early in the novel Marcus's online handle is 'W1n5t0n' – 'pronounced "Winston"' (2008: 9) – an obvious reference to *Nineteen Eighty-Four*'s Winston Smith. Thematic resonances between *Little Brother* and *Nineteen Eighty-Four* emerge from both narratives pitting a free-thinking dissident against a security state with panoptic surveillance capabilities. Moreover, much of Marcus's character development turns on his romantic, eventually sexual, relationship with a coconspirator, named Ange: as with Winston's relationship with fellow Outer Party traitor, Julia, for Marcus the political and the sexual intertwine. Like Julia to Winston, Ange is more sexually experienced than Marcus. Yet, unlike Orwell's misogynistic depiction of Julia, Ange is equally committed to the political cause and is as proficient with technology as is Marcus. Not unlike *Orwell's Revenge*, then, *Little Brother* simultaneously honours and revises Orwell's novel.

Central to *Little Brother*'s representation of Big Tech is its depiction of the San Francisco Bay Area. Cohen calls the internet 'a Bay Area baby' (2008: 5) and Fred Turner's *From Counterculture to Cyberculture* (2008) details the relationships between the Bay Area's 1960s hippie scene and its then-nascent digital technologies industries. San Francisco's status as a signifier of US counter-culture, progressiveness and youth culture informs Big Tech's 'individualistic, anti-authoritarian ideas' (Cohen 2017: 45) about itself and its project. Similarly, *Little Brother*'s teen hero Marcus not

JACKSON AYRES

only embraces his own rebelliousness, but he also soliloquises on his city's bohemian history. Ironically, Marcus laments gentrification's erosion of various local cultures and ethnic communities, a process notoriously intensified and accelerated by Silicon Valley. Still, the novel's allegiances reside with the Bay Area as an entity: in simplest terms, the conflict of the narrative pits San Francisco, as a haven for cultural liberalism and free expression, against an aggressive, overweening US security state, represented by the DHS. On this point, Marcus's father is 'a mild-mannered librarian' who had 'been a real radical in the sixties' (2008: 77). Anxiety over terrorism prompts him to waver on his commitments and support DHS security measures, creating a personal disagreement with Marcus that replicates the narrative staging of a national crisis to preserve professed values amid a climate of fear.

Other conflicts and tensions structure the narrative of *Little Brother*. For instance, Doctorow presents an inter-dependent relationship between individual and collective, recalling how *Nineteen Eight-Four* makes plain that Winston's insistence on a private mental life and autonomy depends on his ability to find others who share and affirm his conception of the human. Such a negotiation between the individual and the collective appears in *Little Brother* when Marcus and his friends organise teen hackers into what he calls an online 'web of trust' that can coordinate resistance against DHS. This picture of underground youth rebellion reconciles solidarity and mutual trust with privacy and anonymity. At the same time, however, *Little Brother* also positively represents the competitive and meritocratic values of these teen hackers, who frequently contrast each other's technical proficiencies and rank themselves in a hierarchy of talents. This dynamic chimes with Cohen's profiles of Silicon Valley figures, in which he emphasises how they simultaneously competed with and assisted each other, noting that 'there is something jarring about a group of self-styled survival-of-the-fittest free-marketeers committed to a strategy of collective risk and mutual support' (2017: 166). Similarly, Marcus and other hackers share a purpose and project, but they also measure themselves against each other in a spirit of rivalry. *Little Brother* thus seems to credit a youthful, counter-culture capitalism that resonates with Big Tech's favoured vision of itself.

TECHNOPHILE POLITICS

If digital technologies' compatibility with counter-cultural projects in *Little Brother* subtly registers Silicon Valley's mythopoeia, Big Tech's fantasies of itself fully suffuse *Orwell's Revenge*. Although expressed to different extents, the books' shared resonances with Big Tech's techno-utopian myths align these otherwise politically divergent appropriations of Orwell. Both books endorse a core tenet of Big Tech mythology: the inevitability of new technologies. This axiomatic commitment to technological advancement, for Big Tech, is wedded to an ideological commitment to free-market capitalism. Wendy Liu distills the dogma:

> The dominant narrative within Silicon Valley is that technology is inseparable from capitalism, and so innovation requires letting the free market run roughshod over every aspect of our lives. Anyone who suggests otherwise comes off as a Luddite, opposed to much-needed progress due to malice or ignorance. … Silicon Valley is the harbinger of the future, and anyone who opposes it is stuck in the past (2020: 4).

Orwell's Revenge embraces this ethos, whereas *Little Brother*'s relationship with it is more vexed and nuanced.

Despite their differences, a shared starting point for both novels is a rejection of Orwell's alleged techno-phobia. Huber rehearses Orwell's hatred of the innovations of the 'machine age': gramophones, films, telephones and radio. Observes Huber: 'Orwell dislikes all machines, but he hates instruments of electronic communication the most' (2015: 34) for 'the electronic media are ugly, oppressive, mind-numbing – the enemies of quiet and the wreck of civilization' (ibid: 35). Huber cites Orwell himself to conclude, '*The machine itself may be the enemy*. That's what Orwell believes, first and last' (ibid: 30). Though Doctorow does not offer commentary on Orwell and technology in *Little Brother* itself, in a 2010 interview he says: 'Orwell saw technology in a fairly one-sided way. He was brilliant and insightful and gifted, and a wonderful writer. But there is no inkling in *1984* of the notion that technology cuts both ways and actually cuts harder against the establishment than it does against the anti-establishment' (Bernick et al. 2010: 438). Such myopia, Doctorow notes, reflects the fact that 'Orwell existed in an era in which technology had not yet gotten to the most important part of its life cycle: the part at which it becomes not just a tool for people who have power, but also a tool for people who lack it' (ibid). This second sentiment echoes Huber's comment that Orwell wrote his last novel 'when primitive, one-way television was the high-tech marvel of the day. All of the technological props and gadgets that Orwell describes were, in fact, made possible by the transistor. Yet the transistor was discovered at Bell Laboratories only in 1947, the year Orwell completed his first draft of *1984*' (2015: 71). Doctorow and Huber temper admiration for Orwell by lamenting what they see as his shortsightedness, and this scepticism toward Orwell's disdain for technology necessarily informs their respective portraits of Big Tech and its political valences.

PAPER

Of the two, Huber's libertarian techno-utopianism adheres closer to Big Tech's dominant political position. Reflecting on the opportunities created by the telescreen, Smith's journal asserts: 'The secret of the telescreen is the power of choice' (ibid: 166). The space for this newfound choice to occur is 'their market' (ibid: 172), no longer delimited by distance and access, so in a telescreened society, 'free markets will be irrepressible' (ibid: 173). Markets expanded online will drive a meritocratic capitalism: 'Labor supplied over the network – which is to say, most labor – will be valued with scrupulous precision. People who really produce will be in high demand, and no one will care at all about their race or religion, their sex, social graces, physical appearance, or how they smell' (ibid: 174). By 'correcting' the technical details of the telescreen and inverting *Nineteen Eighty-Four*, Huber imagines a libertarian utopia that ironically even transcends Orwell's notorious fixation on the reputed odour of the working classes.

Despite the undermining of social hierarchies that Huber attributes to his online market, culturally reactionary sentiments intrude into Huber's text in ways that speak to a contemporary integration of social conservatism and Big Tech's free-market economistic vision. Analysing the Party's inculcation of ignorance, Smith's journal explains: 'The Party's pursuit of ignorance began in schools, which were staffed by loyal Party drones. … Our universities studied the oral traditions of lesbian headhunters in New Guinea, not the great classics on human freedom' (ibid: 149). A reference point to explain this seeming non sequitur is Stanford University. A hub for computer science research and entrepreneurism, Stanford has long been a chief 'source for Silicon Valley's values' (Cohen 2017: 10). According to Cohen, by the 1950s, Stanford 'had turned itself into an explicitly pro-business research institution' (ibid). At the time of *Orwell's Revenge*, Stanford was also a site for university-based 'culture wars'. Stanford's institutional decision, in 1988, to replace its required Western Civilisation course with a new one featuring a more diverse syllabus became a flashpoint in disputes over education that extended into mainstream discourses. Huber's dismissive contrast reflects the language used in these debates. A *New York Times* article covering the Stanford controversy of January 1980 cites Saul Bellow's remark in an issue of *The New York Times Magazine* that he did not know 'the Tolstoy of the Zulus, the Proust of the Papuans'. Even a defender of the new curriculum, also quoted in the *Times*'s coverage, evinces such ethnocentric chauvinism:

> 'Plato will not be banned from our republic of letters,' said Barry M. Katz, a historian [at Stanford]. 'Freshmen will not emerge from their first year steeped in the lore of Eskimos and Pygmies but ignorant of English composition' (Bernstein 1988).

Peter Thiel, the libertarian Silicon Valley entrepreneur who invested early in Facebook and PayPal, attended Stanford at the time of these curricular changes, an experience that radicalised him. In addition to reactionary provocations while a student, in 1995 he and David O. Sacks – another Stanford alumni and technology investor – co-wrote *The Diversity Myth*, which focused on their experiences at Stanford in order to attack multiculturalism and so-called political correctness. During the 2016 US presidential campaign, Thiel emerged as an early major backer of Donald Trump, defending the inflammatory, racist rhetoric of the politician eventually known, among other things, as 'the first Twitter President'. *Orwell's Revenge*, in other words, provides glimpses of how, despite its libertarian reputation, Big Tech comprises culturally reactionary attitudes.

Similarly, Huber anticipates Big Tech's recent interventions in debates over free speech. In the Smith diary, a passage muses on the supposed contradictions of free speech:

> Speech is truly free only when there is mutual consent to it on both sides. … But half a loaf of consent is easier to find than a whole. My handbill is your litter, my political soundtrack your interrupted rest, my radio broadcast your static, my street art your ugly graffiti, my cross burning your intimidation, my inept wooing your sexual harassment, my copyright your right to publish denied, my privacy your inability to listen, my pillow talk your vulgarity, my autoerotic flashing your indecent exposure (2015: 167).

These startling conflations – as if 'cross burning' can be a politically neutral activity – propose a symmetry of all forms of speech that accommodates if not justifies public expressions of hatred and acts of harassment. A line from Huber's false equivalences goes to the failures, or reluctance, of Big Tech social media companies to regulate speech on their platforms. Richard Seymour, in *The Twittering Machine* (2019), connects the purported free speech absolutism common within Big Tech to cultural patterns of online abuse, or 'trolling'. Seymour writes: 'Social industry platforms prize their self-image as a technology of freedom. And they have at times been used for progressive ends … [b]ut in generalizing the troll-vigilante dialectic, they have also provided an ideal tool for the convocation of new, reactionary masses' (ibid: 130). Huber serves as an antecedent for this dynamic. Not only does *Orwell's Revenge* appropriate *Nineteen Eighty-Four* to morph Orwell's democratic socialism into laissez-faire capitalism, but also it mobilises Orwell's status as a paragon of truth and free speech to launder reactionary views on race and gender.

PAPER

JACKSON AYRES

Little Brother features none of *Orwell's Revenge*'s reactionary strands nor its celebrations of unleashed free enterprise, yet it pairs its celebration of computer technologies as essential, inevitable and emancipatory with positive images of digital entrepreneurs. A character, Trudy Doo, is punk musician and founder of an internet service provider called Pigspleen. Her ISP extends her punk ethos in that it acts as a tool for musicians to evade copyright restrictions. In a key scene, Doo's band reunites for an illegal concert, organised by Pigspleen, to protest at DHS overreach, making this punk tech innovator an exemplar of Big Tech 'disruption'. While on stage at the protest concert, Doo implores her audience *not* to trust her, for her age, 32, inherently undercuts her credibility. Relatedly, Marcus's friend Jose-Luis works at Pigspleen while still in high school, dovetailing counter-cultural distrust of elders with capitalist tapping of a youth labour pool. To be sure, *Little Brother* does not validate capitalism's transactional relationships as the only ones of meaning or possibility. Marcus participates in file-sharing and co-operative software development projects that eschew profit and propriety, and a live-action roleplaying sub-culture that fosters community. Still, characters like Jose-Luis and Trudy Doo validate Big Tech's idealised youthful, radical entrepreneur.

Beyond its images of punk tech entrepreneurs, *Little Brother* more generally celebrates youthfulness and presents online networking and digital technologies as in step with an insurgent, cool youth culture. Doctorow's decision to create teenagers as his heroic characters makes practical sense, given that he is writing in the genre of young adult fiction. Nonetheless, Doctorow's associations of youthfulness with political rebellion resonates with Big Tech's own youth obsession. To this point, despite being now middle-aged or older, several of the prominent Big Tech pioneers profiled by Cohen maintain affectations or signifiers of adolescence: take Elon Musk's brazen public persona, for instance, or Mark Zuckerberg's collegiate wardrobe consisting primarily of jeans, tee shirts and hooded sweatshirts. As Cohen amusedly writes, these titans of Big Tech 'bring to mind a precocious teenager who is sure he knows more than he does, slamming the door to his room and muttering about the "phonies" and "dummies" ruining the world' (2017: 14). Doctorow's Bay Area youth are less petulant than righteous, however, so his presentation of teenaged hacker rebels implicitly casts Big Tech as the forward-thinking underdogs engaged in a generational conflict against an authoritarian establishment.

Of course, complicating this picture is Doctorow's unmistakable emphasis on civil liberties and non-capitalist forms of social relations. These aspects make clear that the future Marcus and the other youthful characters fight on behalf of does not at all resemble the libertarian paradises fantasised by Big Tech. Writing on Orwell's 'literary offspring', Adam Stock notes that a 'key message of Doctorow's text is that if the online world is democratizing and a potential means of holding those in power to account, it is also a potential means for those in power to marshal and manufacture dissent simply to increase their own power and tyranny' (2015: 73). Hollie Johnson, similarly, frames the novel as a depiction of a potential dystopia in the making. Consequently, *Little Brother* is 'representative of a recent and more openly utopian wave of young adult dystopian fiction which, in the shadow of *Nineteen Eighty-Four*, responds to Orwell as a more hopeful vision of what the public and what young people, in particular, can do to fight back against state oppression enforced in the name of security and order' (2010: 128). To return to Doctorow's views on Orwell's techno-phobia, in which he stresses technology's role in any fight against authoritarianism, *Little Brother* depicts digital technologies as neutral tools.

The supposed neutrality of digital tools does nothing, however, to change their apparent necessity and inevitability – the latter being a fundamental plank of Big Tech mythopoeia. On this point, a key aspect of *Little Brother* is its inclusion of actual technical details and user strategies to protect digital privacy. Along these lines, in a passage that reads like a direct address to the reader *qua* aspiring hacker, the narration tellingly instructs: 'You can learn to write simple code in an afternoon. … Even if you only write code for one day, one afternoon, you have to do it. Computers can control you or they can lighten your work – if you want to be in charge of your machines, you have to learn to write code' (2008: 120). Coincidentally, shortly after *Little Brother*'s 2013 release the phrase 'learn to code' became a fraught political expression and cudgel in debates about Big Tech's role in the economy. High-profile Democratic politicians in the US, including President Barack Obama and, later, President Joe Biden, as well as 2016 presidential candidate Hillary Clinton, publicly recommended that coal miners laid off under green energy policies should 'learn to code'. Later, in 2019, that phrase became a sneering insult used by the online alt-right to harass journalists fired amid a wave of media layoffs. The fluke that *Little Brother* includes this phrase does not suggest any political affinities between Doctorow and either neoliberal politicians or alt-right trolls; rather, it signals how the book's co-optations of *Nineteen Eighty-Four* complicate its politics in ways that risk validating Silicon Valley's view of itself as revolutionary, liberatory engineers of the future.

CONCLUSION

What, ultimately, do *Orwell's Revenge* and *Little Brother* reveal about the ongoing discursive relationship between Orwell and Big Tech? Apple's Orwell-inspired commercial from 1984, with which this essay began, actually points the way. If that advert posits the Macintosh personal computer as a tool of resistance against totalitarian conformity and control, Apple founder Steve Jobs properly contextualises its message when he debuted the commercial to employees and shareholders in a 1983 forum. In his introductory remarks, Jobs recounts a history of personal computing, casting rival company IBM as the villain. IBM, in Jobs's account, dismissed the viability of personal computing until visionary companies, chief among them Apple, refined the technology and proved the market demand. Exploiting the innovations of others, alleges Jobs, IBM has been investing its resources into their home computing products because it 'wants it all'. Casting Apple as 'the only hope to offer IBM a run for its money', Jobs avers that 'dealers … fear an IBM-dominated and -controlled future. They are increasingly and desperately turning back to Apple as the only force that can ensure their future freedom' (2013: 3:51). Jobs's remarks hit their crescendo when he refers to IBM by its nickname: 'Will Big Blue dominate the entire computing industry, the entire Information Age? Was George Orwell right about 1984?' (ibid: 4.22). On its own, Apple's *Nineteen Eighty-Four* ad evokes digital technologies' possibilities for personal expression as well as political and social revolution, but Jobs's presentation equates IBM with Big Brother for industry monopoly is totalitarianism and consumer choice is resistance. The contours of this reasoning remain the parameters for Big Tech's conceptions of freedom and empowerment.

Residing on opposite sides of this boundary drawn by Big Tech, *Orwell's Revenge* and *Little Brother* provide distinct additions to the expansive discourse constellating Big Tech and Orwell's many legacies. Typically, journalistic or political invocations of Orwell to criticise Big Tech function as a pithy shorthand for accusing Big Tech of panoptic invasiveness, excessive disciplining of its users, spreading misinformation or stifling speech or simply possessing too much power. Far more sophisticated and nuanced meditations on the relationships between Orwell and Big Tech occur in Orwell criticism, such as Lynskey's careful unpicking of rhetorical deployments of Orwell in the context of digital technologies. Scholarship on Big Tech itself, moreover, frequently deploys Orwell in meaningful ways: for example, Zuboff's riffing term 'Big Other' evocatively characterises the 'networked, computational infrastructure' (2019: 20) underpinning what she deems 'surveillance capitalism'. Huber and Doctorow, however, offer something different. *Orwell's Revenge* and *Little Brother* stand apart from these other instances of writing not only because they are novels, but also because they contend with the proposition coming from Big Tech: as Rebecca Solnit says of Apple's landmark commercial, Silicon Valley imagines itself 'as the solution, not the problem – a dissident rebel, not the rising new Establishment' (2014). Huber embraces this fantasy, while Doctorow projects an alternate version of it.

In *Orwell's Revenge*, Huber effectively writes *for* techno-capitalism and *against* democratic socialism, as Orwell understood it. Essential to this endeavour is the inevitable triumph of Big Tech. As Huber insists: 'The world of Stalin filled with Apple computers belongs to Apple, not Stalin' (2015: 234). This declaration pitches itself as the victory of technological progress over oppressive political ideology, and this logic underpins the entire text. *Orwell's Revenge* operates from the assumption that Orwell's politics contained a bug and, therefore, required a technical fix. Solving the technical matter of how telescreen devices would and could operate necessarily eliminates the conditions that Orwell's socialism, in Huber's view, imperfectly addresses. This technocratic conviction disguises its own ideological commitments and implications. In this way, Huber's book fits neatly within the neoliberal consensus, consecrated around the time of its publication, which also sought to depoliticise liberal democracies and global capitalism. Big Tech, of course, exists as a product of and ongoing purveyor of that neoliberal consensus. By reversing the politics of *Nineteen Eighty-Four* in order to advocate for Big Tech's model of neoliberal capitalism, Huber in a sense proposes a technical solution to the problem of Orwell for Big Tech: Huber attempts to show that despite digital technologies' resemblances to Orwell's telescreen, Big Tech does not resemble Big Brother. Instead, in Huber's account – one whose echoes we hear in Silicon Valley rhetoric now – telescreens eliminate, rather than facilitate, authoritarian power.

Doctorow, by contrast, imagines a sort of alternate version of Big Tech. On this point, unlike Huber, Doctorow disputes Big Tech's image of itself and its brand of neoliberal techno-capitalism. Recent work, like the 'guidebook' *The Internet Con: How to Seize the Means of Computation* (2023) reflect Doctorow's hostility to Big Tech as it currently exists. The historical context of *Little Brother*, moreover, prompts Doctorow's attention towards the US federal government's deployment of digital tools made possible by Big Tech, as opposed to Big Tech itself. However, in Doctorow's account of Marcus, his fellow hackers, the punk entrepreneurialism of Trudy Doo and other supporting characters, as well as the romanticised portrait of San Francisco counter-culture, a different system of technological development and dissemination emerges. Doctorow

JACKSON AYRES

refers to *Nineteen Eighty-Four* and, by extension, taps the talismanic reputation of Orwell, to propose an alternate and more just, but not utopian, technology sector.

Putting these two texts in conversation with each other, and contrasting them with other invocations of Orwell *vis-à-vis* Big Tech, gives attention to two novels largely overlooked in Orwell scholarship and clarifies how each of them utilises Orwell to comprehend and represent Big Tech. First, Huber's *Orwell's Revenge* acknowledges that Orwell's views on technology and markets conflict with Big Tech's widespread libertarianism and techno-utopianism. However, it revises – 'corrects' – Orwell's depiction of the telescreen in *Nineteen Eighty-Four* in order to claim Orwell's reputation as an anti-authoritarian and a paragon of objective truth for Big Tech mythopoeia. In so doing, *Orwell's Revenge* also telegraphs how reactionary cultural attitudes inflect Big Tech's understanding of freedom and free speech. For its part, Doctorow's *Little Brother* shares Orwell's socialist distrust of markets and market logics, filtering references to Orwell through its representations of alternative, non-profit forms of production and dissemination as well as more ethical ('punk') forms of capitalist entrepreneurialism.

If at times these depictions reflect Big Tech's own preferred images of itself as youthful, insurgent, and disruptive, Doctorow's rejection of Silicon Valley libertarianism amounts to a vision of what Big Tech could look like if it were to embody, in actuality, its professed radical values. These two novels serve as interesting counterpoints, given their competing appropriations of Orwell. Yet, given their shared rejection of Orwell's techno-phobia, they also act together as a contrast with mainstream discourses that conjure Orwell's name and legacy to disparage Big Tech. *Orwell's Revenge* and *Little Brother* demonstrate that the persistent discursive relationship between Orwell – *Nineteen Eighty-Four* especially – and Big Tech is not strictly oppositional: the former a rhetorical bludgeon against the latter. These two texts complicate our sense of the vast discourse entangling Orwell's afterlife with digital technologies.

REFERENCES

Bernick, Philip, Steele, Rhonda and Bernick, Galen (2010) Interview with Cory Doctorow about *Little Brother*, *Journal of Adolescent and Adult Literacy*, Vol. 53, No. 5 pp 434-439

Bernstein, Richard (1988) In dispute on bias, Stanford is likely to alter Western culture program, *New York Times*, 19 January. Available online at https://www.nytimes.com/1988/01/19/us/in-dispute-on-bias-stanford-is-likely-to-alter-western-culture-program.html, accessed on 15 July 2023

Bradford, Richard (2020) *Orwell: A Man of Our Time*, London: Bloomsbury Caravel

Cohen, Noam (2017) *The Know-It-Alls: The Rise of Silicon Valley as a Political Powerhouse and Social Wrecking Ball*, New York: The New Press

Doctorow, Cory (2008) *Little Brother*, New York: Tor Books

Doctorow, Cory (2023) *The Internet Con: How to Seize the Means of Computation*, London: Verso

Eggers, Dave (2013) *The Circle*, New York: Knopf

Gleason, Abbott, Goldsmith, Jack and Nussbaum, Martha C. (eds) (2005) *On Nineteen Eighty-Four: Orwell and Our Future*, Princeton: Princeton University Press

Harris, Robert (2012) *The Fear Index*, New York: Knopf

Jobs, Steve (2013) History versus Hollywood: Steve Jobs introduces the famous '1984' Apple commercial, *YouTube*. Available online at https://www.youtube.com/watch?v=zlQvMp5rB6g, accessed on 1 July 2023

Huber, Peter (2015 [1994]) *Orwell's Revenge: The 1984 Palimpsest*, New York: The Free Press

Johnson, Hollie (2020) Orwell's literary inheritors, 1950-2000 and beyond, Waddell, Nathan (ed.) *The Cambridge Companion to Nineteen Eighty-Four*, Cambridge: Cambridge University Press pp 123-137

Lessig, Lawrence (2005) On the internet and the benign invasions of *Nineteen Eighty-Four*, Gleason, Abbott, Goldsmith, Jack and Nussbaum, Martha C. (eds) *On Nineteen Eighty-Four: Orwell and Our Future*, Princeton: Princeton University Press pp 212-221

Liu, Wendy (2020) *Abolish Silicon Valley: How to Liberate Technology from Capitalism*, London: Repeater Books

Lynskey, Dorian (2020) *The Ministry of Truth: The Biography of George Orwell's 1984*, New York: Doubleday

Marshall, Roger (2021) Big Tech is behaving more like Big Brother, *Washington Examiner*, 29 January. Available online at https://www.washingtonexaminer.com/opinion/op-eds/big-tech-is-behaving-more-like-big-brother, accessed on 2 February 2022

Maughan, Tim (2019) *Infinite Detail*, New York: Farrar, Straus and Giroux

NPR (2012) *The Fear Index* trades in thrills, *Morning Edition*, 6 February. Available online at https://wamu.org/story/12/02/06/the_fear_index_trades_in_thrills/, accessed on 1 July 2023

Orwell, George (2009 [1949]) *Nineteen Eighty-Four*, New York: Plume

Sacks, David O. and Thiel, Peter (1998 [1995]) *The Diversity Myth: Multiculturalism and Political Intolerance on Campus*, Oakland: Independent Institute

Seymour, Richard (2019) *The Twittering Machine*, London: Indigo Press

Solnit, Rebecca (2014) Poison apples, *Harper's*, January. Available online at https://harpers.org/archive/2014/12/poison-apples/, accessed on 2 February 2022

Stock, Adam (2015) Little nephews: Big Brother's literary offspring, Keeble, Richard Lance (ed.) *George Orwell Now!*, New York: Peter Lang pp 63-80

Turner, Fred (2006) *From Counterculture to Cyberculture: Stewart Brand, the Whole Earth Network, and the Rise of Digital Utopianism*, Chicago: University of Chicago Press

Zuboff, Shoshana (2019) *The Age of Surveillance Capitalism: The Fight for a Human Future at the New Frontier of Power*, New York: Public Affairs

JACKSON AYRES

NOTE ON THE CONTRIBUTOR

Jackson Ayres is an associate professor of English at Texas A&M University-San Antonio, where he teaches courses on modern and contemporary British literature as well as on comics and graphic literatures. He is the author of *Alan Moore: A Critical Guide* (Bloomsbury, 2021). His writing appears in *Contemporary Literature*, *Modern Fiction Studies*, *Journal of Modern Literature*, *Public Books*, among other journals and venues. Currently, he is working on several projects related to Orwell's legacy.

The Essayist's Velvet Fist

MIR ALI HOSSEINI

Orwell the essayist is often understood primarily in relation to his self-assigned anti-totalitarianism, as an embodiment of a 'liberal' ethos. One reason is that Orwell portrayed himself as, above all, a relentless fighter against totalitarianism – which for him was, besides a system of governance, an attitudinal tendency. Another reason is that the essay form (and more broadly the practice of 'writing') has been – not incidentally, since the mid-twentieth century – generally theorised in terms of a set of affective attributes such as scepticism and openness, associated also with liberalism. In this paper, I offer a more nuanced understanding of Orwell as an essayist by discussing him in relation to an aesthetically and philosophically – though not necessarily politically – rich mid-century liberalism and by drawing attention to how certain features of Orwell's essays attributed to his persona could be understood as rhetorical strategies.

Key words: Orwell, anti-totalitarianism, liberal ethos, writing, the essay form, mid-twentieth century

Whether they are favourable to him or not, literary critics tend to rank Orwell a better essayist than a novelist.[1] Yet, overshadowed by his last two works of fiction, Orwell as an essayist is often cast in terms of his strong literary-political commitment to anti-totalitarianism. Somewhat ironically, then, Orwell's essays are considered superior to his later fiction because they more effectively embody his fight against totalitarianism. The irony here can be explained by distinguishing two meanings of the word 'totalitarianism' for him. Orwell, it seems, may not have been the most patient expositor of totalitarianism as a system of governance (as he does in *Animal Farm* and *Nineteen Eighty-Four*), but was seemingly excellent at detecting (or 'sniffing', to use his own metaphor) totalitarianism as an 'outlook' or attitudinal tendency, particularly among the left (as he frequently does in his essays). In exposing 'the smelly little orthodoxies' of his contemporaries – that is, the perceived heterodoxies of the left which have, in turn, become orthodoxies – Orwell's essays, especially because he nominally belonged to the same political camp which he targets, embody par excellence a liberal ethos of scepticism.[2] The word 'liberal' here should be used cautiously. 'Liberal' in Orwell's conception, before and beyond any specific policies or economic doctrines, denoted a certain attitude and disposition of openness, diametrically opposed to that of totalitarianism – a conception which indicates how Orwell's allegiance to 'liberalism' was more fundamental than, for instance, his commitment to specific socialist policies. Early on in his career, Orwell diagnosed that this fundamentally liberal attitude was in a sharp decline among the left. 'The sin of nearly all left-wingers from 1933 onwards,' he claimed, 'is that they have wanted to be anti-Fascist without being anti-totalitarian' (Orwell 1998c: 394). He, thus, chose as his life-long mission to attack the left on their illiberal positions and tendencies — or what he perceived as their totalitarian outlook.

Beyond the impact of Orwell's self-assigned mission of fighting totalitarianism on our understanding of his essays, the essay form is itself generally associated with broadly liberal attributes such as scepticism and openness. As much as thinking of Orwell's essays in terms of a fundamental commitment to promoting an anti-totalitarian liberal attitude illuminates certain features of his writing, however, it tends to obscure others. How can, for instance, attributes such as self-scepticism, an appreciation for ambiguity and a sense of openness, associated with the essay form be reconciled with, respectively, Orwell's outspoken and assertive persona, his so-called 'plain speech' and his at times bitterly polemic language? To appreciate the complexities of Orwell's essays, I propose to move beyond viewing them in relation to a thinly conceived anti-totalitarianism. The politics of Orwell's essays, I argue, is best understood in relation to a philosophical and aesthetically – though not necessarily politically – rich mid-century liberalism, developed across the Atlantic by figures such as Reinhold Niebuhr, Lionel Trilling and Isaiah Berlin.[3]

The idea of the essay as an 'inherently' anti-totalitarian form is itself a mid-twentieth-century construct. Many key texts in mid-century political thought, especially on totalitarianism, were produced by writers who, like Orwell, had either a background in literary criticism specifically or received, more broadly, a classic humanistic education – think, for instance, of the so-called 'New York intellectuals' (such as Mary McCarthy, Dwight Macdonald, Lionel Trilling and Susan Sontag). Being by virtue of their background highly conscious of the formal features of their politico-philosophical output, these writers utilised and valorised for their political purpose the very form which was not entirely a matter of their choice but dictated by the 'little magazine' format and the fast-paced political environment of the mid-twentieth century. The essay's perceived openness, scepticism and lack of systematicity, they thought, embodied a quintessentially 'liberal' subjectivity. In this way, they conceived the essay predominantly *vis-à-vis* the writer's subjectivity, as an embodiment of the authorial persona. According to Orwell: 'When one reads any strongly individual piece of writing one has the impression of seeing a face somewhere behind the page' (Orwell 1998b: 56). Pushing against this conception of the essay – which arguably still largely shapes our understanding of the genre – I draw attention to the complicated dynamic, in Orwell's work, between the authorial persona implied in his essays and his use of rhetorical strategies. The essay, I seek to remind us, is an exercise in persuasion — and by persuasion I do not refer to a rational 'force of the better argument', but persuasion by every means at the writer's disposal.

'PROFOUNDLY LIBERAL'

In 1937, at a Barcelona hotel during the Spanish Civil War, a scruffy, tall English man with a pair of giant boots on his shoulders approached a Scottish miner's daughter who had, a few years earlier, become the first female Labour MP for North Lanarkshire at the age of only 24, in an election in which she herself, as a woman in 1929 Britain, was too young to vote. The man introduced himself as 'George Orwell', primed and eager to step into the fray. At first, she was rather suspicious, for he had no credentials on him. The man's audacious charm and giant boots, however, eventually won her over.

This is how Jennie Lee recalls her first encounter with Orwell in a 1950 letter, shortly after his death. Lee, who in 1945 took over Orwell's famous *Tribune* column 'As I Please' while he served as a war correspondent for David Astor's *Observer* in France and Germany, describes 'George' as 'a deeply kind man and a creative writer … a satirist who did not conform to any orthodox political or social pattern … not only a socialist but profoundly liberal' (quoted in Orwell 1998a: 5). Lee's use of the word 'profoundly' here affords us an insight into Orwell's liberalism: that it is at once deep and deep-seated. Orwell's liberalism, she implies, rather than being a choice, is a kind of disposition that comes naturally to a 'creative writer'. The idea that creative writing and the liberal attitude are fundamentally linked is a mid-century myth that Orwell himself helped construct. Frequently in his critical pieces, Orwell refers to how the rise of totalitarianism threatens the very existence of prose.[4] I will return to this briefly, but for now let us further discuss in what sense Orwell is a 'liberal'.

Given Orwell's important role in promoting anti-totalitarianism, it is not surprising that intellectual histories of mid-century liberal anti-communism feature him prominently. Yet, by advancing a rather reductive interpretation of Orwell's 'anti-totalitarianism' – an interpretation, nonetheless, which Orwell's way of writing at times encourages – these narratives tend to overlook the complexities of Orwell's literary output. Consider, for instance, Louis Menand's *The Free World: Art and Thought in the Cold War* (2021), which explains Orwell's liberal anti-communism in terms of shaping 'an unofficial anti-totalitarianism directed at tendencies within the liberal democracies' that simply 'replicated' the 'official anti-totalitarianism directed at Communist states' (ibid: 50). Similarly, Duncan White's *Cold Warriors: Writers Who Waged the Literary Cold War* (2019) accepts, without further complication, Orwell's self-portrait as having turned into a relentless anti-totalitarian after his experience in the Spanish Civil War.[5] White arguably dramatises this turn even more so than Orwell allowed himself to do, tying it to the single event of him being shot in Spain: 'Since he was hit but not killed, Orwell entered a new trajectory, into a confrontation with a force he would come to despise as deeply as fascism: Stalinism. The coming weeks and months offered up an unexpected education in the virulent spread of totalitarianism' (ibid: 18).

Both Menand and White refer to the influence of James Burnham's *The Managerial Revolution* (1941) on Orwell's thought. In his book, Burnham proposed that with the advent of the planned economy, which was superior in its efficiency to *laissez-faire* capitalism, power was increasingly concentrated in the hands of an emerging managerial class, who would dominate both the traditional bourgeoisie and the working class (Burnham 1941: 71-76). There was much that Orwell despised about Burnham's work, as he expressed in a 1944 'As I Please' column (Orwell 1998c: 60-61). He rebuked Burnham for his deterministic attitude, especially his thesis that, as Orwell paraphrases, 'A totalitarian society … *must* be stronger than a democratic one' (Orwell 1998c: 61, italics in the original). This theory was falsified, Orwell believed, as the tides of the war shifted course since the publication of Burnham's book in 1941. Despite his attack on Burnham, however, as Menand and White observe, some of the ideas in *The Managerial Revolution* influenced Orwell (Menand 2021: 45-51; White 2019: 665). Particularly, the idea that the post-totalitarian world will be divided between a few superpowers seems to have inspired Orwell's *Nineteen Eighty-Four*.[6] Furthermore, as Menand shows, in *Nineteen Eighty-Four*, Orwell satirises Burnham's book: *The Theory and Practice of Oligarchical Collectivism*, the fictional political treatise which Winston receives from O'Brien, parodied *The Managerial Revolution* (Menand 2021: 48).

While studying Orwell's engagement with Burnham's work can help illustrate the complexities of Orwell's liberal anti-totalitarianism,

Menand's and White's commentaries stop short of fleshing out these complexities. For instance, if the crux of Orwell's critique of Burnham is that he deemed totalitarianism inevitable, how is it that *Nineteen Eighty-Four*, which supposedly satirises Burnham, is often itself read as extremely pessimistic? Indeed, after the novel's publication, Orwell emphasised that his goal was not to argue that a dystopian future is inevitable, but to warn that 'something resembling it *could* arrive' (Orwell 1998g: 135, italics in the original). Orwell may not want to be read as a pessimist in the final analysis, but he does appeal to pessimism or even fatalism, in his essays as well as his fiction, to elicit a certain response in the reader. Similarly, Orwell's critique of collectivism is not as unequivocal as it seems. Consider, for instance, how he summarises Burnham's observation about collectivism – an observation which Orwell finds reasonable: 'The fact that collectivism is not inherently democratic, that you do not do away with class rule by formally abolishing private property, is becoming clearer all the time' (Orwell 1998c: 61). Instead of arguing that collectivism is inherently undemocratic – as we would expect from the arch-'anti-totalitarian liberal' which Orwell is at times portrayed – he phrases the thesis negatively, implying that there *can* be forms of collectivism which are democratic and liberal. Orwell's ambivalence towards collectivism is further evinced in how he criticised the left for both ignoring individual liberty and for neglecting 'primal things such as patriotism and religion' – that is, a fundamental need in human nature for belonging (Orwell 1998b: 102).

For another point of complexity, consider Orwell on fear. Upon reading Emmanuel Goldstein's *The Theory and Practice of Oligarchical Collectivism*, Winston realises that the book was 'the product of a mind similar to his own, but enormously more powerful, more systematic, less fear-ridden' (Orwell 1997: 208). How can Orwell at once attribute fearlessness to the totalitarian mind and valorise plain speech as thinking fearlessly? 'To write in plain, vigorous language,' Orwell emphasises, 'one has to think fearlessly, and if one thinks fearlessly one cannot be politically orthodox' (Orwell 1998d: 376). Could it be that Orwell *also* believed that fear in a certain dose can help immunise one against the totalitarian outlook? A similar ambivalence in Orwell is displayed in his rebuke to Burnham for assuming that 'the expert's opinion *must* be worth more than the ordinary man's' (Orwell 1998c: 61, italics in the original). This, indeed, conforms with what is generally perceived as Orwell's valorisation of the 'ordinary man' and the accessibility of ordinary speech. But again, going back to Orwell's 1946 essay, 'Politics and English language', published two years before his piece on Burnham, one comes across a hypothesis that is fundamentally elitist: it is

MIR ALI HOSSEINI

upon a select few who have the means to stop the language from what he perceived as a trend towards deterioration. 'Silly words and expressions have often disappeared,' Orwell states, 'not through any evolutionary process but owing to *the conscious action of a minority*' (Orwell 1998d: 429; emphasis mine).

The complexities and ambivalences I have highlighted in Orwell's engagement with Burnham point to how his liberal anti-totalitarianism is not as unequivocal and reductive as his tone and self-presentation at times suggest. To appreciate the complexities of Orwell's literary-political legacy, I propose to place him in a philosophically and existentially oriented – or 'profound', to borrow Jennie Lee's word – liberalism at the mid-twentieth century. This existential mid-century liberalism has been, since the emergence of the New Left, largely dismissed by intellectual and cultural historians as an embrace of an overtly pessimistic and tragic attitude, which resulted in a politically impoverished state of 'apathy'. I am borrowing the word 'apathy' here from the title of the first publication in the 'New Left Book' series, *Out of Apathy* (1960), in which a new generation of left-wing thinkers provided a diagnosis of the legacy of Cold War liberal intellectuals. E. P. Thompson, the collection's editor, has a chapter in the book which incidentally analyses Orwell as an example of the mid-century intellectuals whose 'profound political pessimism' contributed significantly to the general post-war mood of apathy' (Thompson 1978: 223).

Pushing against this somewhat standard, New Left critique of mid-century liberalism as unproductively pessimistic, Amanda Anderson's *Bleak Liberalism* (2016) proposes that mid-century liberalism displays not an unequivocal embrace of despair, but 'an interplay between hope and skepticism'. For Anderson, what is perceived as mid-century liberalism's overtly pessimistic attitude, rather than signifying an abandonment of progressive goals, signals an 'existential density' through which mid-century liberals attempted to reconcile liberal aspirations with the historical and philosophical conditions which threaten those aspirations (ibid: 24).

While Anderson's book does not discuss Orwell as a mid-century liberal specifically, as my brief discussion of the ambivalences and complexities in Orwell shows, 'an interplay between hope and skepticism' describes Orwell's work better than a 'profound political pessimism'.[7] Besides its descriptive aspect, Anderson's argument in *Bleak Liberalism* has indeed a normative aspect. For Anderson, 'bleak liberalism' is politically productive in that it cultivates complex subjectivities that can better appreciate the discrepancies between lived experience and political ideals and, hence, less susceptible to become politically disengaged (in complete contrast to Thompson's critique). While I think Anderson's argument better (though by no means perfectly) captures the complex affective qualities of mid-century liberalism, I do not agree with the normative aspect of her judgement. A complex subjectivity may be more in tune with how messy life is in 'reality', capable of appreciating how we inevitably fall short of reaching our ideals, and hence less likely not to commit to action – at least action in a vaguely broad sense. For this very reason, however, a complex subjectivity could be also less conducive to specific, concrete forms of action and organisation – because 'action always fails' and 'organisations become inevitably tyrannical'. It is from this latter point, I believe, that the legacy of liberalism has been enduringly damaged during the Cold War era.

In the case of Orwell, for instance, one can think of how he did not want *The Lion and the Unicorn* (1941), where he advocated for specific socialist policies, to be reprinted (Orwell 1998g: 226). Only five years after the publication of *The Lion and Unicorn*, Orwell stated that, as the history of committed literature in the 1930s shows, 'a writer does well to keep out of politics. For any writer who accepts or partially accepts the discipline of a political party is sooner or later faced with the alternative: toe the line, or shut up' (Orwell 1998b: 105). In making this remark, Orwell, indeed, does not wish to promote apolitical writing, but he implies that getting involved in the messy world of actual political work is below the dignity of a writer *qua* writer. A good writer, Orwell believed, advances their writing from a profound level: they may take action by writing against this or that specific policies or ideas (orthodoxies, as he liked to call them) occasionally, but they should never become involved in political organisation. Another name for this 'profound' position, as Thompson correctly diagnoses, is the post-ideological position.[8] Yet, in ascribing this position to a 'profound political pessimism', Thompson misses the appeal of Orwell's way of writing: although in the final analysis Orwell's writing may result in a self-conscious state of detachment, it convinces the reader of its position precisely by not being apathetic – that is, by exhibiting a passionate care for the world and affirming the possibility of change.

MIRROR OR TYPEWRITER?

In April 1948, Orwell published a review of a recent anthology of contemporary US-American writing, which in a letter he had called 'a rather dreadful anthology of recent American stuff' (Orwell 1998f: 282). Entitled *Spearhead*, the anthology, edited by James Laughlin, was intended to give an overview of the experimental, avant-garde writing in the US from the mid-1930s to mid-1940s. Orwell found it doubtful whether American literature in this period was as 'experimental' as Laughlin claimed. He believed that the editor's 'selection is less interesting than it might have been, since it consists almost entirely of "creative" writing – that is, poems and stories' (ibid: 312). Orwell's addition of inverted commas to the word 'creative' here is a critique of Laughlin's assumption that there exists a rigid distinction between non-fiction prose and other forms of literary writing (otherwise Orwell himself believed that there is something essentially creative about 'writing', as a by-product of bourgeois liberal democracies).[9] Orwell explains: 'Much of the best and liveliest American writing of the past ten years has been done by literary critics and political essayists' (ibid). He then lists American writers such as Lionel Trilling, Dwight Macdonald and Mary McCarthy who, he says, produced excellent 'political and sociological essays' (ibid: 316). As Orwell's remarks on mid-century American writing show, he was neither unaware of the literary value of the essay form nor believed non-fiction prose to be secondary to fiction. Orwell, even when he writes a memoir such as *Homage to Catalonia* (1938), where he commits himself to representing facts as objectively as possible, writes with 'a regard for form' (Orwell 1998e: 320).

As Robert Lane Kauffmann shows in his study of the essay form, influential theorists of the essay, most remarkably Adorno, consider 'the essay as a function of the cognitive experience of a writing subject' (Kauffmann 1981: xi). In reflecting the contingency inherent in 'the *actual* process of thought', the essay form for Adorno is a means of combatting what he perceived as a Platonist, instrumental mode of thinking inherent in the Enlightenment, the dominance of which led to totalitarianism in the twentieth century (Adorno 1984: 157; emphasis mine).[10] Adorno's theorisation of the essay form was shaped by a post-war, post-totalitarian moment shared with Orwell, as well as the American essayists whose exclusion from the *Spearhead* anthology upset the British writer.[11] Adorno's 'The essay as form' appeared originally in 1958, eight years after Orwell's death, and was translated into English years later. Even if Orwell had had a chance to read the English translation of Adorno's piece, it is hard to imagine how he would not have been at once disgusted by its obscure, sophisticated language. Yet, Adorno's valorised conception of the essay form as an antidote to totalitarian thinking is remarkably close to Orwell's idea of 'writing'. Compare, for instance, how Adorno concludes his piece on the essay form and a concluding remark from Orwell's 'Writers and Leviathan' (1948):

> ... the law of the innermost form of the essay is heresy. By transgressing the orthodoxy of thought, something becomes visible in the object which it is orthodoxy's secret purpose to keep invisible (Adorno 1984: 171).

> He [a writer] should never turn back from a train of thought because it may lead to heresy, and he should not mind very much if his unorthodoxy is smelt out, as it probably will be (Orwell 1998f: 292).

The advice given here by Orwell, echoed in Adorno's theorisation, is one which Orwell, unsurprisingly, in his own writing follows. In Orwell's writing, a thought at times appears to lead him spontaneously to another, giving the impression that the movement between ideas has not been planned. This feature of Orwell's writing is illustrated perhaps best in his 'As I Please' columns for *Tribune* (1943-1947) which often begin with a random observation, instilling in the reader the perception that something has *occurred* to the writer: 'Looking through the photographs in the New Year Honours List, I am struck (as usual) by the quite exceptional ugliness and vulgarity of the faces displayed there' (Orwell 1998c: 55); 'The other night a barmaid informed me that if you pour beer into a damp glass it goes flat much more quickly' (Orwell 1998c: 81); 'I have just found my copy of Samuel Butler's *Note-books*, the full edition of the first series, published by Jonathan Cape in 1921' (Orwell 1998c: 292).[12] These random observations, occasioned seemingly by happenstance than by design, appear then to kick off a train of thought.

Consider, for instance, the very 'As I Please' piece where Orwell discusses Burnham (Orwell 1998c: 60-61). The text starts with a seemingly random observation about how the custom of binding up magazines in the book form is dying out. Orwell's reminiscence about the pleasure of reading old magazines in the book form leads him to discuss various magazines which he has collected over the years. Meandering away from this initial observation, Orwell then discusses seemingly unrelated topics like historical war scares and the British intelligentsia's attitude towards totalitarianism. At this point, as a regular reader of the column may have expected, the central topic of the text starts to become clear – in this case, James Burnham's *Managerial Revolution* and his assumption, in Orwell's reading, that totalitarianism is inevitable. As these examples show, the tangential connections and lack of strict structure in how Orwell develops his writing – besides his casual tone, personal anecdotes and an apparently unrehearsed language – turn the essay form for him, just like for Adorno, to a representation of the act of thinking as it occurs in the writing subject.

It should thus be no surprise that a piece of writing is, for Orwell, beyond all, a reflection of its author's attitude towards the world: 'When one reads any strongly individual piece of writing, one has the impression of seeing a face somewhere behind the page' (Orwell 1998b: 55). That 'writing' is primarily a reflection of the writer's

MIR ALI
HOSSEINI

attitude was a belief shared by the American essayists whom Orwell admired. In a 1969 piece, Irving Howe re-examines the style of 'the essay cultivated by the New York writers': 'its strategy of exposition was likely to be impersonal ... but its tone and bearing were likely to be intensely personal'; he further clarifies: 'The audience was to be made aware that the aim of the piece was not judiciousness, but, rather, a strong impress of attitude, a blow of novelty, a wrenching of accepted opinion' (Howe 1968: 41). Howe's remark not only captures some features which Orwell's essays have in common with American essays associated with mid-century liberalism, but incidentally also clarifies what Orwell means by 'any strongly individual piece of writing'. By 'individual' here Orwell does not mean a writing that is reflective of the author's biographical facts or is unique, but a writing in which the 'face' of the writer – his attitude and fundamental motivations – is not disguised under a veneer of linguistic manoeuvres and 'ready-made phrases' (Orwell 1998d: 426).

The belief in Orwell, as well as in many other mid-century essay writers, that the essay form represents the act of thinking – and thus the attributes – of the writing subject is often coupled with another belief: if creative writing flourishes in liberal democracies and perishes under totalitarian tyranny, then the more an essay embodies a 'liberal' attitude, the greater is the literary merit of that essay. These normative assumptions about the essay form and writing have, over time and with the influence of writers like Orwell, become ingrained in our understanding of the genre. As a result, studies of Orwell's essays, and of the essay form in general, seldom question these assumptions. Consider, for instance, the book-length study of Orwell by Alex Woloch: *Or Orwell* (2016) includes fine-grained, sophisticated close-readings of Orwell, but its thesis – that Orwell's writing embodies 'a pervasive, stubborn skepticism about ... consummated expression' – as interesting as it is, reinforces the assumption that writing is a representation of the act of thinking (ibid: 53). In *George Orwell the Essayist* (2011), Peter Marks contributes to our understanding of Orwell's essays by a much-needed historical study of some Orwell pieces that, after years of anthologising and republishing in different formats, appear in complete isolation from the concrete contexts in which they were written. Marks's historical approach leads him to consider Orwell's essays in relation to their specific reading publics. Yet, from this consideration, Marks draws a conclusion about the formal features of Orwell's essays that falls back into the same persistent theory of the essay:

> For a polemicist like Orwell the essay could provide a vital tool for communicating unorthodox or provocative opinions that … could activate responses and reactions. … The personal voice central to many (although not all) essays advertised and simultaneously helped cultivate Orwell's own take on the world, reflecting the changes, subtleties, variety, bias and occasional contradictions of that voice. Because no topic is prohibited, essays can roam freely across all terrain, restricted only by the inquisitiveness of the essayist (Marks 2015: 10).

To push our understanding of Orwell's essays besides the valorised set of beliefs about the essay form which we have inherited (mostly) from the mid-twentieth century, we need to think of the essay beyond a supposed 'symbiotic relationship' with a thinly conceived anti-totalitarian, liberal temperament (Lopate 2021: xv). In their fight against 'totalitarian' thinking, mid-century liberals adopted the essay form very consciously, over-emphasising the genre's unsystematic and anti-dogmatic features at the expense of its more imaginative, creative, affirmative elements – but this does not mean that they themselves did not exploit such possibilities. One way in which our established theoretical frameworks for understanding the essay can be productively challenged is by thinking of the genre in relation to the reader. What does an essay do to the reader besides a mere activation of scepticism and openness? How does a 'strongly individual piece of writing' persuade us? What rhetorical strategies does an essay draw upon? This line of inquiry should not imply that we must think of the essay's use of rhetorical strategies in isolation from the authorial persona or the implied attitude of the writer – to the contrary: the persona of the essayist can itself be seen as a rhetorical strategy, working in concert with other elements in the text, to influence the reader. This dynamic is particularly interesting in Orwell's case.

HOW ORWELL WRITES

'Why I write' is probably Orwell's most famous essay on the topic of his undertaking as a writer. As Peter Marks correctly reminds us, however, Orwell did not intend this piece as a manifesto nor a statement of purpose to his entire oeuvre (Marks 2015: 167). The privileged status given to 'Why I write' is rather the result of many volumes of Orwell's selected essays and anthologies which have, at times, anachronistically presented this essay as an introduction to Orwell's prose in general. That said, being a piece of writing about writing, the essay illustrates vividly certain formal features of Orwell's writing that relate to the 'profoundly liberal', self-reflective attitude, which he sought to cultivate. Here I want to suggest that attending to the ways in which 'Why I write' seeks to persuade the reader in relation to the persona the essay embodies can productively complicate our understanding of both Orwell's essays and mid-century liberalism.

The title as well as the way Orwell starts the piece set the reader's expectation to discover why he decided to become a writer. Yet, it remains deliberately unclear throughout the text whether Orwell's pursuit of a writing career (and more specifically writing politically) is a result of his environment or of his free will. 'From a very early age, perhaps the age of five or six,' Orwell begins, 'I knew that when I grew up I should be a writer' (Orwell 1998e: 316). If we swap the word 'should' in this sentence with 'would', the difference may seem subtle; from the rest of the essay, however, we gather that the word 'should' has been selected here cautiously, since further in the essay, Orwell seems to want to avoid implying a kind of Socratic intellectualism – that the knowledge of the good results in doing the good. A few lines into the essay, Orwell refers to an adolescent habit which was formative in his writing career – of constantly describing in his head whatever he sees or does. 'I seemed to be making this descriptive effort,' Orwell remarks, '*almost* against my will, under a kind of compulsion from outside' (Orwell 1998e: 317; emphasis mine). The word 'almost' here is a careful addition that creates a tension between agency and necessity – a tension which is sustained throughout the essay. Few sentences later for instance, Orwell states that an author's 'subject-matter *will be determined* by the age he lives in', adding immediately between dashes: '*at least* this is true in tumultuous, revolutionary ages like our own' (Orwell 1998e: 318; emphases mine). The dissonance here between the certainty of 'will be determined' and the uncertainty of Orwell's qualifier added between the dashes ('at least…') is further intensified in the rest of the sentence: 'but before he ever begins to write he will have acquired an emotional attitude from which he will never *completely* escape' (Orwell 1998e: 318; emphasis mine). A short decisive sentence then follows, in which Orwell seems to suggest that the influence of the environment is not an immutable destiny: 'It is his job, *no doubt*, to discipline his temperament' (Orwell 1998e: 318; emphasis mine); for what purpose does self-discipline serve if we lack any semblance of control? Despite this momentary release, however, the essay immediately continues to dramatise the tension between agency and necessity. Orwell lists four motives behind every writer (beyond the need to earn a living), which determine their literary output: 'sheer egoism', 'aesthetic enthusiasm', 'historical impulse' and 'political purpose' (Orwell 1998e: 318). He then emphasises the role of both internal and external factors in determining his own writing career: '*By "nature"* … I am a person in whom the first three motives would outweigh the fourth. In a peaceful age I might have written ornate or merely descriptive books … As it is I have been *forced* into becoming a sort of pamphleteer' (Orwell 1998e: 318-319; emphases mine). Briefly after this, however, Orwell affirms his agency stressing how his experiences culminated in a 'decision', which he initially failed to make, but eventually did make in 1936 (Orwell 1998e: 319). This tension between agency and necessity in 'Why I write' is represented also, and more subtly perhaps, on a formal level. Consider these two sentences which have become two of the most memorable Orwell quotes:

> Every line of serious work that I have written since 1936 has been written, directly or indirectly, *against* totalitarianism and *for* democratic Socialism, as I understand it.

> What I have most wanted to do throughout the past ten years is to make political writing into an art (Orwell 1998e: 319, italics in the original).

Orwell's shift from passive to active voice in these sentences, which appear only a few lines apart and basically convey the same message (that Orwell's writing is highly politically informed), encapsulates the interplay between external influences and personal decision in his journey as a political writer. The sustained tension in 'Why I write' between agency and necessity – reflected prominently in the certainty and uncertainty of Orwell's language – correlates neatly with what Amanda Anderson describes as mid-century liberalism's 'interplay between hope and skepticism', for hope can arise from our certainty about the possibility of change, and scepticism, whether directed towards ourselves or our environment, from our uncertainty to have control. In a way then, Orwell's 'Why I write' highlights an essential quandary (or 'bleakness') of the human condition. Besides this broadly philosophical reading, we can also interpret the sustained tension between certainty and uncertainty in Orwell, as Alex Woloch argues (2016), as an enactment of a political commitment.

In 'Why I write', Orwell memorably states: 'Every line of serious work that I have written since 1936 has been written, directly or indirectly, *against* totalitarianism and *for* democratic socialism, as I understand it.' Woloch argues that Orwell's statement here, rather than a conclusive expression, is a dramatic enactment of a fundamental political commitment, as the uncertainties in his language suggest: 'directly or indirectly', 'as I understand it' and 'every line of *serious* work' (ibid: 4; Woloch's emphasis). As brilliant as these lines of inquiry are, I want to suggest that we would miss key features of Orwell's writing if we read the tension in his work between hope and scepticism, between uncertainty and certainty, as only a representation of the human condition or an enactment of a fundamental political commitment – and not in relation to the reader.

As I have so far shown, throughout 'Why I write', Orwell sustains a tension between agency and necessity. This tension, I want to further suggest, becomes at pivotal points in the essay momentarily reconciled (though not completely resolved), and such moments of reconciliation are designed in a way that lends credibility to Orwell's authorial persona. Consider, for instance, the following passage towards the end of the essay where Orwell reflects on how he was compelled to include a chapter in *Homage to Catalonia* which was of little literary value but especially important politically:

> A critic whom I respect read me a lecture about it. 'Why did you put in all that stuff?' he said. 'You've turned what might have been a good book into journalism.' What he said was true, but I could not have done otherwise. I happened to know, what very few people in England had been allowed to know (Orwell 1998e: 320).

The remark about turning a potentially good book into journalism highlights a conflict between Orwell's desire for artistic accomplishment (agency) and demands imposed on his writing that are beyond his control (necessity). While the notion of transforming a work into 'journalism' implies a negation of the writer's creative control, the very act of foregoing this control – even if it may not be readily apparent – implies that Orwell has exercised his agency. On the surface, it seems that Orwell's action has been guided by an incidental alignment between the external circumstances ('I *happened* to know') and an inner drive for justice ('I could not have done otherwise'), which is also beyond his control. As we recall, however, earlier in the text Orwell introduced himself as a person whose 'nature' happens to draw him more to artistic pleasures than to political purpose – 'I am a person in whom the first three motives would outweigh the fourth' (Orwell 1998e: 317-318).

Therefore, while by including an aesthetically damaging chapter, Orwell has not acted against all his inner compulsions, in forgoing his 'aesthetic enthusiasm' for an inner impulse in him which is 'naturally' less strong, he has indeed acted with free will. But Orwell's presentation of his decision as *mostly* a matter of necessity than of his agency makes his intellectual integrity appear less a heroic accomplishment and, hence, more sincere: Orwell may be a great writer with noble political ends, but admittedly this has been almost, though not completely, due to his nature and environment. The sincerity of Orwell's acknowledgment here is reinforced by other formal elements in the passage. Notice, for instance, how the remark about turning a good book into journalism is first filtered through the objectivity of an observer (the critic) and followed by an almost perfunctory admission by the author ('What he said was true'). That Orwell needed to be confronted by a critic to realise the consequence of his decision implies how the question of artistic success, in this instance, almost did not even cross his mind. His cursory admission of the desire for success, on the other hand, while signalling his honesty and reminding the reader of his strong 'aesthetic enthusiasm', lets the emphasis lie on the second part of the sentence, which as I discussed – indirectly though decisively – affirms his agency: 'What he said was true, but I could not have done otherwise.'

The tension between agency and necessity in 'Why I write', as I previously mentioned, is reflected in the oscillations between certainty and uncertainty in Orwell's tone. I want to suggest that on this level, too, the essay attempts to persuade the reader through the author's persona. The authorial persona of 'Why I write' comes across overall as very assertive and outspoken. This assertiveness, however, is carefully tempered to not extend beyond the point of making Orwell seem overtly uncertain and sceptical, but to signal an added level of detachment and self-consciousness, which makes his otherwise brazen assertiveness far more agreeable. Consider, for instance, how the same passage can be read differently, depending on where the emphasis lies:

> It seems to me *nonsense*, in a period like our own, to think that one can *avoid* writing of such [public] subjects. *Everyone* writes of them in one guise or another.

> It *seems to me* nonsense, *in a period like our own*, to think that one *can* avoid writing of such [public] subjects. Everyone writes of them *in one guise or another* (Orwell 1998e: 320; emphases mine).

On the one hand, Orwell uses a strong noun like 'nonsense' (rather than weaker alternatives like 'absurd' or 'foolish'), a quantifier which makes his claim universal ('Everyone'), and a strong verb like 'avoid' (rather than, for instance, 'stay away from' or 'escape') which, against the essay's sustained emphasis on the role of the environment on a writer's career, implies bad faith. All these characteristic choices make Orwell's statement boldly assertive. On the other hand, there are various elements in the passage that temper Orwell's tone: the personal conjecture ('seems to me') makes the statement less definitive (than the verb 'is' would, for instance), the descriptive qualifiers ('in a period like our own' and 'in one guise or another') limit the scope of the claim, and the addition of a modal verb ('can') further tones down the claim. Yet, the tension between uncertainty and certainty, and by implication agency and necessity, is reconciled in the sentence that immediately follows: 'It is *simply* a question of which side one takes and what approach one follows' (Orwell 1998e: 319; emphasis mine). With the addition of this sentence, Orwell himself 'simply' (albeit momentarily) takes sides with agency: as understanding and judicious as Orwell portrays himself, he is by no means interested in letting those whom he perceives to be morally and politically wrong (very often intellectuals on the left) off the hook because of a lack of agency. This position is already embedded in the choice of the word 'avoid', but is made explicit only in a concluding sentence, for its rhetorical effect establishes Orwell as someone who is deeply understanding but whose sense of justice – if he wants – would override his empathy and judiciousness.

CONCLUSION

As I hope my discussion here shows, Orwell's alterations between agency and necessity, between certainty and uncertainty, besides representing a specific philosophical outlook or enacting a certain political commitment, serve the rhetorical function of establishing the author's credibility and charisma. As I proposed in the first part of the paper, considering Orwell in relation to the philosophically and aesthetically dense mid-twentieth-century liberalism illustrates overlooked aspects of his writing. Orwell is known to have despised philosophy. He once stated, albeit satirically, that 'philosophy should be forbidden by law' and took pride in 'the lack of philosophical faculty, the absence in nearly all Englishmen of any need for an ordered system of thought' (Orwell 1998g: 52; Orwell 1998b: 399). As I discussed, however, his work exhibits profound philosophical concerns. Accordingly, Orwell's aesthetics is more complicated than his use of 'plain speech' and his intolerance for 'humbug' may at first sight suggest. In turn, I hope my discussion of Orwell's essays has complicated the somewhat standard explanation of mid-century liberalism in terms of anti-totalitarianism besides what critics like Amanda Anderson have proposed – for as I have already emphasised, as much as mid-century liberalism seems philosophically and aesthetically rich, this does not mean that its political achievements were as remarkable. In sustaining a tension between agency and necessity, for instance, Orwell's 'Why I write' may gesture towards the idea that political responsibility is at once individual and collective, but clearly fails to draw that conclusion.

NOTES

[1] For instance: Lionel Trilling believes that Orwell's fiction, especially *Animal Farm*, is overrated, but 'His critical essays are *almost always* very fine' (Trilling 1952: 221); John Rodden argues that Orwell's 'compelling ethos' is best captured in his use of the essay form (Rodden 2001: xviii); Harold Bloom thinks that insofar as his aesthetic achievements are concerned, 'is a far better essayist than a novelist' (Bloom 2009: 1)

[2] The phrase 'smelly little orthodoxies' appears in Orwell's description of Dickens (Orwell 1998b: 56). In a 1949 unfinished essay on Evelyn Waugh, Orwell writes: 'To a great extent, what is still loosely thought of as heterodoxy has become orthodoxy. It is nonsense to pretend, for instance, that at this date there is something daring and original in proclaiming yourself an anarchist, an atheist, a pacifist, etc' (Orwell 1998g: 74-75)

[3] While I do not focus on these specific thinkers in this paper, studies on mid-century liberalism discuss these, among others, as key figures in shaping what can be called liberalism's existential turn at the mid-twentieth century. See, for instance: Müller 2008, Anderson 2016 and Cherniss 2021

[4] The best example here is perhaps Orwell's essay 'The prevention of literature' (1945)

[5] Orwell famously dramatises the year 1936 as a watershed moment in his life narrative: 'Every line of serious work that I have written since 1936 has been written, directly or indirectly, *against* totalitarianism and *for* democratic Socialism, as I understand it' (Orwell 1998e: 319, italics in the original)

[6] In a 1948 letter, however, Orwell claimed that the idea occurred to him after the Tehran Conference of 1943, the first of a series of conferences in which the three leading Allies (Britain, the United States and the Soviet Union) divided up the world into 'zones of influence' (Orwell 1998f: 487)

[7] For Anderson, mid-century liberalism rather than being an anomaly is a heightened expression of a 'bleakness' which had been continuously cultivated in the liberal tradition (Anderson 2016: 20). One of Anderson's protagonists, Charles Dickens, happens to be for Orwell a literary maverick, though not without his own limitations, with whom Orwell closely identified

[8] Thompson calls it 'Natopolitan' ideology: 'that there is in fact *no* orthodoxy but only an infinite variety of opinions among which each man is free to choose' (Thompson 1978: 213)

[9] Orwell uses 'creative writer' to refer to himself. For instance, in 'Writers and Leviathan' Orwell writes: 'To suggest that a creative writer, in a time of conflict must split his life into two compartments, may seem defeatist or frivolous' (Orwell 1998f: 292)

[10] In *Dialectic of Enlightenment*, Adorno and Horkheimer famously announced that 'enlightenment is totalitarian' (Adorno and Horkheimer 1975 [1947]: 24)

[11] To borrow from Samuel Moyn, in this post-war moment, the Frankfurt School had turned into 'a kind of Cold War liberalism within Marxism' (McAteer and Moyn 2022). For a similar critique of the Frankfurt School's Marxism, see also Morley 2023

[12] This is by no means the only literary strategy adopted by Orwell in the 'As I Please' columns. In 'The lasting in the ephemeral', Richard Keeble analyses a myriad of literary strategies employed in Orwell's 'As I Please' columns

REFERENCES

Adorno, Theodor W. (1984) The essay as form, *New German Critique*, Vol. 32 pp 151-171

Adorno, Theodor W. and Horkheimer, Max (1975 [1947]) *Dialectic of Enlightenment*, London: Verso

Anderson, Amanda (2016) *Bleak Liberalism*, Chicago: The University of Chicago Press

Bloom, Harold (2009) Introduction, Bloom, Harold (ed.) *George Orwell's 1984*, New York: Infobase Publishing pp 1-7

Burnham, James (1941) *The Managerial Revolution: What Is Happening in the World*, New York: Van Rees Press

Cherniss, Joshua L. (2021) *Liberalism in Dark Times: The Liberal Ethos in the Twentieth Century*, Princeton: Princeton University Press

Howe, Irving (1968) The New York intellectuals: A chronicle and a critique, *Commentary*, Vol. 46, No. 4 pp 29-51

Kauffmann, Robert Lane (1981) *The theory of the Essay: Lukács, Adorno, and Benjami*n, University of California San Diego, dissertation

Keeble, Richard (2007) The lasting in the ephemeral: Assessing George Orwell's As I Please columns, Keeble, Richard and Wheeler, Sharon (eds.) *The Journalistic Imagination: Literary Journalists from Defoe to Capote and Carter*, London: Routledge pp 100-115

Lopate, Phillip (2021) Introduction, Lopate, Phillip (ed.) *The Golden Age of the American Essay: 1945-1970*, New York: Anchor Books pp xi–xxiii

Marks, Peter (2015) *George Orwell the Essayist: Literature, Politics and the Periodical Culture*, London: Bloomsbury Publishing

McAteer, Daniel and Moyn, Samuel (2022) A conversation with Samuel Moyn: The Cold War and the canon of liberalism, *Centre for Intellectual History Blog*, 1 April. Available online at https://intellectualhistory.web.ox.ac.uk/article/a-conversation-with-samuel-moyn-the-cold-war-and-the-canon-of-liberalism, accessed on 9 August 2023

Menand, Louis (2021) *The Free World: Art and Thought in the Cold War*, New York: Farrar, Straus and Giroux

Morley, Daniel (2023) The Frankfurt School's academic 'Marxism': 'Organised hypocrisy', 21 April, *In Defence of Marxism*. Available online at https://www.marxist.com/the-frankfurt-school-s-academic-marxism-organised-hypocrisy.htm, accessed on 9 August 2023

Müller, Jan-Werner (2008) Fear and freedom: On 'Cold War liberalism', *European Journal of Political Theory*, Vol. 7, No. 1 pp 45-64

Orwell, George (1997) *The Complete Works of George Orwell, Vol. IX: Nineteen Eighty-Four*, Davison, Peter (ed.) London: Secker & Warburg

Orwell, George (1998a) *The Complete Works of George Orwell, Vol. XI: Facing Unpleasant Facts, 1937-1939*, Davison, Peter (ed.) London: Secker & Warburg

Orwell, George (1998b) *The Complete Works of George Orwell, Vol. XII: A Patriot after All, 1940-1941*, Davison, Peter (ed.) London: Secker & Warburg

Orwell, George (1998c) *The Complete Works of George Orwell, Vol. XVI: I Have Tried to Tell the Truth, 1943-1944*, Davison, Peter (ed.) London: Secker & Warburg

Orwell, George (1998d) *The Complete Works of George Orwell, Vol. XVII: I Belong to the Left, 1945*, Davison, Peter (ed.) London: Secker & Warburg

Orwell, George (1998e) *The Complete Works of George Orwell, Vol. XVIII: Smothered under Journalism, 1946*, Davison, Peter (ed.) London: Secker & Warburg

Orwell, George (1998f) *The Complete Works of George Orwell, Vol. XIX: It Is What I Think, 1947-1948*, Davison, Peter (ed.) London: Secker & Warburg

Orwell, George (1998g) *The Complete Works of George Orwell, Vol. XX: Our Job Is to Make Life Worth Living, 1949-1950*, Davison, Peter (ed.) London: Secker & Warburg

Rodden, John (2001) *George Orwell: The Politics of Literary Reputation*, New Brunswick: Transaction Publishers, revised edition

Thompson, E. P. (1978) Outside the whale, *The Poverty of Theory and Other Essays*, London: Merlin Press pp 211-243

Trilling, Lionel (1952) George Orwell and the politics of truth, *Commentary*, Vol. 13 pp 218-227

White, Duncan (2019) *Cold Warriors: Writers Who Waged the Literary Cold War*, London: Little, Brown

Woloch, Alex (2016) *Or Orwell: Writing and Democratic Socialism*, Cambridge, Massachusetts: Harvard University Press

NOTE ON THE CONTRIBUTOR

Mir Ali Hosseini is a PhD candidate at the University of Regensburg, studying mid-twentieth-century political writing and liberal thought. He was introduced to Orwell by his Persian literature teacher who recommended, slightly rebelliously and wittingly, his students to read *Animal Farm* as an illustration of how revolutions, despite their noble goals, disastrously fail. It took him quite a while to find out that the first Persian translation of Orwell's book was commissioned for anti-communist propaganda purposes by the British, who later conspired with the Americans to overthrow the popular, liberal government of Mohammad Mosaddegh, who had just nationalised the oil industry.

PAPER

George Orwell's Gandhi

DOUGLAS KERR

M. K. Gandhi and George Orwell were not only leading political thinkers and actors, but iconic national figures in the years that saw the beginning of the end of the British Empire around the world. In their beliefs and political aims, Gandhi and Orwell had a good deal in common. Both were born into different kinds of allegiance to Britain and what it stood for, but both in due course became implacable enemies of the injustice of imperial rule and worked to change the minds of those who sustained it. This campaign came to a climax with the end of British rule in India, which both lived to see. Both embraced a practical socialism, and worked in different ways to improve the conditions of the poor. So what was it that prevented Orwell from seeing in Gandhi a kind of ally, even a hero? Through his career, in which he wrote a good deal about Gandhi, he expresses suspicion, hostility, irritation, 'a sort of aesthetic distaste' and at best a grudging respect for the older man. Why? This paper looks for answers to this question.

Key words: Orwell, Gandhi, India, Burma, British Empire, anti-imperialism

From the end of 1925 to February 1929, M. K. Gandhi's autobiography, later given the title *The Story of My Experiments with Truth*, was serialised in two publications in India devoted to the promotion of his ideas and principles: the Hindi-language *Navajivan* and the English-language *Young India*. Gandhi was the most famous person in India and had a huge following amongst Indians. In neighbouring Burma, which for administrative purposes came under the government of India and had a large Indian population, an instalment of Gandhi's autobiography came into the hands of a young English officer of the Indian Imperial Police. In his later 'Reflections on Gandhi', a year after Gandhi's death, in 1948, he was to remember reading it with mixed feelings:

> At about the time when the autobiography first appeared I remember reading its opening chapters in the ill-printed pages of some Indian newspaper. They made a good impression on me, which Gandhi himself, at that time, did not (*CWGO* XX: 50).

It is no surprise that Gandhi himself was not popular with British officials in the Raj. He, and the Congress Party with which he was associated, had for years been a thorn in the side of the imperial authorities and were in the vanguard of the movement to force the British to quit India. While the anti-British cause in Burma was less well-organised and less formidable than in India, there was considerable anti-colonial disaffection in Burma throughout the nineteen-twenties.[1] Burmese nationalists looked to India for inspiration and sometimes support in their own struggle. Every imperial policeman in Burma would have been aware of Gandhi as the figurehead of this rebellious spirit, as well as a wily political operator with an international reputation, who kept finding new ways to get under the skin of the government of British India and its disciplinary forces.

If Gandhi did not make a good impression on the young policeman, whose name was Eric Blair, that hostile perception was maintained, for the most part, throughout the subsequent career of George Orwell, the writer. The aim of this paper is to explain why and how this was so. To answer these questions we need to explore the contradictions of Orwell's political beliefs about empire, a complex matter which may be most simply expressed as a conflict between forces already present in the young police officer reading that Indian newspaper in Burma, an Anglo-Indian professional who was also an anti-imperialist.[2]

On the face of it, this hostility is surprising. In their beliefs and political aims, Gandhi and Orwell had a good deal in common. They were both born into different kinds of allegiance to Britain and what it stood for. Orwell belonged not only to the governing class, but specifically to the Anglo-Indian imperial service class. The young Gandhi was, by his own description, a most amenable colonial subject. 'Hardly ever have I known anybody to cherish such loyalty as I did to the British Constitution,' he remembered in his autobiography, adding: 'In those days I believed that British rule was on the whole beneficial to the ruled' (1949: 142). On this basis it might even be possible to make an argument for the young Gandhi as a kind of Anglo-Indian like Orwell. He came from a professional family, trained in London, and made his career in the Empire for 21 years, in South Africa. Like Orwell, he later turned his back on imperial loyalties.

In the light of experience and of growing intellectual conviction, both men in due course became implacable enemies of the injustice of imperial rule and worked to change the minds of those who sustained it. This campaign came to a climax with the end of British rule in India, which both lived to see. Both embraced a practical socialism and worked in different ways to improve the conditions

PAPER

DOUGLAS KERR

of the poor. Gandhi was a nationalist and Orwell a patriot, but both men understood that justice recognised no boundaries. 'Either we all live in a decent world,' Orwell wrote, in March 1943, to an Indian friend, 'or nobody does' (*CWGO* XV: 33). Gandhi was a universalist in the same way: Ashis Nandy puts it elegantly: 'As Gandhi was to so clearly formulate through his own life, freedom is indivisible, not only in the popular sense that the oppressed of the world are one but also in the unpopular sense that the oppressor too is caught in the culture of oppression' (Nandy, Ashis, *The Intimate Enemy: Loss and Recovery of Self under Colonialism*, Delhi, Oxford University Press, 1988: 63).

Before his death in the case of Gandhi and after his death in the case of Orwell, both acquired a kind of aura as the embodiment of political and moral values that seemed to transcend their particular time and circumstances. They became, to use a much-abused word, iconic. So what was it that prevented Orwell from seeing in Gandhi a kind of ally, a comrade in arms, even a hero? Through his career, in which he wrote a good deal about Gandhi, he expresses suspicion, hostility, irritation, 'a sort of aesthetic distaste' (*CWGO* XX: 10), and at best a grudging respect for the older man. Why?

Gandhi first starts to appear in Orwell's writing in the 1940s, and it is the Second World War that supplies the crucial context for Orwell's antipathy. Either during or soon after his time in Burma (he left in 1927), Orwell had become convinced that the British Empire was a despotism that could not be justified. It was a view he shared with Gandhi and his allies, and he never deviated from it. But now the world had come under the more menacing shadow of Nazi Germany and, in the East, Germany's ally Japan. The game had changed, and Orwell now found himself advocating something like the classic British liberal position on Indian independence: yes, but not yet. He set this out in *The Lion and the Unicorn*, early in 1941. In military, economic, and administrative terms, the British had made themselves indispensable to India. 'If India were simply "liberated", i.e. deprived of British military protection, the first result would be a fresh foreign conquest, and the second a series of enormous famines which would kill millions of people within a few years' (*CWGO* XII: 425).[3] When the Japanese entered the war and quickly overran British possessions in South East Asia, the situation became extremely urgent. Their advances in Burma brought them to the gates of British India. Among their forces was the Indian National Army, under Subhas Chandra Bose, a fighting force whose mission was to liberate India from the imperial European occupier.

The Churchill government in London was sufficiently alarmed by these developments to send Sir Stafford Cripps, Leader of the House of Commons, to India in late March 1942 to talk with the

Indian nationalist leaders. Cripps, one of the few members of the National government that Orwell admired, was sympathetic to Indian self-rule. To the leaders of the Congress (including Gandhi) and the Muslim League, Cripps promised full self-government, with Dominion status, after the war was over. In exchange, he asked for the loyalty of Indians for the duration of hostilities. This was not far from what Orwell had advocated in *The Lion and the Unicorn* a year earlier: 'Immediate Dominion status for India, with power to secede when the war is over' (ibid: 422).

Meanwhile, in August 1941, Orwell had gone to work in the Indian section of the Eastern Service of the BBC, writing and making programmes for broadcast to India. While the corporation had a reputation for independence and the reliability of its news service, in wartime it was, in fact, a state apparatus, though it retained its autonomy to schedule programmes. Policy directives were issued from time to time by the Ministry of Information, under its interestingly initialled minister Brendan Bracken, and all broadcasts were censored in conformity to government requirements (see Briggs 1961-1995 and Bateman 2022).[4] Part of Orwell's brief at the BBC was to produce regular newsletters or commentaries: he wrote two hundred of these between November 1941 and his departure from the BBC in November 1943. The newsletters were to be a vehicle to 'put across the British view of the news, without sacrificing the reputation that has been carefully built up for veracity and objectivity in news presentation'.[5] Orwell was naturally worried that his own views might be compromised, but late in 1942 he was able to say that the weekly commentaries he wrote for broadcast to Asia 'in fact have contained very little that I would not sign with my own name' (*CWGO* XIV: 101).

In the commentaries he writes enthusiastically about Stafford Cripps – 'recognised as the ablest man in the British Socialist movement' (*CWGO* XIII: 224) – and his talks with Gandhi (whom Orwell often calls Mahatma Gandhi) and the other Indian leaders. 'Everyone in Britain is delighted to see such an important mission as the one which Cripps is now undertaking, conferred upon a man whom even his critics admit to be gifted, trustworthy and self-effacing' (ibid: 225). In his diary, in April 1942, Orwell was less sanguine about the Cripps Mission. 'Gandhi is deliberately making trouble,' he had heard. 'Impossible to be quite sure what his game is' (ibid: 259). The Corporation had to be very circumspect about Gandhi, especially in these critical months as negotiations dragged on. In July Orwell was commissioning a talk on pacifism from an Indian writer. 'This should, of course, have some reference to India and to the special Indian situation of this moment, but you will of course understand that we are not anxious to tread on any toes, and particularly it would be undesirable to make anything in the nature of an attack on Mr Gandhi at this moment' (ibid: 409). This was in accord with an internal BBC directive on 'lines to get across' in broadcasts to India: broadcasts should emphasise that the British offer of independence to India after the war was sincere, but also that the defence of India could not be assured by yielding to the Congress demands, because 'Congress is dominated by Gandhi who is utterly and completely committed to pacifism' (ibid: 411).[6] Orwell would have had no difficulty with this position, which coincided with his own.

But negotiations collapsed, and Gandhi launched the Quit India movement in August 1942, demanding what he called an orderly British withdrawal from India. This was a huge setback not just for British policy, but also for Orwell's own hopes that Britain and India might enter into 'alliance, partnership – in a word, equality' (*CWGO* XII: 424). He saw this move as reckless, totally unrealistic, and a potential threat to the whole war effort across the globe. At a time when the war was going badly, with German advances in the Soviet Union and North Africa, he felt this was a betrayal; certainly many Anglo-Indians, military and civilian, saw ingratitude at the least in the Quit India movement. Most of the Congress leaders were immediately imprisoned; acrimony, widespread protests and violence followed. There is no doubt that Orwell held Gandhi himself responsible, while also expressing his disgust at the British response. In August 1942, he wrote: 'It is strange, but quite truly the way the British Government is now behaving upsets me more than a military defeat' (*CWGO* XIII: 458) The ending of empire had been Orwell's chief political ambition for more than ten years. Now the sides that would need to co-operate to bring this about were further apart than ever.

The Quit India movement, Orwell and others felt, was of material and moral assistance to the Japanese. If its advocates had been successful, they might have brought about the transfer of India from British rule to the authority of a different empire, that of Japan, albeit in the beguiling disguise of the Greater East Asia Co-Prosperity Sphere. But Orwell's anger at Gandhi's long campaign dated from years before the Japanese entered the scene. In Burma where, he recorded in his celebrated essay 'Shooting an elephant', he was 'hated by large numbers of people' (*CWGO* X: 501), his life as a policeman had been made difficult by widespread nationalist anti-British resentment, though this never broke out into open rebellion while he was there.[7] At the time of the incident evoked in 'Shooting an elephant', Orwell says he had already made up his mind that the Raj was an evil thing.

With one part of my mind I thought of the British Raj as an unbreakable tyranny, as something clamped down, in saecula saeculorum, upon the will of prostrate peoples; with another part I thought that the greatest joy in the world would be to drive a bayonet into a Buddhist priest's guts. Feelings like these are the normal by-products of imperialism; ask any Anglo-Indian official, if you can catch him off duty (ibid: 502).

Already, the anti-colonial convictions were warring with the Anglo-Indian instincts of the imperial policeman. In a sense we can see this sort of contradiction still alive in Orwell's response to the Quit India movement, but the ambivalence was already there in the young officer's reaction to reading Gandhi's memoirs in an Indian newspaper in Burma. It is part of a wider blindness in Orwell's thinking. As we shall see, it might, indeed, be called doublethink.[8] Sincere and passionate anti-imperialist though he was, he could not bring himself to believe in the capacity of colonised peoples to liberate themselves. He knew that empire could only be ended by the action of imperial subjects, but he consistently under-estimated the power of liberation movements across the world to bring this about. (There is some similarity in Orwell's belief in the need for a socialist revolution in Britain, but his disbelief in the capacity of British socialists to accomplish anything like it.)

This started with Gandhi. First of all, in Orwell's view, Gandhi's methods did not have universal application. He was fortunate in his opponent, the British government of India. He never had to deal with a totalitarian power. Orwell wrote in October 1948 that Gandhi was dealing with 'an old-fashioned and rather shaky despotism which treated him in a fairly chivalrous way and allowed him to appeal to world opinion at every step'; his tactics of fasting and civil disobedience could not be applied 'in a country where political opponents simply disappear and the public never hears anything that the Government does not want to hear' (*CWGO* XIX: 452, 453).

Few states were as forbearing as the British Raj. In an exchange about pacifism in *Partisan Review* in 1942, Orwell stated that in Germany and Japan, the penalty for pacifist activities was beheading (*CWGO* XIII: 397). Gandhi's success in India, he believed, relied on the mildness of the government and its tolerance of his brilliant exploitation of public opinion, in India and beyond.

But not only was Gandhi's success owed to the obligingness of his opponent, in Orwell's view. His campaigns were actually counter-productive. Here Orwell, in the same debate about pacifism in *Partisan Review*, cited his own experience again. 'As an ex-Indian civil servant, it always makes me shout with laughter to hear, for instance, Gandhi named as an example of the success of non-violence. As long as twenty years ago it was cynically admitted in Anglo-Indian circles that Gandhi was very useful to the British Government. So he will be to the Japanese if they get there' (ibid: 397).[9] He was repeating an argument he had made a year earlier that, while no doubt Gandhi was personally honest and unaware of being used, for the past twenty years he had been regarded by the government of India as one of its right-hand men. 'I know what I am talking about – I used to be an officer in the Indian police. It was always admitted in the most cynical way that Gandhi made it easier for the British to rule India, because his influence was always against taking any action that would make any difference' (*CWGO* XII: 467).

Here again we seem to see Orwell finding it difficult to think straight about Gandhi. Gandhi was successful because the government of India was a shaky despotism that treated him with leniency. But the government of India treated him with leniency because his activism was unsuccessful, and they could see that his influence always worked against translating anti-British resistance into any effective action. (Another doublethinkful moment!) Gandhi had not brought the end of empire nearer: he had 'alienated the British public by his extremism and aided the British Government by his moderation' (*CWGO* XV: 215). As an anti-imperialist, Orwell found Gandhi's actions disappointing and ineffectual. As an Anglo-Indian, he found them dangerous but naïve.

At the core of Orwell's quarrel with Gandhi was the question of non-violence. 'I grew up in an atmosphere tinged with militarism, and afterwards I spent five boring years within the sound of bugles,' he recalled in 1940; but now in wartime he discovered in himself and his country 'the spiritual need for patriotism and the military virtues, for which, however little the boiled rabbits of the Left may like them, no substitute has yet been found' (*CWGO* XII: 272).[10] Patriotism and the military virtues were qualities more likely to be found in the Anglo-Indians Orwell had tried to leave behind than among the leftists to whom he had attached himself, and the conditions of wartime brought these Anglo-Indian attitudes back to the surface, rather to his surprise. From their perspective, it was clear non-violence could not be a realistic option in times of extreme peril. Pacifism barely existed, he claimed, except in places where people had no reason to fear invasion or conquest. Governments could not be pacifist, because a government which refused to use force could be overthrown by anyone who *was* willing to use force; meanwhile 'pacifists think always as people who will never be in a position of control, which is why I call them irresponsible' (ibid: 467). In September 1943 he wrote:

The idea put forward by Gandhi himself, that if the Japanese came they could be dealt with by sabotage and 'non-co-operation', is a delusion, nor does Gandhi show any very strong signs of believing in it. Those methods have never seriously embarrassed the British and would make no impression on the Japanese (*CWGO* XV; 212).

Gandhi was reported in an interview as recommending unadulterated non-violent non-co-operation, should the Japanese invade India. 'That involves the determination of India not to give quarter on any point whatsoever and to be ready to risk the loss of several million lives. But I would consider that cost very cheap and victory won at that cost glorious' (see Fielden, *Beggar My Neighbour* 1943: 63-64).

Gandhi's central principle was *Ahimsa*, from the Sanskrit word meaning non-injury: you should not use violence, even if the alternative is defeat. What, then, about the fate of European Jewry? The American Louis Fischer, in a book broadly sympathetic to the Indian leader, *Gandhi and Stalin*, tackles this question (Fischer 1948: 48-51). He reports that, after the war, Dr Judah L. Magnes, Chancellor of the Hebrew University of Jerusalem, took Gandhi up on an article in *Harijan* in which he had advised the Jews of Germany to offer *Satyagraha* or non-violent opposition to Hitler. Magnes rejected this out of hand, pointing out that the slightest sign of resistance would have resulted in murder or deportation to a concentration camp. Fischer raised the question with Gandhi himself, and Gandhi denied that he had said the Jews should offer 'passive resistance', a term he disliked. There was nothing passive about *Satyagraha* (which means 'holding firmly to truth' or 'truth-force').[11] He thought the Jews of Germany had made a mistake in submitting to Hitler. 'But the Jews should have offered themselves to the butcher's knife. They should have thrown themselves into the sea from cliffs.'

> 'You think,' I [Fischer] said, 'that the Jews should have committed collective suicide?'

> 'Yes,' Gandhi agreed, 'that would have been heroism. It would have aroused the world and the people of Germany to the evils of Hitler's violence, especially in 1938, before the war. As it is, they succumbed anyway in their millions' (ibid: 50).

In his *Observer* review of the book, Orwell calls this 'an answer which seems to embarrass even Mr Fischer' (*CWGO* XIX: 453).

After all, Orwell had a history of his own with pacifism. In 1938 he had joined the Independent Labour Party, which was anti-war, but he left soon after war started because, he said, 'they were talking nonsense and proposing a line of policy that could only make things easier for Hitler' (*CWGO* XII: 148).[12] After the war, Orwell tried, as Peter Marks says in *George Orwell the Essayist: Literature, Politics and the Periodical Culture*, 'to distinguish Gandhi from left-wing Westerners who would claim him for pacifism and anarchism' (2011: 181).[13] *Ahimsa* was not pacifism on the Western model. And writing in 1949, in some desperation under the looming shadow of a war waged with atomic weapons, Orwell conceded that it was possible that Gandhi's path might after all represent mankind's last and only hope. 'It seems doubtful whether civilization can stand another major war, and it is at least thinkable that the way out lies through non-violence' (*CWGO* XX: 10).

Through much of his career, Gandhi served Orwell not only as a useful antagonist but as something like an intellectual catalyst, resolving and clarifying his views on difficult issues, and sometimes simply exposing his self-contradictions. So it is with the issue of war. Although his thinking about Gandhi could be muddled, there is evidence that Gandhi's *Ahimsa* helped to clarify Orwell's own conviction that some things were worth fighting for. For him the Spanish Civil War had meant defeat and disillusion, and in 1942 the outcome of the war with Hitler was still uncertain. But in his essay 'Looking back on the Spanish War' (1942), he maintained in a spirited declaration that both wars, whatever their setbacks and degradations and compromises, were part of a long struggle undertaken to improve the living conditions of ordinary people at a time when 'the average human being is either drudging like an ox or shivering in fear of the secret police'.

> Understand that, and the long horror that we are enduring becomes at least intelligible. All the considerations that are likely to make one falter – the siren voices of a Pétain or of a Gandhi, the inescapable fact that in order to fight one has to degrade oneself, the equivocal moral position of Britain, with its democratic phrases and its coolie empire, the sinister development of Soviet Russia, the squalid farce of left-wing politics – all this fades away and one sees only the struggle of the gradually awakening common people against the lords of property and their hired liars and bumsuckers. The question is very simple. Shall people like that Italian soldier be allowed to live the decent, fully human life which is now technically achievable, or shall he not? (*CWGO* XIII: 510).[14]

Neither Gandhi's commitment to non-violence, nor the cynical defeatism of the collaborationist Marshal Pétain, should stand in the way of this purpose.[15] (Gandhi, to be sure, might have argued that he was pursuing the same end by different means.)

It will be useful at this point to take a look at Gandhi's methods, his application of the principle of *Satyagraha*, his dealings with the government of India, his popular support and his use of publicity, all of which greatly interested Orwell. For this, we can travel to Motihari, the headquarters of the Champaran district of Bihar, at the foot of the Himalayas. This was the site of one of Gandhi's most successful campaigns, known as the Champaran Satyagraha, in 1917.[16] Another of the town's claims to fame is that it was the birthplace, fourteen years earlier, of George Orwell, the son of an official in the opium department of the government of India.[17]

Gandhi had been invited to Champaran to intervene on behalf of the workers or *ryots* who complained of exploitation by the 'planters', on whose land indigo was cultivated. In his autobiography he tells the story of how he used his experience in South Africa to organise peasant *Satyagraha* in Champaran. He was known to be a troublemaker; soon after arriving, he was served with a notice to leave the district, and when he refused, he was served a summons for trial. He offered no resistance to this, but a huge crowd gathered round the house where he was staying. The local authorities were thoroughly disconcerted.

> A sort of friendliness sprang up between the officials – Collector [district officer], Magistrate, Police Superintendent – and myself. I might have legally resisted the notices served on me. Instead I accepted them all, and my conduct towards the officials was correct. They thus saw that I did not want to offend them personally, but that I wanted to offer civil resistance to their orders. In this way they were put at ease, and instead of harassing me they gladly availed themselves of my and my co-workers' co-operation in regulating the crowds. But it was an ocular demonstration to them of the fact that their authority was shaken. The people had for the moment lost all fear of punishment and yielded obedience to the power of love which their new friend exercised (1949: 343).

By this stage Gandhi had, in effect, already won. In the Motihari courthouse it was the government that was on trial. He happily pleaded guilty to the charge of disobeying the order to leave Champaran, and eloquently justified his action in the courtroom. Meanwhile he scrupulously wired full details of the case to the Viceroy in New Delhi.[18] Congress was the *bête noire* of the government and the planters, so he had been careful not to mention his affiliation with Congress either to the magistrate or to the peasants whose cause he had taken up. He wanted to prevent the struggle from assuming a political aspect.

No political work had yet been done amongst them [the peasants]. The world outside Champaran was not known to them. And yet they received me as though we had been age-long friends. It is no exaggeration, but the literal truth, to say that in this meeting with the peasants I was face to face with God, *Ahimsa* and truth (ibid: 344).

The provincial Lieutenant Governor wrote to the magistrate ordering that the case against Gandhi be withdrawn, and the Collector informed him that he was free to conduct his proposed inquiry into the grievances of the *ryots*, and that he could count on whatever help he needed from officials. 'The country thus had its first object-lesson in Civil Disobedience' (ibid: 346). Gandhi's activities and his inquiry brought about significant improvements in the lives of the peasants, and later he was made a member of an official committee of inquiry looking into the peasants' complaints, which in due course recommended the abolition of the *tinkathia* system.[19] Meanwhile, Gandhi also took care to control the news. He wrote to the editors of the principal newspapers telling them not to trouble to send any reporters: he himself would send them whatever might be necessary for publication and keep them informed.

The story of Gandhi in Motihari confirms Orwell's analysis: the determination to improve the material conditions of the poor, the populism, the political skill, the appeal to the better instincts of relatively mild government authorities, the clever use of publicity.[20] The point is that there is nothing in Gandhi's aims, methods, or results that Orwell could not have thoroughly approved, unless it be the slightly messianic tone of Gandhi's account.

And yet it is this that points to what it was that probably above all alienated Orwell from the Gandhi project. For, of course, Gandhi was not just a political activist but also a religious figure. Orwell had no problem with mysticism though he was not much interested in it. But he thought that Gandhi's teachings 'make sense only on the assumption that God exists and that the world of solid objects is an illusion to be escaped from' (*CWGO* XX: 7). In particular, this entails a shrinking or withdrawal from the life of the body. Even early on in Gandhi's autobiography, there is a great deal of discussion of the demands of the spirit, of his many temptations (when he goes to London as a young student he sometimes sounds like the young Augustine in Carthage), of scriptural injunctions of self-denial, of the necessity of vegetarianism and other bodily disciplines. In 1906, having become convinced that procreation and the consequent care of children are inconsistent with public service, he takes the vow of *Brahmacharya* (self-restraint, particularly sexual): 'I had not shared my thought with my wife until then, but only consulted her at the time of taking the vow' (1949: 174).

His treatment of his long-suffering wife Kasturba (or Kasturbai) will seem to many people highly problematic. They married very young and had children, but after his return from Europe, they lived very little together. 'Our love could not yet be called free from lust, but it was getting gradually purer' (ibid: 85-86). On one occasion, in Durban, she becomes critically ill and emaciated. The doctor insists she be given beef tea, but Gandhi forbids it, saying he would never allow his wife to be given meat or beef, even if the denial meant her death, unless of course she desired to take it. He speaks to her, although he says she was really too weak to be consulted in this matter. 'I pleaded with her. I told her that she was not bound to follow me. I cited to her the instances of Hindu friends or acquaintances who had no scruples about taking meat or wine as medicine' (ibid: 270). Essentially he is telling her: I forbid it, but feel free to disobey me. (This, in turn, may be construed as Gandhian doublethink, or at the least doublespeak.) She refuses the beef tea, but eventually recovers anyway. 'To her the scriptural texts were a sealed book, but the traditional religion of her forefathers was enough for her' (ibid: 271). Commenting on Gandhi's behaviour, Orwell says: 'This attitude is perhaps a noble one, but, in the sense which – I think – most people would give to the word, it is inhuman' (*CWGO* XX: 8).

Gandhi 'weaponised' his own body. Often emaciated and on display, it was the visible symbol of its owner's willingness to deny it, as well as of his simplicity of living and his embrace of poverty. To some, Gandhi's non-violence was bizarrely unmasculine, to others he seemed childlike, even comic, and he was sometimes unkindly compared to Charlie Chaplin or Mickey Mouse.[21] Orwell found him ugly, 'with his long sly nose and huge bat's ears' (*CWGO* XVI: 55). He confessed he had never been able to feel much liking for him. 'One may feel, as I do, a sort of aesthetic distaste for Gandhi,' he wrote, in January 1949, after Gandhi's death (*CWGO* XX: 10). Here we might remember his vehement insistence, in *The Road to Wigan Pier*, that middle-class socialists are all ugly, and his irrational rage at what he called faddists – sandal-wearing pacifists and vegetarians – a class which, it could be said, certainly included the sandal-wearing Gandhi, with his homespun cloth and strange diet, his talk of soul forces and his enthusiasm for spinning-wheels, and what Orwell, in his essay 'Reflections on Gandhi' for the American *Partisan Review* in January 1949, called his unviable 'medievalist program' (*CWGO* XX: 5).[22]

The combination of spiritualism and nationalism in Gandhi was suspect to Orwell, and he was impatient with those followers who declared the Mahatma a kind of saint. This is the explanation of his intemperate response to Lionel Fielden's book *Beggar My Neighbour*, which he reviewed in 1943 under the odd title 'Gandhi in Mayfair' (*CWGO* XV: 209-216).[23] Fielden had quoted an imaginary Indian extolling the superiority of Indian over European culture (op cit: 20-21). Orwell found this offensive, and counter-productive to the cause of Indian independence. Fielden's hero was Gandhi, and in his book, Orwell says, he 'upholds the East against the West on the ground that the East is religious, artistic and indifferent to "progress", while the West is materialistic, scientific, vulgar and warlike' (*CWGO* XV: 211). But this Orientalist stereotype of a spiritual India, embodied in Gandhi, was harmful to the interests of Indian people. 'Now, one of the finest weapons that the rich have ever evolved for use against the poor is "spirituality". Convince the working man that a desire for better living standards is materialistic, and you have him where you want him' (ibid: 215). Orwell's own socialism was materialist, indeed bodily. 'How right the working classes are in their "materialism"! How right they are to realise that the real belly comes before the soul, not in the scale of values but in point of time!' (*CWGO* XIII: 510).

Spirituality, like pacifism, could get in the way of practical action. Interestingly, Orwell twice likened Gandhi to Frank Buchman, the charismatic American evangelist of Moral Re-Armament, who preached a spiritual revolution in revivalist terms. Buchman had an influential following in America and Europe, with his campaign 'to restore moral standards and the guidance of God to men and nations' (Lean, Garth, *Frank Buchman: A Life*, London: Constable p. 329). Others considered him a cult leader and in wartime there were rumours that he was being subsidised by Goebbels.[24]

Gandhi was much on Orwell's mind in the late 1940s, the turbulent years of the independence of India and Pakistan and of Gandhi's own assassination. He acknowledged that Gandhi's main political objective, the ending of British rule, had after all been attained (*CWGO* XX: 10). In 1943, he had described this as 'the only large scale decent action that is possible in the world at this moment' (*CWGO* XV: 213), but, as we have seen, he had always found it hard to believe it could ever be achieved. Yet he remained lukewarm in his admiration. He was suspicious of Gandhi's allies, the Congress party which he had claimed had considerable resemblances to the Nazi party and was backed by sinister businessmen with pro-Japanese leanings (*CWGO* XVI: 447), the Indian millionaires who liked Gandhi because he asked for their repentance and not their money, the adoring women disciples. Even after Gandhi's death Orwell said he retained 'dark suspicions' about him, 'based only on gossip, but such a lot of gossip that I think there must be something in it' (*CWGO* XIX: 322). (This gossipmongering about Gandhi momentarily makes Orwell sound like an Anglo-Indian clubman.)

But it was not Gandhi's associations that alienated Orwell so much, as it were, as his disassociations.

This aspect of his understanding of Gandhi is explored in another of his late essays, 'Lear, Tolstoy and the fool' (*CWGO* XIX: 54-67).[25] Ostensibly this is about Tolstoy's attack on Shakespeare in a pamphlet of 1906, hardly a topic of pressing contemporary relevance, but one that enables Orwell to explore his feelings about forms of spiritual authority, and which brings him round, later in the essay, to Gandhi. The root of Tolstoy's hostility to Shakespeare, in Orwell's view, was his objection to Shakespeare's interest in the actual process of life. 'It is the quarrel between the religious and the humanist attitudes towards life' (ibid: 60). Even the tragedies like *King Lear* start out with the humanist assumption that life is worth living, he says, but Tolstoy did not share this view. 'Tolstoy was no saint, but he tried very hard to make himself into a saint, and the standards he applied to literature were other-worldly ones' – unlike Shakespeare, who manifestly 'loved the surface of the earth and the process of life' (ibid: 63, 64).[26] He continued: 'A sort of doubt has always hung round the character of Tolstoy, as round the character of Gandhi' (ibid: 65). But where earlier Orwell had claimed that spirituality like Gandhi's acted as a distraction from the need to get things done, he now advances a more subtle, psychological critique. He finds something bullying, even tyrannical, in both Tolstoy's and Gandhi's deployment of spiritual authority.

> Creeds like pacifism and anarchism, which seem on the surface to imply a complete renunciation of power, rather encourage this habit of mind. For if you have embraced a creed which appears to be free from the ordinary dirtiness of politics – a creed from which you yourself cannot expect to draw any material advantage – surely that proves that you are in the right? And the more you are in the right, the more natural that everyone else should be bullied into thinking likewise (ibid: 66).

For the saint, or the would-be saint, is not just an unusually good person, trying to work an improvement in earthly life: he (or she) is a utopian, who wants to bring earthly life to an end and replace it with something better. Orwell found something inhuman in the apostles of utopia. Who would want to live in the utopia of Tolstoy, or Swift or William Morris or H. G. Wells? 'All "favourable utopias" seem to be alike in postulating perfection while being unable to suggest happiness' (*CWGO* XVI: 40).[27] Gandhi preached 'friendship with the world' in general, but for such seekers after goodness, Orwell writes, 'there must be no close friendships and no exclusive loves whatever' (*CWGO* XX: 7).[28] Utopia, being a form of perfection, does not tolerate difference or distraction. Tolstoy abjured violence and coercion, yet he was an uncompromising bully, and not just to those around him. 'The distinction that really matters is not between violence and non-violence, but between having and not having the appetite for power' (*CWGO* XIX: 65).

It might be argued that Gandhi exercised this kind of coercion in a powerfully passive-aggressive way in the story of Kasturbai and the beef tea, or in the invention of the hunger strike as an instrument to coerce his own followers. This came about when he had organised a strike of textile workers in Ahmedabad in 1918: when their resolve seemed to weaken, Gandhi declared in a meeting that henceforth he would touch no food. He reports the mill-hands' reaction with satisfaction. 'The labourers broke out, "Not you but we shall fast. It would be monstrous if you were to fast. Please forgive us for our lapse, we will now remain faithful to our pledge to the end"' (op cit: 359).[29]

In the Tolstoy essay Orwell articulated the humanist quarrel with the religious attitude to life, which may be the fundamental cause of his antipathy to Gandhi.[30] In the last sentence of 'Reflections on Gandhi' he is still thinking in this way, when he talks of rejecting sainthood as an ideal and, therefore, feeling that 'Gandhi's basic aims were anti-human and reactionary' – even though he adds, in characteristic terms, 'compared with the other leading political figures of our time, how clean a smell he has managed to leave behind!' (*CWGO* XX: 10).

His troubled response to Gandhi reflects some of the complications of the feelings of Orwell, the Anglo-Indian anti-imperialist, towards India, empire and resistance. He shared Gandhi's vision of the freeing of India, but struggled to believe that it could actually be brought about, by Indians or anyone else. India's achievement of independence, and Pakistan's, is not marked by any mention in Orwell's surviving writing. He would acknowledge Gandhi's extraordinary achievement, the ending of the British Raj which would lead to the dismantling of the Empire itself. But in the years after the war, and after *Nineteen Eighty-Four* took shape in his imagination, his attention was shifting away from the despotism of formal empire and towards a different use of power, that of a coercive utopia.

NOTES

[1] In Burma in that decade, 'racial tension became more acute, crime increased and disaffection spread' (Furnivall, J. S., *Colonial Policy and Practice: A Comparative Study of Burma and Netherlands*, New York: New York University Press, 1956 p. 165)

[2] It is uncertain at what point Orwell turned against empire. In *The Road to Wigan Pier* he wrote that he hated imperialism bitterly by the end of his service in the Imperial Police, suggesting that this conviction built up gradually, but also that 'every Anglo-Indian is haunted by a sense of guilt which he usually conceals as best he can' (*CWGO* V: 134, 135). For Orwell, empire, and Anglo-India, see Kerr, Douglas, *Orwell & Empire*, Oxford: Oxford University Press, 2022

[3] British rule, however, did not prevent the Bengal famine two years later, in which two to three million people died

[4] Asa Briggs was the author of the five-volume *The History of Broadcasting in the United Kingdom* (Oxford: Oxford University Press, 1961-1995). Ron Bateman's *The Radio Front: The BBC and the Propaganda War 1939-45*, was published by the History Press, 2022

[5] Memorandum from the assistant controller of overseas programmes, February 1942, quoted in C. Fleay and M. L. Sanders, Looking into the Abyss: George Orwell at the BBC, *Journal of Contemporary History*, Vol. 24, No. 3, July 1989, p. 508

[6] Michael Barkway's memorandum, coincidentally dated on the same day as Orwell's letter to Chinna Durai (above), is marked for distribution to the Eastern Service

[7] The tragic Saya San rebellion against British rule in Burma broke out in 1930 and was finally crushed in 1932

[8] In *Nineteen Eighty-Four*, doublethink means 'to hold simultaneously two opinions which cancelled out, knowing them to be contradictory and believing in both of them' (*CWGO* IX: 37)

[9] Here 'twenty years ago' would be 1922, the year Eric Blair arrived in Burma

[10] It was not just Hitler's war that prompted 'one kind of loyalty to transmute itself into another' (*CWGO* XII: 272); he found the same virtues in John Cornford, the young communist who died fighting in the International Brigade in the Spanish Civil War

[11] '*Satyagraha* in the political sphere assumes the form of Civil Disobedience.' Bharatan Kumarappa, 'Editor's Note', in Gandhi, M. K., *Satyagraha (Non-Violent Resistance)*, Ahmedabad: Navajivan, 1951 p. iii. *Satyagraha* meant what Gandhi said. He described himself as 'the sole authority on *Satyagraha*' (ibid: 300)

[12] See also 'Why I join the ILP' (*CWGO* XI: 167-69) and Bowker, Gordon (*George Orwell*, London: Little Brown pp 241, 264). For Orwell's association with, and repudiation of, pacifism in 1938-40, see Rai, Alok, *Orwell and the Politics of Despair*, Cambridge: Cambridge University Press, 1988 pp 83-93

[13] See also Orwell, 'Reflections on Gandhi' (*CWGO* XX: 7)

[14] The Italian soldier mentioned is the subject of the poem 'The Italian soldier shook my hand' with which Orwell ends the essay (*CWGO* XIII: 510-511)

[15] Orwell said Pétain had attributed France's defeat in 1940 to the common people's 'love of pleasure' (*CWGO* XIII: 509)

[16] See Gandhi, Rajmohan, *Gandhi: The Man, his People and the Empire*, London: Haus Books, 2008pp 190-205, and Guha, Ramachandra, *Gandhi: The Years that Changed the World*, London: Allen Lane 2018 pp 44-49

[17] Some of the implications of this strange coincidence have been explored in Pai, Gita V., 'Orwell's reflections on Saint Gandhi', *Concentric: Literary and Cultural Studies*, Vo. 40, No. 1, March 2014 pp 51-77, and in Mishra, Astik, 'The relevance of George Orwell's ideas in the promotion of global citizenship education', a paper given at the 'Critical Orwell' conference in 2022. I am very indebted to both these scholars

[18] At the same time he said that he felt obliged to return his Kaiser-i-Hind medal (R. Gandhi 2008: 192)

[19] By the operation of this system, the peasant was obliged to plant three out of every twenty parts of his land with indigo for his landlord

[20] Michael Edwardes gives a more cynical account of Gandhi's Champaran triumph. 'With the departure of the magician and his assistants, the ensorcelled were released from the spell, and the farmers and peasants of Champaran went back to their old ways. There is no reliable evidence that Gandhi thought constructively about them again' (Edwardes, Michael, *The Myth of the Mahatma: Gandhi, the British and the Raj*, London: Constable, 1986 p. 194)

[21] See Nandy, p. 104. Nandy has a fascinating discussion of Gandhi's unsettling impact on the Orientalist tropes of feminisation and infantilisation of India

[22] Describing himself as 'a crank', Gandhi insisted that his experiments in dietetics were 'dear' to him as a part of his researches in *Ahimsa* (1949: 377, 379)

[23] Orwell seriously misrepresents both Gandhi and Fielden in this review. Fielden pointed this out in 'Toothpaste in Bloomsbury', a dignified response in *Horizon*. 'But, when all that is said, there remains in Mr Orwell's writing a rancour which is hard to explain' (*CWGO* XV: 221)

[24] See Lean, 302. Tom Driberg wrote that Buchman would be remembered for his egregious statement: 'I thank God for a man like Adolf Hitler' (quoted in Lean p. 530)

[25] The relevance of this essay to Orwell's Gandhi is interestingly discussed in Pai, Gita V. (op cit: 57-58)

[26] Orwell's own investment in this debate can be judged from his words in the essay 'Why I write' a year earlier. 'So long as I remain alive and well I shall continue to feel strongly about prose style, to love the surface of the earth, and to take a pleasure in solid objects and scraps of useless information' (*CWGO* XVIII: 319-20)

[27] According to Peter Davison (*CWGO* XVI: 38), 'John Freeman', the credited author of 'Can Socialists be happy?' seems to have been another of Eric Blair's pen names

[28] For a good discussion of Orwell, Gandhi and utopia, see Dwan, David (*Liberty, Equality and Humbug: Orwell's Political Ideals*, Oxford: Oxford University Press, 2018 pp 105, 190-97)

[29] See also R. Gandhi op cit: 198-200

[30] 'Actually, some of what I said in it ['Lear, Tolstoy and the fool'] I also said apropos [sic] of Gandhi' (*CWGO* XX: 124)

NOTE ON THE CONTRIBUTOR

Douglas Kerr is the author of *Orwell & Empire* (Oxford: Oxford University Press, 2022) and of *Wilfred Owen's Voices* (Oxford: Oxford University Press, 1993), *George Orwell* (Writers and their Work series, Northcote House Publishers, 2003), *Eastern Figures: Orient and Empire in British Writing* (Hong Kong University Press, 2008) and *Conan Doyle: Writing, Profession and Practice* (Oxford: Oxford University Press, 2013). He was Professor of English and Dean of Arts at Hong Kong University and is Honorary Research Fellow at Birkbeck College, London University.

PAPER

What Was Orwell's Conception of Free Speech?

MARK SATTA

Orwell's views on the nature of free speech are significantly more complex than is often recognised. This paper examines what he had to say about freedom of speech and intellectual freedom. It seeks to provide a philosophical analysis of his understanding and use of these concepts and to address some apparent tensions in his thought. In so doing, the paper identifies five dominant aspects of Orwell's account of free speech. He viewed free speech as closely related to intellectual freedom, which he highly valued; he treated free speech as primarily about the ability to say what one believes to be true; he thought that both government and various kinds of private actors posed serious threats to free speech; he believed that free speech required social safeguards, in addition to legal protection; and he recognised that free speech was a right with limits. He wrote little about the freedom of speech for liars. The paper concludes with the observation that he, therefore, left us with a number of crucial questions to discuss and think about for ourselves.

Key words: Orwell, free speech, intellectual freedom, freedom of the press, truth, philosophy

Modern thinkers often turn instinctively to Orwell when delivering warnings about perceived threats to free speech. Such appeals tend to bypass the nuance and complexity in Orwell's thinking about free speech in favour of gumming together long strips of evocative Orwellianisms from *Nineteen Eighty-Four*. One might worry that such appeals use Orwell's prose less like a windowpane and more like a mirror. That is to say, one might worry such commentary often uses the cultural force of Orwell's vocabulary to bolster the commentator's pre-existing views rather than using Orwell's own ideas as a lens through which to examine assumptions about the nature of free expression and a free society.

The paper's primary goal is to illuminate how Orwell conceived of free speech by studying what he had to say about it, especially in his essays. Thus it aims to make sense of and to untangle various tensions in his thought about freedom of speech and related concepts such as freedom of the press and intellectual freedom. This

MARK SATTA

paper's secondary goal is to map Orwell's conception of free speech onto some issues and debates about free speech occurring today.

As will be shown, in some ways, Orwell's conception of free speech is broader than many modern conceptions, while in other ways it is narrower. Orwell's conception of free speech is broad in the sense that Orwell viewed free speech as requiring both legal and social protection. It is also broad in the sense that he was keenly aware of how a free speech culture could be threatened not only by government but also by private entities, such as monopolies. Orwell's conception of free speech is narrow in the sense that he interpreted free speech specifically as protecting people's right to say what they believed was true. This contrasts with a common modern perspective on which freedom of speech includes both the right to lie and the right to say things without regard for truth, even when doing so results in demonstrable harm.

Because of the narrowness in Orwell's conceptions of free speech, his defences of free speech sometimes fail to defend, or even address, certain contemporary standards for free speech. But because of the broadness in Orwell's conception of free speech, modern defences of free speech sometimes fail, in turn, to defend or address aspects of free speech about which he was deeply concerned. One need not view any of this as a weakness in Orwell's conception of free speech. Perhaps his conception of free speech is superior to those that predominate today. This paper provides reasons to think that such a favourable assessment of his understanding of free speech has merit.

This examination of Orwell's views on free speech focuses on five key points central to his thought about free speech. For Orwell, free speech is closely related to intellectual freedom, which he valued highly. He conceived of it as primarily about the ability to say what one believes to be true. He thought that both governmental and private actors – especially socially and economically powerful ones – posed a threat to free speech. He also thought, therefore, that free speech required social safeguards, in addition to legal protection. Finally, he did not view freedom of speech as an unlimited right.

INTELLECTUAL FREEDOM AND FREE SPEECH

Orwell's writing reveals that he considered intellectual freedom – which he sometimes referred to as 'freedom of the intellect' or 'freedom of thought' – to be vitally important for a flourishing human life. Crucially, for purposes of this paper, Orwell treated intellectual freedom as closely tied to both intellectual honesty and freedom of speech. This is perhaps best exemplified in his claim that 'Freedom of the intellect means the freedom to report what one has seen, heard, and felt, and not to be obliged to fabricate imaginary facts and feelings' (*CEJL* 4: 62). Here Orwell treats the relationship between intellectual freedom and free speech as so close that he seems to *define* intellectual freedom as a type of speech freedom – namely a freedom to report. Importantly, it is not just any kind of freedom to report, but a freedom to report what one has experienced, rather than fabrications. Thus, he seems to define intellectual freedom in terms of a right to speak with intellectual honesty. But this does not make his concept of intellectual freedom narrower than his conception of free speech because, as will be argued in the next section, Orwell conceives of free speech as itself limited to an ability to speak what one believes to be true – i.e., to speak with intellectual honesty.

It seems unlikely that Orwell's considered view was that intellectual freedom actually meant freedom to report with honesty and nothing else. Elsewhere, he was quite clear about at least the conceptual distinction between language and thought. However, given the close interconnection he consistently posits between speech and thought (and, more generally, between language and thought), it is easy to see why in many contexts he did not thoroughly distinguish freedom of speech from freedom of thought. Arguably, a key point in both in his *Horizon* essay 'Politics and the English language' (1946) and *Nineteen Eighty-Four* (1949) is that free thought cannot exist without free speech and vice versa (cf Satta 2022).

Starting from the perspective of Orwell's commitment to intellectual freedom, one can better understand many of his other commitments. And understanding these commitments can, in turn, help explain his fierce commitment to intellectual freedom and its inextricably intertwined companions, intellectual honesty and free speech. Take two examples: (i) his commitment to preserving the conditions under which good literature could be written, and (ii) his opposition to all forms of totalitarianism.

For Orwell, intellectual freedom was a precondition for the creation of literature – or at least good literature. Consider, for example, his claim in his 1940 essay 'Inside the whale' that 'Literature as we know it is an individual thing, demanding mental honesty and a minimum of censorship' (*CELJ* 1: 518). He expands on this idea in 'Literature and totalitarianism' (1941), writing that 'The whole of modern European literature – I am speaking of the literature of the past four hundred years – is built on the concept of intellectual honesty, or, if you like to put it that way, on Shakespeare's maxim, "To thine own self be true"' (*CELJ* 2: 134). For Orwell, expressing oneself in this intellectually honest way is at the heart of intellectual freedom. It is also at the heart of European literature. Thus, he saw preserving the one as necessary for preserving the other.

MARK SATTA

As will be shown later, Orwell identified a wide variety of threats to the ability to express oneself honestly. He opposed capitalism, monopoly, bureaucracy, fascism, etc., at least in part, because he viewed them as harmful to the honest self-expression constitutive of free thought. But at least from the time of his fighting alongside a Republican militia in the Spanish Civil War in 1937, Orwell viewed the chief threat to intellectual freedom to be totalitarianism. Take, for example, his diagnosis of the totalitarian threat:

> Totalitarianism has abolished freedom of thought to an extent unheard of in any previous age. And it is important to realize that its control of thought is not only negative, but positive. It not only forbids you to express — even to think — certain thoughts, but it dictates what you shall think, it creates an ideology for you, it tries to govern your emotional life as well as setting up a code of conduct. And as far as possible it isolates you from the outside world, it shuts you up in an artificial universe in which you have no standards of comparison. The totalitarian state tries, at any rate, to control the thoughts and emotions of its subjects at least as completely as it controls their actions (*CELJ* 2: 135).[1]

Given this perspective, it is unsurprising that the chief totalitarian character in *Nineteen Eighty-Four*, O'Brien, makes eliminating free thought the cornerstone of his attempt to break completely the protagonist Winston Smith.

If one accepts, as Orwell did, both that totalitarianism seeks to eliminate intellectual freedom and that writing literature requires intellectual freedom, one might naturally conclude that totalitarianism is a threat to writing literature. This is exactly how he reasons, concluding that 'If totalitarianism becomes world-wide and permanent, what we have known as literature must come to an end' (ibid). This reveals that Orwell's pessimism about the ability to continue producing literature was rooted in his lack of confidence about the ability to stave off totalitarianism. This is exemplified in his reasoning in 'Inside the whale':

> [ind]Almost certainly we are moving into an age of totalitarian dictatorships — an age in which freedom of thought will be at first a deadly sin and later on a meaningless abstraction. The autonomous individual is going to be stamped out of existence. But this means that literature, in the form in which we know it, must suffer at least a temporary death (*CELJ* 1: 525).

By understanding the significance Orwell placed on intellectual freedom and the close conceptual connection he made between intellectual freedom and free speech, one can learn much about why free speech was such a central notion for him.

SAYING WHAT ONE BELIEVES TO BE TRUE

One of Orwell's most powerful and pithy descriptions of his conception of free speech comes in his claim that 'the controversy over freedom of speech and of the Press is at bottom a controversy of the desirability, or otherwise, of telling lies' (*CELJ* 4: 61). The larger content of the passage from which this quotation comes reveals that, on his account, the defender of speech and press freedom does not think telling lies is desirable, while the enemy of speech and press freedom does. From a twenty-first century perspective, this may seem like a mysterious claim. This is because today it is often the case that neither the truth nor falsity of speech nor whether a speaker believes what they are saying is true or false plays any role in whether speech receives protection under freedom of speech and freedom of the press.[2] This is exemplified in, for example, the commitment of the US judiciary to 'viewpoint neutrality' – i.e., a commitment to banning regulation of speech based on the perspective or viewpoint taken by the speaker, even if that viewpoint espoused consists of obvious lies or falsehoods.[3]

But his statement is not at all mysterious once one recognises that he viewed free speech as the right to say what one believes to be true. He makes this clear in the larger passage from which the above quotation comes:

> Although other aspects of the question are usually in the foreground, the controversy over freedom of speech and of the press is at bottom a controversy of the desirability, or otherwise, of telling lies. What is really at issue is the right to report contemporary events truthfully, or as truthfully as is consistent with the ignorance, bias and self-deception from which every observer necessarily suffers. In saying this I may seem to be saying that straightforward 'reportage' is the only branch of literature that matters: but I will try to show later that at every literary level, and probably in every one of the arts, the same issue arises in more or less subtilized forms (ibid: 61).

For Orwell, free speech – which at least in this passage seems to be used interchangeably with freedom of the press – is, in brief, 'a right to report contemporary events truthfully'. This is remarkably similar to the description encountered in the previous section of intellectual freedom as 'the freedom to report what one has seen, heard, and felt'. The subtle difference is that the former seems to concern a right to report the *truth*, while the latter seems to concern a right to report what one *believes* to be true. But this gap is bridged by Orwell's clarification that free speech is a right to report 'as truthfully as is consistent with the ignorance, bias and self-deception from which every observer necessarily suffers'. Orwell recognises the many limitations of the human psychological condition. We are highly epistemically fallible. Moreover, freedom of speech cannot protect *only* the right to say true things. This could squash expression by anyone humble enough to recognise that they may be mistaken on a matter about which they wish to speak. It is not viable – nor, in Orwell's view, desirable – for freedom of speech to cover only true speech. But he seems to think it is both viable and desirable for freedom of speech to cover only speech that aims at truth, or at the very least only cover speech that does not aim at telling lies or falsehoods.

At this point one might object that this makes freedom of speech far too narrow a freedom, for much of our speech seeks to do things other than report. Orwell seems to foresee this objection. Presumably, this is part of why he specifies that the freedoms of speech and press cover more than 'straightforward "reportage"'. Rather, he has a capacious conception of what kind of speech and writing can aim at expressing what we have seen, heard and felt and what we believe to be true. Indeed, he thinks this kind of speech extends to 'every literary level' and likely to 'every one of the arts', presumably including highly abstract forms of artistic expression.

One may provide another objection, however, that this makes freedom of speech far too narrow a freedom because it does not protect lies nor other forms of reporting that aim to conceal or show deliberate indifference to the truth. Here, the Orwellian response seems to be quite different. Orwell seems to accept that free speech does not protect such things but to deny that this is a bad thing. This is the perspective he seems to have in mind when he says: 'What is needed is the right to print *what one believes to be true*, without having to fear bullying or blackmail from any side' (*CWGO* XVIII: 443; emphasis added) and: 'What matters is that in England we do possess juridical liberty of the press, which makes it possible *to utter one's true opinions fearlessly* in papers of comparatively small circulation' (*CELJ* 4: 241-242; emphasis added).

David Dwan has noted how this same perspective on the importance of being able to say what one thinks is true underlies the famous Orwellian aphorism from *Nineteen Eighty-Four* that 'Freedom is the freedom to say that two plus two make four. If that is granted, all else follows.' Dwan puts the matter as follows:

> The key thing here, some argue, is that we should be free to say our sums, not that they should be correct. But this seems to miss Orwell's point. Free speech is important but it is not enough; as the trolls and the cyber-thugs reveal each day, freedom of expression is a dangerous licence when it is severed

from any commitment to truth. Such freedom erodes freedom itself, undermining our ability to account for ourselves and to hold others to account. Orwell was wrong about many things, but he was right to suggest that a world that turns its back upon truth also gives two fingers to freedom (Dwan 2018a).

I agree with Dwan, especially if we read him as using the terms 'free speech' and 'freedom of expression' in a common twenty-first century manner as meaning something like the ability to say whatever one wants. However, from the perspective of trying to elucidate Orwell's conception of free speech, another way of putting a similar point presents itself: freedom to say what one wants is important, but protecting speech severed from a commitment to truth is not what freedom of speech is about. On the Orwellian conception, freedom of speech, at its core, is about protecting the ability to say and write what one believes to be true, or more generally protecting the ability to say and write that which honestly expresses or reflects one's perspectives, feelings or experiences.

As is the case of intellectual freedom, there are close connections between Orwell's ideas about free speech and his views about the nature of literature and the role of writers. This shows up in some of his most important works on literature, such as his statement in 'Literature and totalitarianism' that 'The first thing that we ask of a writer is that he shall not tell lies, that he shall say what he really thinks, what he really feels. The worst thing we can say about a work of art is that it is insincere' (*CELJ* 2: 134). Similarly, in 'The prevention of literature', he writes: 'Everything in our age conspires to turn the writer, and every other kind of artist as well, into a minor official, working on themes handed down from above and never telling what seems to him the whole of the truth' (*CELJ* 4: 60). Glenn Burgess illuminates the underlying logic connecting Orwell's views on free speech and on the responsibilities of writers: 'It was freedom, especially the freedom to write and say what you thought, that mattered most to Orwell, in part because this sort of freedom was fundamental for someone who lived by writing and cared to write with integrity' (Burgess 2023: 122).

While I think a holistic look at Orwell's corpus makes it fairly clear that he took the freedom to say what one believes to be true to be at the heart of free speech, that observation alone risks making his thoughts on free speech tidier than they in fact were. There is sometimes a second conception of free speech in his writing. This second conception is more frequently promoted by those quoting Orwell's claim that 'If liberty means anything at all, it means the right to tell people what they do not want to hear' ('The freedom of the press'). Granted, this is a statement about the value of liberty

PAPER

generally, not specifically freedom of speech. But surely Orwell saw freedom of speech as a, if not the, crucial component of liberty. Besides, he elsewhere said, in a very similar vein, that 'freedom of the press, if it means anything at all, means the freedom to criticize and oppose' (*CELJ* 4: 59).

But sometimes what people do not want to hear are lies and one can criticise and oppose the truth just as one can falsehoods. This seems to suggest that at least freedom of the press, if not also freedom of speech, includes the right to lie and to criticise and oppose the truth. But this seems to be in tension with the Orwellian ideas covered earlier that 'the controversy over freedom of speech and of the Press is at bottom a controversy of the desirability, or otherwise, of telling lies' and that 'What is needed is the right to print what one believes to be true, without having to fear bullying or blackmail from any side.' What is the best way to understand what is going on here?

One option would be to conclude that this is merely an instance of Orwell being inconsistent. Orwell's brilliance is not typically thought to rest on his consistency or systematic thinking. Indeed, it should not surprise us if he had various narrower and broader conceptions of liberty, intellectual freedom and free speech in mind when he wrote at different times. Given his love of individualism and unorthodoxy, it is at least plausible to think that he believed that, on some level, even the liar deserved some speech and press freedom – especially when that liar was unorthodox and unpowerful. Perhaps this is part of the answer.

But there is a better way of resolving the apparent tension in Orwell's writing about free speech and about freedom more generally. This solution begins by taking seriously his claim in 'Why I write' (1946) that 'Every line of serious work that I have written since 1936 has been written, directly or indirectly, *against* totalitarianism and *for* democratic socialism, as I understand it' (*CELJ* 1: 5). It seems that, in so doing, he wrote with a constant enemy in mind: totalitarianism. If we have that enemy in mind when reading all of his claims about liberty, free speech and the free press, his thinking appears more consistent. What does the totalitarian not want to hear? Criticism, opposition, the truth. These are antithetical to totalitarianism's need for complete control at the expense of truth. The totalitarian does not want people reporting matters truthfully or as they have seen, heard and felt them. The totalitarian wants people to report matters as the totalitarian says they are, regardless of what people have heard, seen or felt. In short, the totalitarian does not want people to say what they believe to be true. This is to show loyalty to truth over loyalty to the totalitarian state. Similarly, the ability to criticise and oppose the totalitarian – who rejects the concept of objective truth in favour of ultimate power – is the ability to tell the truth despite pressure to speak, instead, the totalitarian's lies. This helps explain the apparent tension in Orwell's claims about free speech. In resolving the tension this way, it gives priority to the view that his central understanding of free speech was an ability to speak what one believes to be true. Burgess summarises the matter well: 'Free speech was, in Orwell's eyes, the willingness to speak frankly, to speak one's mind, to refuse orthodoxy of any sort. When this honesty of speech was characteristic of a culture, accountability would follow. The lie could not escape exposure' (Burgess 2023: 6).

NON-GOVERNMENTAL THREATS TO FREE SPEECH

If the core of Orwell's conception of free speech is the ability to say what one thinks is true, then it would be natural for him to find anything that hinders the ability of people to say what they think is true to be a hindrance to free speech. His writings reveal that he thought a great many forces hindered the ability of people to say what they think is true. Thus, unsurprisingly, he also had a long list of forces that he thought hindered free speech. This is significant because traditional defences of free speech often implicitly, if not explicitly, treat government as the sole real threat to free speech. He saw the government as just one of many threats to free speech.

This section uses Orwell's own words to identify a set of entities beyond the government that he viewed as threats to free speech. Notably, many of these threats are associated with capitalist economic structures. Thus, identifying what Orwell considered the full set of threats to free speech helps show the consistency in his fight for both a free speech society and a democratic socialist society.

The existence of multifarious threats to intellectual liberty and free speech is a key theme in his essay, 'The prevention of literature'. Orwell puts the matter bluntly writing that 'in England the immediate enemies of truthfulness, and hence of freedom of thought, are the press lords, the film magnates, and the bureaucrats, but that on a long view the weakening of the desire for liberty among the intellectuals themselves is the most serious symptom of all' (*CELJ* 4: 64). Once again, he shows how a commitment to truthfulness is central to his notion of intellectual liberty. The enemies of truth are the enemies of free thought. Here he identifies four discrete threats to free thought (and, given his other commitments, thus also threats to free speech): the press lords, film magnates, bureaucrats and intellectuals with their weakening desire for liberty. Orwell provides a more detailed explanation of why these forces are threats to free thought and speech:

> In our age, the idea of intellectual liberty is under attack from two directions. On the one side are its theoretical enemies, the

apologists of totalitarianism, and on the other its immediate, practical enemies, monopoly and bureaucracy. Any writer or journalist who wants to retain his integrity finds himself thwarted by the general drift of society rather than by active persecution. The sort of things that are working against him are the concentration of the press in the hands of a few rich men, the grip of monopoly on radio and the films, the unwillingness of the public to spend money on books, making it necessary for nearly every writer to earn part of his living by hackwork, the encroachment of official bodies like the M.O.I. and the British Council, which help the writer to keep alive but also waste his time and dictate his opinions, and the continuous war atmosphere of the past ten years, whose distorting effects no one has been able to escape (ibid: 59-60).

As shown elsewhere in his corpus, Orwell saw totalitarianism as the most significant threat to free speech in the sense that it sought to eliminate free speech and thought *completely*. But here he identifies another sense in which monopoly and bureaucracy were a greater threat to free thought because they were forces that were actually operating in his own time and country. Thus, monopoly and bureaucracy were the 'immediate, practical enemies' of free speech given their current power, even if the level of suppression they threatened was less than the total suppression of successful totalitarian rule.

It is noteworthy but unsurprising that Orwell pivots directly from the threats to intellectual liberty to threats to the integrity of a writer or journalist. No doubt the kind of integrity he has in mind here is integrity through intellectual honesty. All the threats to free thought that he identifies here have in common that they exert pressure on the writer to say what the writer thinks others want them to say rather than what they really think. When the gatekeeping is strong enough or the economic pressures significant enough, Orwell recognises that this pressure can come to have a coercive function.

As already shown, Orwell did not perceive all threats to free speech and thought to be of the same kind. It is useful to distinguish at least three levels of threat that he generally kept separate. There were threats to:

(i) the ability to reach an audience,

(ii) the ability to say things freely at all, and

(iii) the ability even to think freely.

Orwell saw totalitarianism as a threat to all three. Many of the other threats he identified were only to (i) or, occasionally, to (i) and (ii). Thus, the other threats were less extreme but more proximate. Orwell expresses some of these differences writing that:

> ... totalitarianism has not fully triumphed anywhere. Our own society is still, broadly speaking, liberal. To exercise your right of free speech you have to fight against economic pressure and against strong sections of public opinion, but not, as yet, against a secret police force. You can say or print almost anything so long as you are willing to do it in a hole-and-corner way' (*CELJ* 4: 70).

Orwell acknowledges that, despite economic and social pressure, one can engage in (ii) and (iii), but by being required to voice certain views in 'a hole-and-corner way', economic and social pressure may remove one's ability to do (i). These distinctions track contemporary debates over the nature and scope of free speech. There is disagreement, for example, about when, if ever, removing someone's access to a platform from which to speak violates freedom of speech (cf Chemerinsky and Gillman 2017; Simpson and Srinivasan 2018; Satta 2021).

Orwell also distinguishes how bureaucratic and market forces in England secure a limited form of free speech while suppressing a more robust form of free speech:

> What matters is that in England we do possess juridical liberty of the press, which makes it possible to utter one's true opinions fearlessly in papers of comparatively small circulation. It is vitally important to hang on to that. But no Royal Commission can make the big-circulation press much better than it is, however much it manipulates the methods of control. We shall have a serious and truthful popular press when public opinion actively demands it. Till then, if the news is not distorted by businessmen it will be distorted by bureaucrats, who are only one degree better (ibid: 241-42).

Here Orwell recognises the vital importance of 'juridical liberty of the press', which seems to amount to a legal freedom to say as you want, while simultaneously recognising the limiting effects forces like monopoly capitalism and bureaucracy have on free expression. But he is still keenly aware of the significant ways in which market forces shape our ability to think and speak freely. This is shown clearly by his reasoning in 'Poetry and the microphone' (1945):

> Broadcasting is what it is, not because there is something inherently vulgar, silly and dishonest about the whole apparatus of microphone and transmitter, but because all the broadcasting that now happens all over the world is under the control of governments or great monopoly companies which

are actively interested in maintaining the status quo and therefore in preventing the common man from becoming too intelligent. Something of the same kind has happened to the cinema, which, like the radio, made its appearance during the monopoly stage of capitalism and is fantastically expensive to operate. In all the arts the tendency is similar. More and more the channels of production are under control of bureaucrats, whose aim is to destroy the artist or at least to castrate him (*CELJ* 2: 334-335).

Orwell's recognition of the threat that 'great monopoly companies' pose to intellectual freedom and freedom of speech has proven remarkably prescient. His insights are highly relevant to those worried about the power that social media companies and mammoth news conglomerates play in shaping public thought and public discourse. His work can be viewed as a forerunner to political economy approaches to journalism, communication studies, law, philosophy, and elsewhere about the significance of attention and controlling what it is that people attend to (cf. McCombs and Shaw 1993; Wu 2016; Castro and Pham 2020). For, according to Orwell: 'The freedom of the Press in Britain was always something of a fake, because in the last resort, money controls opinion; still, so long as the legal right to say what you like exists, there are always loopholes for an unorthodox writer' (*CELJ* 1: 337).

LEGAL AND SOCIAL FREEDOM TO SPEAK

In examining the wide range of what Orwell considered threats to free speech – including many non-governmental organisations and persons – it becomes clear that he viewed free speech as more than just a legal right. For Orwell, it seems, true freedom of thought and speech required participating in a society that permitted one to think and speak views that were unpopular. This understanding of free thought and speech helps explain his disdain for 'orthodoxy sniffers' and others who required conformity of thought or speech on matters of importance. It is deeply in line with his views that 'What is needed is the right to print what one believes to be true, without having to fear bullying or blackmail from any side' (*CWGO*, XVIII: 443) and that 'To exercise your right of free speech you have to fight against economic pressure and against strong sections of public opinion' (*CELJ* 4:70).

Given that Orwell extended his conception of free speech to include cultural and social freedom to speak and think freely, it is natural to apply Orwell's thinking to questions raised in current debates over 'cancel culture' and 'no platforming' campaigns (cf Romano 2021; Srinivasan 2023). However, it is less clear when Orwell might consider cancelling someone or depriving them of a platform to be a restriction on free speech. On the one hand, he railed against those who sought to control the public narrative through economic or social coercion. This might suggest he would have been wary of using social pressure through cancelling or no platforming to limit the reach of speech or ideas. But there are several other considerations that suggest he might see cancelling or no platforming as permissible, depending on the substance of the views and the modes by which such cancellation or deplatforming might occur.

First, Orwell had little tolerance for lying or indifference to truth. Often those who are denied platforms or who lose sponsorship for their speech experience these consequences because they are liars, ill informed, or indifferent to truth. Orwell's deep commitment to allowing people to say, in good faith, what they believe to be true does not seem to extend to facilitating the speech of those acting in bad faith. Second, Orwell thought there was at least some room for platform providers, such as newspapers, magazines and book publishers, to make editorial judgements as to what kind of content they would approve. For example, from his perspective as the literary editor at *Tribune*, Orwell wrote: 'Obviously we cannot print contributions that grossly violate *Tribune's* policy. Even in the name of free speech a Socialist paper cannot, for instance, throw open its columns to antisemitic propaganda' (*CELJ* 3: 312). It seems natural to use this line of reasoning to suggest that it is obvious that democratic institutions, including universities or publishing houses committed to liberty and democracy, should not throw open their doors to propaganda rooted in antisemitism, Islamophobia, racism, sexism or other pernicious ideologies.

Significantly, Orwell combined his position about the need for *Tribune* to exclude certain views based on content (e.g., antisemitic propaganda), with a general policy of trying to include a wide range of viewpoints and perspectives. Still writing about *Tribune*, he noted: 'Looking through our list of contributors, I find among them Catholics, Communists, Trotskyists, Anarchists, pacifists, left-wing Conservatives, and Labour Party supporters of all colours' (ibid). Orwell combines a commitment to ideological diversity with a recognition that platforms that have a guiding purpose or perspective must use some editorial discretion in declining to provide platforms for certain objectively odious views.

Orwell's position is not without its internal tensions. How can one both promote a culture of free speech where people are neither afraid to say what they believe nor restricted to doing so in a 'hole-and-corner way' while also granting the powers that be the editorial discretion to deny a platform for views antithetical to their purposes? I know of no place where he clearly resolves this tension.

But, in this context, it is useful to acknowledge his commitment to the idea of objective truth (cf *CELJ* 2: 258). Orwell was not a pure proceduralist. That is to say, Orwell did not think that fair procedure alone was all that mattered. He thought that, as a matter of substance, some views were better than others. And he seemed to think in one's role as the custodian for a platform – such as *Tribune* – it was appropriate to make some substantive judgements about what content should be permitted. This does not mean on its own, of course, that he thought there were views that should be banned from *all* platforms, even those with small circulations or from public forums open to all-comers. Generally, he was highly tolerant of dissident, unpopular and odious speech, so long as the speaker was sincere. But even this tolerance was subject to limitation.

LIMITS ON FREE SPEECH

While Orwell's conception of free speech varies in some important ways from many popular modern conceptions, it is no doubt still fitting to call him a champion of free speech. But like any reasonable champion of free speech, Orwell did not see the free speech right as completely unlimited. As shown in the previous section, he allowed that the social and cultural dimension of free speech could be limited in certain narrow ways based on the editorial discretion of those who controlled access to various platforms. But he also seems to allow for even legal restrictions on free speech. For example, Orwell wrote in 'The freedom of the press' that 'If the intellectual liberty which without a doubt has been one of the distinguishing marks of western civilisation means anything at all, it means that everyone shall have the right to say and to print what he believes to be the truth, provided only that it does not harm the rest of the community in some quite unmistakable way.' Noting this, David Dwan aptly concludes that while 'Orwell was certainly an advocate of free speech' this 'support for the principle was not unqualified' such that Orwell saw freedom of speech as 'constrained by the notion of harm – and what constituted harm was left open' (Dwan 2018b: 258-259).

Orwell did, indeed, leave this matter open. He never explained what types of harms would allow for speech restrictions in which sort of way. But it was clear that he thought some restrictions were warranted, although he probably condoned fewer restrictions than many of his contemporaries. This is exemplified by the position he takes in 'The freedom of the press' about the imprisonment of the British fascist leader Oswald Mosley in the 1940s: 'In 1940 it was perfectly right to intern Mosley, whether or not he had committed any technical crime. We were fighting for our lives and could not allow a possible quisling to go free. To keep him shut up, without trial, in 1943 was an outrage.' Glenn Burgess summarises the matter nicely: 'Orwell consistently defended a minimalist view of what limits should be placed on free expression, and he consistently defended the right to be heard even of those who disgusted or appalled, whether morally or politically' (Burgess 2023: 147).

CONCLUSION

Orwell was a staunch defender of the freedoms of speech, press and thought. But his conception of those freedoms is much more nuanced and counter-cultural than is often acknowledged by the pundits who mine small chunks of his writing to bolster their pre-existing views. The essence of free speech for Orwell was the freedom to say what you believed to be true, without fear of legal sanctions and without undue social or economic pressure. Because he typically thought of free speech in these terms, his writing about free speech says little about the speech of the liar or the wilfully ignorant speaker. Thus, a simple appeal to Orwell cannot answer the complex contemporary questions about the extent to which free speech should protect even prevaricators and the epistemically insouciant.

Orwell was not a particularly systematic thinker – although he did have a consistent set of themes and ideas that he wrote about. Nor was he particularly consistent in how he used terms. Nor was he inclined to provide clear definitions of those terms. These features of his thought and writing make critical philosophical analysis of Orwell challenging, including philosophical analysis of his conception of free speech. But this paper rests on the assumption that the challenge is worth it.

ACKNOWLEDGEMENTS

Thanks to the Wayne State University Humanities Center, which helped fund this research through a faculty fellowship, to Ryan Biehl for valuable research assistance, to Richard Lance Keeble and Tim Crook for helpful editorial suggestions, and to Nathan Waddell for the invitation to contribute to this issue.

NOTES

[1] While Orwell sees totalitarianism as a threat to free thought, he seems to view free thought and socialism as highly compatible. For example, Orwell claims that 'we believe that anyone who upholds the freedom of the intellect, in this age of lies and regimentation, is not serving the cause of Socialism so badly either' (*CELJ* 3: 312). For a detailed and compelling case for the compatibility between Orwell's commitments to socialism and free speech, see Burgess 2023

[2] There are exceptions to this generalisation, of course, such as laws against perjury, defamation and false advertising. But they are just that: exceptions

[3] A notable example of this position can be found in the 2012 Supreme Court decision in *United States v. Alvarez*, 567 US 709 (2012)

MARK SATTA

REFERENCES

Burgess, Glenn (2023) *George Orwell's Perverse Humanity: Socialism and Free Speech*. New York: Bloomsbury Academic

Castro, Clinton and Pham, Adam K. (2020) Is the attention economy noxious?, *Philosophers' Imprint*, Vol. 20, No. 17 pp 1-13

Chemerinsky, Erwin and Gillman, Howard (2017) *Free Speech on Campus*. New Haven: Yale University Press

Dwan, David (2018a) Orwell was right: Free speech is important but it is not enough, *Guardian*, 21 October. Available online at https://www.theguardian.com/commentisfree/2018/oct/21/orwell-free-speech-important-not-enough

Dwan, David (2018b) *Liberty, Equality, and Humbug: Orwell's Political Ideals*, Oxford: Oxford University Press

McCombs, Maxwell E. and Shaw, Donald L. (1993) The evolution of agenda-setting research: Twenty-five years in the marketplace of ideas, *Journal of Communication*, Vol. 43, No. 2 pp 58-67

Orwell, George (1968) *The Collected Essays, Journalism, and Letters* (*CEJL*), 4 Vols, Orwell, Sonia and Angus, Ian (eds) New York: Harcourt, Brace & World (reprinted by Godine Publishing in 2000)

Orwell, George (1972) The freedom of the press, *Times Literary Supplement*. Available online at https://www.orwellfoundation.com/the-orwell-foundation/orwell/essays-and-other-works/the-freedom-of-the-press/

Orwell, George (1998) *The Complete Works of George Orwell* (*CWGO*), XX Vols, Davison, Peter (ed.) London: Secker & Warburg

Romano, Aja (2021) The second wave of 'cancel culture', *Vox*, 5 May. Available online at https://www.vox.com/22384308/cancel-culture-free-speech-accountability-debate

Satta, Mark (2021) Multi-forum institutions, the power of platforms, and disinviting speakers from university campuses, *Public Affairs Quarterly*, Vol. 35, No. 2 pp 94-118

Satta, Mark (2022) George Orwell, *The Internet Encyclopedia of Philosophy*. Available online at https://iep.utm.edu/george-orwell/

Simpson, Robert Mark and Srinivasan, Amia (2018) No platforming, Lackey, Jennifer (ed.) *Academic Freedom*, Oxford: Oxford University Press pp 186-210

Srinivasan, Amia (2023) Cancelled, *London Review of Books*, Vol. 45, No. 13, 29 June. Available online at https://www.lrb.co.uk/the-paper/v45/n13/amia-srinivasan/cancelled

Wu, Tim (2016) *The Attention Merchants: The Epic Scramble to Get Inside Our Heads*, New York: Knopf

NOTE ON THE CONTRIBUTOR

Mark Satta is Assistant Professor of Philosophy and Linguistics at Wayne State University. His research interests include epistemology, philosophy of language, philosophy of law, free speech law, and social and political philosophy. He is interested in how Orwell's writing addresses these and other areas in philosophy.

PAPER

The Labyrinths of *Nineteen Eighty-Four*

SELINA-MARIE SCHOLZ
GEOFF RODOREDA

The labyrinth is mentioned five times in George Orwell's Nineteen Eighty-Four, *drawing attention to distinct metaphorical and material structures that the protagonist, Winston Smith, encounters, puzzles over and becomes lost in. These labyrinths function, as the trope of the labyrinth does in literary texts generally, to signal disorientation, impenetrability, the inexplicable and the complex. But* Nineteen Eighty-Four's *labyrinths do more: importantly, each is a construction of the regime, and each, introduced into the text in a specific order, serves to index the regime's all-encompassing control of everything, from small to large, from individual minds to the entire spaces of a city. This paper thus analyses an aspect of Orwell's masterwork that has not been examined to date, its literal as well as its broader literary labyrinths and mazes, offering new readerly insights into the novel's various ambiguities and seeming dead-ends.*

Key words: Orwell, labyrinth, *Nineteen Eighty-Four*, Room 101, maze, O'Brien, Winston Smith, minotaur

In her study of the 'uniqueness, the intensity, the breadth, and the coherence of the vision' that George Orwell communicates in *Nineteen Eighty-Four*, Erika Gottlieb alludes to the labyrinthine nature of Orwell's 'masterpiece' novel (Gottlieb 1992: 6-7). In comparing Orwell's despairing vision to that of Franz Kafka's, Gottlieb argues that most critics seem to 'view the novelist's craft as a kind of game, played in an underground labyrinth, which, unbeknownst to the writer, has several exits … The writer's performance will then be judged acceptable only if he or she finds an approved exit that leads towards a conclusion of hope, acceptance, or affirmation' (ibid). Gottlieb goes on to argue that *Nineteen Eighty-Four* should not be judged as flawed, as it so often has been, merely because of its apparent bleakness. But in her passing allusion to the crafting of a novel as potentially akin to the construction of an 'underground labyrinth', Gottlieb unwittingly establishes a connection between the figure of the labyrinth and the structure of *Nineteen Eighty-Four*: it turns out the labyrinth is quite prominent in Orwell's final novel.

SELINA-MARIE SCHOLZ

GEOFF RODOREDA

In Chapter 3 of *Nineteen Eighty-Four*, Winston is woken from dreams about his mother by the telescreen to do his morning exercises. His mind wanders, so that his dreams, the patchy memories of his boyhood, and his thoughts about the mind games of the regime, become the focus of the chapter. As Winston is ordered to 'Stand easy' and take a short break, he is distracted again: 'His mind slid away into the labyrinthine world of doublethink' (Orwell 2013 [1949]: 40). This is the first mention of labyrinth in the novel. It is repeated (as labyrinth, labyrinthine) four other times hereafter, making labyrinths a conspicuous element of *Nineteen Eighty-Four*, though an element that has not been investigated in the novel to date. Not only is the labyrinth evocative of important and varying imagery at each of its mentions, such imagery also traces a trajectory – a labyrinthine path, as the novel progresses – from the contained and internal geographies of Winston's mind and the conundrums of doublethink to the more expansive spaces of the ministries of the regime and the city of London. That is to say, there are a number of literal and metaphorical labyrinths in this novel: they are labyrinths of the mind, they are physically built into the structure of the various ministries, they exist in the novel's urban spaces. However, beyond these specifically-named labyrinths, there is one central labyrinth built into the plot structure of the novel that Winston wanders through, finally to arrive at a centre, Room 101, to meet his minotaur in the form of O'Brien, the paradoxical monster that Winston fails to slay. This paper investigates the labyrinths that exist within 'a world turned upside down and inside out' that is the storyworld of Orwell's *Nineteen Eighty-Four* (Waddell 2020a: 18). Although first, we need to background the labyrinth as a mythical and architectural construct, and then consider its wide-ranging literal and metaphorical foundations and manifestations in literary texts.

LABYRINTH AS LITERARY INVENTION

The labyrinth is not a construction of the ancient world that has been discovered and definitively named by modern archaeologists; it is first and foremost a literary invention. The earliest structure named as a labyrinth, described by the Greek writer Herodotus in the fifth century B.C., was a large building of some three thousand rooms in Egypt, probably constructed around 4000 years ago (Matthews 1922: 6). Reports of labyrinthine constructions are also found in Etruscan, (other) Italian, British, and Northern European civilisations (ibid). But it is the story of the Cretan labyrinth that has been most widely represented in architecture, art, song and story from ancient times, through the Middle Ages to the present day. In short, according to Greek mythology (Ovid 1958; Plutarch

1914), the labyrinth was a maze-like structure built by Daedalus for King Minos II of Crete in order to imprison a monstrous minotaur, the product of a union between King Minos's wife Pasiphaë and a white bull. This half-human, half-bull creature fed on human flesh and could not be tamed. Children were sacrificed into the labyrinth to appease the minotaur's cravings. That is until the arrival of the hero, Theseus: with the help of a guide, the king's daughter, Ariadne, Theseus entered the labyrinth using a ball of string to mark his pathway to its centre, where he slayed the minotaur and followed the string back out to the labyrinth's entrance (see also Matthews 1922; Kern 1982; Mercatante and Dow 2009). Thus, key elements of the Cretan labyrinth include a circuitous, disorienting, potentially imprisoning, maze-like structure; a traveller involved in a hazardous quest; a guide; and a dangerous, half-human/half-animal creature that lurks within.

In contemporary English, 'labyrinth' and 'maze' are defined synonymously (cf. *The Oxford English Dictionary*, Vol. VIII p. 564 and Vol. IX p. 507) and are often used to mean the same thing (Doob 1992: 1). However, it is important to distinguish between unicursal and multicursal labyrinths. Unicursal describes a single-path structure, comprising a circuitous route but with no dead ends or false alleyways. The pathway of the maze itself becomes 'an infallible guide' for those who commit to endure the laborious journey to its centre (ibid: 3, 48, 50). One enters and exits a unicursal labyrinth at the same location: Daedalus's labyrinth is, therefore, unicursal in structure. For Umberto Eco, this classical Greek labyrinth:

> … does not allow anyone to get lost: you go in, arrive at the center, and then from the center you reach the exit. This is why in the center there is the Minotaur; if he were not there the story would have no zest, it would be a mere stroll. Terror is born … from the fact that you do not know where you will arrive or what the Minotaur will do (Eco 1994: 525).

A multicursal labyrinth, on the other hand, is constructed with many paths, dead ends and blind alleys, built in order to 'confuse and frustrate' (Doob 1992: 3). Such labyrinths model a 'trial-and-error process' (Eco 1994: 525). As Wendy Faris puts it: 'In a unicursal labyrinth, the explorer's powers of endurance are tested; in a multicursal one, [her] ingenuity comes into play as well. The traveler in the unicursal labyrinth feels [herself] subject to a power beyond [her] own; in the multicursal labyrinth [she] also suffers the responsibility of choice' (Faris 1988: 3). The historian Hermann Kern argues that the journey through any labyrinth-like structure is akin to the enactment of an initiation ritual, of a death and a rebirth (Kern 1982: 26-30).

SELINA-MARIE SCHOLZ

GEOFF RODOREDA

Although based on stories thousands of years old, the labyrinth as a design remains beguiling and mysterious, an architectural structure specifically built to challenge, amaze, bewilder and confuse. Theodore Ziolkowski attributes its renewed popularity in the twentieth century to the excavation work begun in 1900 by the archaeologist Arthur Evans at Knossos on Crete (Ziolkowski 2008: 11, 70). Evans unearthed walls, coins and other objects plastered with imprints of labyrinths, motifs of bulls and minotaur-like images, and a palace of complex architecture, which he concluded may well have been the labyrinth of Greek myth (Matthews 1922: 29-35). Ziolkowski argues that reports of Evans's artefactual discoveries on Crete 'captivated the popular imagination to an extent matched by few other works from classical antiquity' (2008: 12), and that from the early decades of the twentieth century, artists, writers and philosophers 'discovered in classical, and specifically Cretan, myth a marvelous vehicle for the exploration and depiction of thoroughly modern concerns' (ibid: 23-24).

For the literary scholar Penelope Reed Doob, the labyrinth, in stories from antiquity to the present day, is often associated with 'enforced circuitousness; disorientation; the idea of planned chaos; the *bivium* or critical choice between two paths; inextricability; intricacy; complexity' (Doob 1992: 2). Faris highlights 'the persistence of the labyrinth as a compelling and versatile literary image', which developed through the twentieth century in close conjunction with the visual arts, 'so that it often mediates conceptually between symbolic and iconic modes of representation' (Faris 1988: 1, 2). Because the labyrinth encompasses opposing forces, such as 'order and confusion, reason and passion, playfulness and fear', it can 'symbolize their combination in a work of art as well as their presence in the exterior world' (Faris 1988: 1). Indeed, Doob points to the ubiquity of the labyrinth in literature more broadly, arguing that all writers are 'maze-treaders' in their research work, 'maze-makers' in their design and construction of a story, and that the text itself is a 'labyrinth of words' through which readers wander (Doob 1992: xii). In a similar manner, Harold Bloom argues that 'all truly literary text is labyrinthine, interwoven, interlaced,' and that all literary thinking 'is akin to walking a labyrinth' (Bloom 2009: xvi). Presumably, this opens up all literary texts to examination for their 'labyrinthicity' (Doob 1992: 2). Faris, in her study of labyrinths in modern fiction, recommends, instead, a narrower approach:

> I have confined my discussion of structural as well as symbolic uses of the labyrinth to works where the term *labyrinth* or a related … reference appears in the text, so that the presence of

a particular pattern is clearly indicated and thus thematized in varying degrees. Otherwise, given too much latitude, the term *labyrinthine* expands to cover all but the simplest narratives (Faris 1988: 12).

This paper applies Faris's methodology to the examination of labyrinths in Orwell's *Nineteen Eighty-Four*, given they are explicitly referenced in the text, and given that such 'clearly indicated' labyrinths allow for the unearthing of more hidden ones.

THE LABYRINTHINE WORLD OF DOUBLETHINK

Holding fast to Faris's thread, we now draw attention to the first of *Nineteen Eighty-Four*'s five specific mentions of labyrinth. As stated, in Chapter 3, as Winston is ordered to take a short break from the exacting physicality of compulsory morning exercises, 'His mind slid away into the labyrinthine world of doublethink' (Orwell 2013 [1949]: 40). Doublethink becomes *Nineteen Eighty-Four*'s most significant of 'antinomies' (Freedman 1984). It is a concept Winston is only fully able to grasp near the end of the novel. Doublethink, 'a form of controlled schizophrenia' (Gottlieb 1992: 117), is the regime's 'most important resource for undermining human freedom' (Martin 1984: 319). As explained more succinctly, later, in Goldstein's book, '*Doublethink* means the power of holding two contradictory beliefs in one's mind simultaneously, and accepting both of them' (op cit: 244). Such a 'reconciling [of] contradictions', admittedly a 'vast system of mental cheating', is foundational to both the regime's 'seizure of power' and its maintaining control (ibid: 246, 245, 247). It is significant that the first explanation of the 'world of doublethink', in Chapter 3, should be described as 'labyrinthine' (ibid: 40), for labyrinths are inextricably linked with doubling and doubleness. They are 'full of ambiguity, their circuitous design prescribes a constant doubling back … [They] encode the very principle of doubleness, contrariety, paradox, *concordia discors*' (Doob 1990: 1, 2). Orwell's doublethink is labyrinthine in structure, but also in the sense that labyrinths may signal disorientation and puzzlement. For Winston, at this stage of his resistance to the regime, doublethink is still puzzling. Such puzzlement is stylistically revealed not only in the *content* of the sentence that immediately follows the one linking labyrinths with doublethink, but also in the perplexity of the sentence, its labyrinthine *form*, wherein Winston ponders the meaning of doublethink:

> To know and not to know, to be conscious of complete truthfulness while telling carefully constructed lies, to hold simultaneously two opinions which cancelled out, knowing them to be contradictory and believing in both of them, to use

SELINA-MARIE SCHOLZ

GEOFF RODOREDA

logic against logic, to repudiate morality while laying claim to it, to believe that democracy was impossible and that the Party was the guardian of democracy, to forget whatever it was necessary to forget, then to draw it back into memory again at the moment when it was needed, and then promptly to forget it again: and above all, to apply the same process to the process itself (Orwell 2013 [1949]: 40-41)

In this twisting, tangled sentence, 106 words long, Orwell artfully reconciles content and form. Constructed as a jumble of phrases, commas, stop-starts and false leads, the sentence itself is a maze. Thus, form speaks to content as the reader slides away with Winston into a sentence whose very labyrinthine structure reflects the disorientations and paradoxes inherent in the concept of doublethink. Indeed, in literary labyrinths, as Faris explains, the 'iconic embodiment of the labyrinth … duplicates the form of the labyrinth in the structural design of the text; the placement of words, sentences, and ideas, and consequently the reader's progressive perception of them, traces a labyrinthine shape' (Faris 1988: 9). In Doob's taxonomy of metaphorical labyrinths, the labyrinth may also be a sign of 'impenetrability or inextricability' (Doob 1990: 6). This is what doublethink is for Winston, for now: a veritable labyrinth of language and thought, full of contradictions and paradoxes, contained in his *mind*. It is important here to note the spatial dimensions associated with the first mention of labyrinth in the novel; it is limited to the confined, internal spaces of Winston's mind. However, *Nineteen Eighty-Four*'s labyrinths are soon to expand and to become more material.

THE LABYRINTHS AT THE MINISTRY OF TRUTH

The second mention of labyrinth is in Chapter 4 of Part 1, which essentially details Winston's work at the Ministry of Truth. Winston puts the corrections he has made to any piece of documentation into a pneumatic tube, to be transported to another part of the Ministry: 'What happened in the unseen labyrinth to which the pneumatic tubes led, he did not know in detail, but he did know in general terms' (Orwell 2013 [1949]: 46). The narrator goes on to describe the elaborate assemblage and collation of documentary texts and sources that exist beyond Winston's office, behind the scenes, as it were, in the 'unseen labyrinth' of the Ministry of Truth. We are confronted with an image of a network of pipes or tubes, invisible and untraceable. The inextricability and impenetrability associated with the labyrinthine world of doublethink extends here to the more expansive architectural spaces of the Ministry: its hidden networks of distribution and filtration are also a conundrum. However, unlike the labyrinth of the mind, this second labyrinth is a mechanical construction, assembled to deliver information from one part of a Ministry to another. As a physical structure it is therefore more than merely associative or metaphorical; the tubes, unicursal by construction (for the documentation is transported to a specific place), more closely resemble the materiality of a real labyrinth. Labyrinths in *Nineteen Eighty-Four* are taking shape and becoming larger.

In the next chapter, Chapter 5, as Winston lunches in the canteen, the labyrinthine structures of the Ministry of Truth are invoked again. Winston drifts off at one point to consider that, 'The little beetle-like men who scuttle so nimbly through the labyrinthine corridors of Ministries … would never be vaporised' (ibid: 70). The *ministries*, now plural, are once again indexed for their labyrinthine or maze-like structure. It is not just information that disappears into the ministries' labyrinths, the corridors within these halls of power provide passage for anonymous and efficient insect-like bureaucrats to scurry to and fro. However, these officials are not lost in any maze; they know how to negotiate the hallways of the ministries. Such talent for maze-wandering would appear to ensure their survival, as they 'would never be vaporised'. But for outsiders like Winston, the 'labyrinthine corridors' of the various ministries 'reflect the mystifying strategies of the officials who govern them' (Waddell 2020b: 172). Later on, in Chapter 5 of Part 2 of the novel, there is a third reference to the labyrinthine nature of the Ministry of Truth when Winston is described as sitting in 'windowless, air-conditioned rooms' within 'the labyrinthine Ministry' (Orwell 2013 [1949]: 170). Three of the five specific mentions of labyrinth, then, are associated with ministries of the regime, emphasising their puzzling intricacy, their uniform knottiness, their indecipherability and their impenetrable reach over the regime's subjects. The labyrinthine features of Orwell's ministries echo the labyrinthine structure of a palace in a Jorge Luis Borges story, where 'corridors that led nowhere, unreachably high windows, grandly dramatic doors that opened onto monk-like cells or empty shafts' evoke repulsion and terror (1999: 423). Borges's narrator concludes that a labyrinth or a maze 'is a house built purposely to confuse men; its architecture, prodigal in symmetries, is made to serve that purpose' (ibid). Nathan Waddell notes that the 'fastidiously calibrated disorder' of the ministries' labyrinthine corridors, along with the dishevelled buildings, walls, streets and landscapes of *Nineteen Eighty-Four* (2020b: 171), amount to muddle and mess by design: 'their very tangledness, seemingly so random and haphazard, can be understood as yet another sign of the Party's grip on its population … In Oceania, mess is control' (ibid: 172).

SELINA-MARIE SCHOLZ

GEOFF RODOREDA

THE LABYRINTH OF THE CITYSCAPE

Orwell's labyrinths expand in dimension and intricacy as the novel proceeds. They exist firstly as the conundrum of doublethink in Winston's mind, then as material structures, principally within the Ministry of Truth, where Winston works. More expansive still, then, is the final, specifically named labyrinth of *Nineteen Eighty-Four*: the streets of the city of London. In Chapter 8 of Part 1, which tells of Winston's meeting with the proles, Winston decides to skip another evening at the Community Centre: 'On impulse he had turned away from the bus-stop and wandered off into the labyrinth of London, first south, then east, then north again, losing himself among unknown streets and hardly bothering in which direction he was going' (2013 [1949]: 95). Unlike the labyrinth of the mind and those of the ministries, this is a much larger labyrinth – that of a cityscape – that Winston wanders into himself. It serves the purpose of a maze in which Winston becomes disorientated and lost as he seeks out the wisdom of the proles. There is a precedent in Orwell's own writing in associating labyrinths with circuitous streetscapes. It suggests that Orwell was aware of and used the imagery of the labyrinth to signal circuitousness and disorientation before applying it strategically in *Nineteen Eighty-Four*.

In *The Road to Wigan Pier* (1937), Orwell writes of becoming lost himself in the labyrinthine back-streets of a northern English mining town. In the opening chapter, he reports that the darker side of British civilisation has produced 'labyrinthine slums and dark back kitchens with sickly, ageing people creeping round and round them like blackbeetles' (Orwell 2001 [1937]: 15). A little later he recounts: 'As you walk through the industrial towns you lose yourself in labyrinths of little brick houses blackened by smoke, festering in planless chaos round miry alleys and little cindered yards where there are stinking dust-bins and lines of grimy washing and half-ruinous wcs' (ibid: 47). The reference to slum dwellers creeping around 'like blackbeetles' in *Wigan Pier* calls to mind the 'beetle-like men who scuttle' through the labyrinthine corridors of the ministries in *Nineteen Eighty-Four*. Descriptions of walking 'round and round' slums and 'round miry alleys' are especially evocative of the circuitous twists and turns of a labyrinth. Significantly, in both *Wigan Pier* and *Nineteen Eighty-Four*, Orwell links the image of a labyrinth with the tangled messiness of the back streets of cities. Further, in both texts, labyrinths are directly associated with becoming lost, as an outsider, among the 'planless chaos' of streets 'unknown' that are principally inhabited by the working poor. However, in contradistinction to Orwell's own labyrinthine wanderings in *Wigan Pier*, Winston is not confronted in Oceania's London with the dark, festering poverty of 1930s northern slums – at least, poor living conditions are not the focus of the text. Although Winston is lost in a labyrinth of London streets, it is not a 'lostness' that invokes any kind of trepidation or fear: his wandering is voluntary, done with abandon. It allows him to embrace a temporary anonymity, to escape the surveillance of the regime and to meet and talk freely with the proles. In this context, Marcella Schmidt di Friedberg points out that in literary texts that connect the city with the labyrinth, 'The metaphor of the labyrinth … becomes a cartographic strategy for finding our way through the complex present-day city, exploring it, getting to know its spaces, overcoming our fears of it, and developing ways of coping with our sense of spatial orientation' (Schmidt di Friedberg 2018: 168).

For other twentieth-century writers like James Joyce, Walter Benjamin and Jorge Luis Borges, who all engage prominently with the architecture of labyrinths in their work, the contemporary city is the labyrinth of modernity, 'albeit a labyrinth that takes on new spatio-temporal forms' (ibid: 167). Again, as for Winston in *Nineteen Eighty-Four*, the streetscape labyrinths of Benjamin and Borges are not foreboding or initially menacing. As pointedly as for Orwell's Winston, Benjamin's city streets are 'the dwelling place of the collective' that effectively 'efface all traces of the individual' (Benjamin 1999: 423, 446): 'they are the newest drug for the solitary … the newest asylum for the reprobate' (ibid: 446). For Benjamin more broadly, 'The city is the realization of that ancient dream of humanity, the labyrinth. It is this reality to which the *flâneur*, without knowing it, devotes himself' (ibid: 429). Happily losing himself in London's streets, with his directionless wandering, the reprobate Winston becomes a Benjaminian *flâneur*, who 'dawdles randomly … about the metropolis, refusing to engage with its rigidly planned layout' (Schmidt di Friedberg 2018: 160). Interestingly, whereas for Benjamin and for Charles Baudelaire (1821-67), the inventor of the *flâneur*, the premier labyrinthine city is Paris, for Borges it is London. In a story collection first published in Spanish in 1949, the same year *Nineteen Eighty-Four* was published, a narrator in one Borges' story synonymises London and labyrinth when listing a sighting in a strange vision: '[I] saw a broken labyrinth (it was London)' (Borges 1999: 641). In another story in the same collection, one character, trying to solve a murder mystery, meets another character in a London pub, and declares:

> A fleeing man doesn't hide out in a labyrinth. He doesn't throw up a labyrinth on the highest point on the coast, and he doesn't throw up a crimson-colored labyrinth that sailors see from miles offshore. There's no need to build a labyrinth when

SELINA-MARIE SCHOLZ

GEOFF RODOREDA

the entire universe is one. For the man who truly wants to hide himself, London is a much better labyrinth than a rooftop room to which every blessed hallway in a building leads (ibid: 590-591).

In these Borges stories, just as in Orwell's novel, London is explicitly cast as a labyrinth and as the ultimate labyrinthine hiding place, 'a much better labyrinth' than any building distinctively constructed as a hideaway labyrinth. Presumably, Winston may have been able to remain anonymous and undetected in the labyrinthine streets of his London for much longer. But he becomes despairing in his conversations with the proles and seeks to exit the maze. He eventually finds himself outside the junk shop, where he bought his diary and is able to re-orient himself and find his way home.

Douglas Kerr has documented the geographies of *Nineteen Eighty-Four*, where refuge might be sought but is never found, from the 'microgeography' of the space inside one's skull, to the 'relatively restricted landscape through which Winston ... moves – basically urban, with one excursion to the countryside' (Kerr 2020: 46, 37). Significantly, these topographies of personal, working and urban space are all marked in the text as labyrinthine. And each of these labyrinths is a construction of the regime: doublethink inside the skull, tubes and corridors within the ministries, the streets of London that control and contain the numerous but docile proles. Each of these labyrinths, introduced into the text in a specific order, serves to index the regime's all-encompassing and ever-expanding control of everything, from small to large, from individual minds to the entire spaces of a city. These specifically named labyrinths in *Nineteen Eighty-Four* expand outwards to pervade the geographies of the text and the whole of Winston Smith's world. However, beyond these more identifiable labyrinths, there is a grander labyrinth, foreshadowed by these early references, that is constructed in Part 3 of *Nineteen Eighty-Four*. It incorporates Winston's journey within the Ministry of Love to the torture chamber at its centre, to Room 101.

THE MAZE AT THE MINISTRY OF LOVE

We have identified the five direct references to the labyrinth in the novel but crucially there is one single mention of its contemporary synonym, the maze. It is found at the very beginning of the novel, in Chapter 1. The narrator recounts that of all the ministries, 'The Ministry of Love was the really frightening one ... Winston had never been inside ... It was a place impossible to enter except on official business, and then only by penetrating through a maze of barbed-wire entanglements, steel doors, and hidden machine-gun nests' (Orwell 2013 [1949]: 7). This earliest reference to a maze, and its particular association with the Ministry of Love, draws attention to the frightening labyrinthine spaces of this particular place, which is where Winston finds himself, arrested and imprisoned, in Part 3. The first sentence of Part 3 is: 'He did not know where he was' (ibid: 259). Disorientation, the key spatialising indicator of a labyrinth, is all pervading here: 'In the Ministry of Love there were no windows. His cell might be at the heart of the building or against its outer wall; it might be ten floors below ground, or thirty above it' (ibid: 263-264). Disorientation is configured here not only horizontally (or laterally), as in the classical labyrinth of Crete, but also vertically. Disorientation is thus exacerbated in being three dimensional. Yet Winston's disorientation is also temporal: '[With] no clocks and no daylight it was hard to gauge the time … At one moment he felt certain that it was broad daylight outside, and at the next equally certain that it was pitch darkness' (ibid: 260, 263). One of Winston's fellow prisoners, Ampleforth, states plainly: 'There is no difference between night and day in this place. I do not see how one can calculate the time' (ibid: 266). As foreshadowed by earlier textual references, we are now inside *Nineteen Eighty-Four*'s most ominous and monolithic of labyrinths, one whose chronospatial structures 'describe both the linearity and the architecture of [labyrinthine] space and time' (Doob 1992: 1), and whose features – 'enforced circuitousness; disorientation; … inextricability; intricacy; complexity' – are most closely associated with significant literary labyrinths (ibid: 2).

Winston is subsequently interrogated, tortured and guided into and along a number of spaces within the labyrinth or maze that is the Ministry of Love, before being led to what must exist in every menacing labyrinth, a dreaded centre, in this case Room 101. Every truly Cretan labyrinth also has its minotaur, lurking somewhere near or at its centre. Although rats are Winston's greatest dread, O'Brien is the novel's minotaur, the monster that every maze-wanderer like Winston must eventually face at the centre of the Ministry of Love. In *Nineteen Eighty-Four* it is O'Brien who metaphorically embodies the essential characteristic of the minotaur which, apart from obvious menace, is that of paradox. The minotaur, both human and animal, a 'hybrid being' (Faris 1988: 4), signifies, as Julie Tallard Johnson puts it, both 'rational and irrational, … good and evil, illusion and reality' (Tallard Johnson 2021: 86). Such contradictory qualities are apparent not only in the character of O'Brien but also in his physicality. Early in the narrative he is introduced in consistently paradoxical terms. He is a 'large, burly man with a thick neck' – in this he could indeed be said to characterise a bull – who appears to be 'formidable' yet charming, 'disarming' yet 'civilised', orthodox yet unorthodox, in possession of both 'urbane' manners

SELINA-MARIE SCHOLZ

GEOFF RODOREDA

and a 'prizefighter's physique', with a 'humorous, brutal face' that exudes a singular 'intelligence' one moment and inscrutability the next (Orwell 2013 [1949]: 13, 20). During his interrogation, Winston is both drawn to and repelled by O'Brien in equal measure. O'Brien both asks questions and suggests answers. Ironically, 'the only person in the novel Winston ever feels any genuine closeness to is his torturer' (Waddell 2020a: 8). In true paradoxical fashion, '[O'Brien] was the tormentor, he was the protector, he was the inquisitor, he was the friend' (Orwell 2013 [1949]: 280).

We even find in O'Brien's name the suggestion of a Cretan minotaur: Brien or Brian is thought to be of Celtic origin, 'to be derived from the root *bri* (force, strength), *brîgh* (valor, strength), or *bruaich* (a hill, steep, high)' (Norman 2003: 97). In the transferred sense, Brien means 'eminence' or 'exalted one' (Hanks et al. 2016: 1983), which characteristically references O'Brien, given he is introduced as a senior Inner Party functionary who holds 'some post so important and remote that Winston had only a dim idea of its nature' (Orwell 2013 [1949]: 13). However, in *Nineteen Eighty-Four* the name is 'O'-Brien, the *son* of someone eminent, the product of a union between an 'exalted one' and another. In the Cretan tale, the minotaur is undoubtedly a creation of eminent parentage. The King's wife, Pasiphaë, is eminent. However, the snow-white bull, the 'father' of the minotaur, sent by the sea god Poseidon to King Minos, is equally distinguished, equally exalted. Orwell's O'Brien, in name, is offspring of eminence just as the minotaur is in the Greek myth. In his study of the 'evil' that is said to lurk in Room 101, Peter Brian Barry also argues that Orwell 'mythologized' O'Brien as 'the evil person in *Nineteen Eighty-Four*', as opposed to basing him on any one historical figure or multiple figures (Barry 2020: 188). Barry does not expand on what mythologies Orwell may have drawn on to construct his O'Brien. He also argues that O'Brien is neither animal nor 'inhuman monster'; that he is, in fact, 'all too human' (ibid: 189). But if O'Brien *is* mythologically constructed, we may well be invited to read him as *half* human, that is to say, as a *human* monster. Waddell has noted the prominence in Orwell's work of the 'slipperiness of the division between human and animal existence', and the numerous 'animal comparisons' that exist in *Nineteen Eighty-Four* (Waddell 2020a: 10, 11): '[We] find running throughout *Nineteen Eighty-Four* a twin emphasis on humans acting, or seeming to act, in other-than-human ways; and on animalistic comparison as a means with which to account metaphorically for human deeds' (Waddell 2020a: 11). Again, in O'Brien we find the paradox of the humane animal, the animalistic human, man and monster united in form. Reading the corridors and chambers within the Ministry of Love as a labyrinth, through which Winston is forced to wander, O'Brien may be read as the feared, monstrous minotaur of *Nineteen Eighty-Four*: half-human, half-beast, a creature of contradictions. O'Brien both embodies *and* signifies reason and unreason, good and evil, the real and the unreal. And, crucially, he is the occupant and keeper of the labyrinth's centre, Room 101.

Much has been written about Room 101, although to date it has not been considered in scholarly analysis as the minotaur's lair. For Barry, Room 101 is, like the minotaur, suffused with contradiction: it *can* contain 'painful and gruesome death', but also something quite trivial (Barry 2020: 185). Room 101 has also been read as a kind of religious confessional (Haldane 2005: 265), as a uterus (Smyer 1979: 159), as Square 101 – and, therefore, off the board – in a game of Snakes and Ladders (Dilworth 2013: 317), and, more recently, as the central space in a panopticon (Roberts 2020: 271). However, given the explicit references to labyrinths in *Nineteen Eighty-Four*, more prevalent than references to confessional boxes, board games, panopticons or uteri, given the additional explicit associations between mazes and ministries, and given the implicit allusions to the Ministry of Love as a type of labyrinth and of O'Brien as a minotaur, we argue Room 101 may be read as the chamber at the centre of a labyrinth where the minotaur devours its prey.

Erika Gottlieb reads Room 101 as 'the dramatic centre of the novel' and what occurs there as the novel's 'climactic scene' (1992: 80, 81), as it brings together 'all the betrayals in a series of symbolic reversals' (Gottlieb 1992: 81). Visually, she argues that the zero in the middle of the number '101' accentuates various readings of the room as suggesting, for instance, 'two parts of the self, face to face through zero: reduced to nothingness through fear and shame' (Gottlieb 1992: 81). The number 101 also suggests 'repetition after reversal: repeating the childhood trial, Winston reverts to another state of childhood' (ibid). But it also suggests the 'links of a chain – that is, not only one, but a whole series of continuous, repeated reversals' (ibid). For Gottlieb, 'Room 101 is at the heart of the novel because it is the centre of the mythical, the political, and the psychological drama of betrayal' (ibid). Inspired by Gottlieb's invitation to read '101' visually, here is our visual allusion to 1-0-1 in the context of our particular reading of Room 101 as the minotaur's lair at the centre of a labyrinth:

I 0 I

A labyrinth has walls and passages enclosed around a centre. It is inscribed here textually and diagrammatically as a simplified labyrinth. This visual allusion is neither anecdotal nor incidental

SELINA-MARIE SCHOLZ

GEOFF RODOREDA

to the broader interpretation we seek to make in this essay; rather, it serves to enhance our reading of a labyrinth in Part 3 of *Nineteen Eighty-Four*, with Room 1-0-1 at its centre.

CONCLUSION

Labyrinths always 'presume a double perspective' (Doob 1992: 1). There is the view of the 'maze-treader', lost and concentrated on the immediacy of puzzle solving, always and anywhere lacking a broader overview (ibid). Beyond this, however, there is the top-down view of the labyrinth's architect who delights in 'an image of order containing and controlling magnificent complexity' (ibid: 52). It is the regime of Oceania that constructs and controls the labyrinths of *Nineteen Eighty-Four*. These labyrinthine spaces are of the mind; they are physically built into the structure of the various ministries; they exist in the novel's circuitous and disorientating urban spaces. Through doublethink, a labyrinth of language and thought control, the regime manages to infiltrate the most private of spaces, the cognitive structure confined to Winston's brain. As the story progresses, the labyrinth of the winding pneumatic tubes at the Ministry of Truth introduces the materiality of labyrinths in dystopian space. This is later expanded to other ministries. The linking of three of the five mentions of the word labyrinth specifically to ministries serves to accentuate the regime's puzzling and indecipherable omnipotence and power. The most expansive labyrinth is that of the cityscape of London, wherein Winston becomes happily disorientated, for a time, in his escapist wanderings. These *literal* labyrinths in Parts 1 and 2 of the novel become our Ariadnes, guiding us towards the discovery of the foremost *literary* labyrinth in Part 3, with its unicursal windings leading inexorably to a terrible centre. The Everyman, Winston Smith, who wanders through the labyrinth in the Ministry of Love, is no hero; he is no Theseus. This is dystopian fiction. In this story, he is destroyed by the minotaur, the burly, bullish, paradoxical O'Brien, who devours all who would seek to defeat him in his lair, in Room 101.

REFERENCES

Barry, Peter Brian (2020) Room 101: Orwell and the question of evil, Waddell, Nathan (ed.) *Cambridge Companion to* Nineteen Eighty-Four, Cambridge: Cambridge University Press pp 181-196

Benjamin, Walter (1999) *The Arcades Project*, translated by Howard Eiland and Kevin McLaughlin, Cambridge: The Belknap Press of Harvard University Press

Bloom, Harold (2009) Into the living labyrinth: Reflections and aphorisms, Bloom, Harold and Hobby, Blake (eds) *Bloom's Literary Themes: The Labyrinth*, New York: Infobase Publishing pp xv-xvii

Borges, Jorge Luis (1999) *Collected Ficciones*, translated by Andrew Hurley, London: Allen Lane/Penguin

Dilworth, Thomas (2013) Erotic dream to nightmare: Ominous problems and subliminal suggestion in Orwell's *Nineteen Eighty-Four*, *Papers on Language and Literature*, Vol. 49, No. 3 pp 296-326

Doob, Penelope Reed (1992) *The Idea of the Labyrinth: From Classical Antiquity through the Middle Ages*, Ithaca: Cornell University Press

Eco, Umberto (1994) *The Name of the Rose*, San Diego: Harcourt Brace

Faris, Wendy B. (1988) *Labyrinths of Language: Symbolic Landscape and Narrative Design in Modern Fiction*, Baltimore: Johns Hopkins University Press

Freedman, Carl (1984) Antinomies of *Nineteen Eighty-Four*, *Modern Fiction Studies*, Vol. 30, No. 4 pp 601-620

Gottlieb, Erika (1992) *The Orwell Conundrum: A Cry of Despair or Faith in the Spirit of Man?*, Ottawa: Carleton University Press

Haldane, John (2005) *Nineteen Eighty-Four*, Catholicism, and the meaning of human sexuality, Gleason, Abbott, Goldsmith, Jack and Nussbaum, Martha C. (eds) *On* Nineteen Eighty-Four*: Orwell and the Future*, Princeton: Princeton University Press pp 261-276

Hanks, Patrick, Coates, Richard and McClure, Peter (eds) (2016) *The Oxford Dictionary of Family Names in Britain and Ireland*, Vol. 1, Oxford: Oxford University Press

Kern, Hermann (1982) *Labyrinthe: Erscheinungsformen und Deutungen 5000 Jahre Gegenwart eines Urbilds* [*Through the Labyrinth: Designs and Meanings over 5,000 Years*], München: Prestel

Kerr, Douglas (2020) The virtual geographies of *Nineteen Eighty-Four*, Waddell, Nathan (ed.) *Cambridge Companion to* Nineteen Eighty-Four, Cambridge: Cambridge University Press pp 37-50

Martin, Mike W. (1984) Demystifying doublethink: Self-deception, truth, and freedom in *Nineteen Eighty-Four*, *Social Theory and Practice*, Vol. 10, No. 3 pp 319-331

Matthews, W. H. (1922) *Mazes and Labyrinths: A General Account of their History and Development*, London: Longmans, Green and Co.

Mercatante, Anthony S. and Dow, James R. (2009) *The Facts on File: Encyclopedia of World Mythology and Legend*, New York: Facts on File

Norman, Teresa (2003) *A World of Baby Names*, New York: Perigee, revised edition

Orwell, George (2013 [1949]) *Nineteen Eighty-Four*, London: Penguin

Orwell, George (2001 [1937]) *The Road to Wigan Pier*, London: Penguin

Ovid (1958) *The Metamorphoses*, translated by Horace Gregory, New York: Viking Press

Plutarch (1914) *Plutarch's Lives*, translated by Bernadotte Perrin, Cambridge: Harvard University Press

Roberts, Adam (2020) Coda: The imaginaries of *Nineteen Eighty-Four*, Waddell, Nathan (ed.) *Cambridge Companion to* Nineteen Eighty-Four, Cambridge: Cambridge University Press pp 265-278

Schmidt di Friedberg, Marcella (2018) *Geographies of Disorientation*, London: Routledge

Smyer, Richard (1979) *Primal Dream and Primal Crime: Orwell's Development as a Psychological Novelist*, Columbia: University of Missouri Press

Tallard Johnson, Julie (2021) *The Clue of the Red Thread: Discovering Fearlessness and Compassion in Uncertain Times*, Brunswick: Nine Rivers

Waddell, Nathan (2020a) Introduction: Orwell's book, Waddell, Nathan (ed.) *Cambridge Companion to* Nineteen Eighty-Four, Cambridge: Cambridge University Press pp 1-20

Waddell, Nathan (2020b) Oceania's dirt: Filth, nausea, and disgust in Airstrip One, Waddell, Nathan (ed.) *Cambridge Companion to* Nineteen Eighty-Four, Cambridge: Cambridge University Press pp 168-80

Ziolkowski, Theodore (2008) *Minos and the Moderns: Cretan Myth in Twentieth-Century Literature and Art*, Oxford: Oxford University Press

NOTE ON THE CONTRIBUTORS

Selina-Marie Scholz is a PhD candidate in the Department of English Literatures and Cultures at the University of Stuttgart, Germany. Her research interests include cognitive narratology and ecocriticism. She is examining disorientation in climate fiction in her doctoral studies.

Dr Geoff Rodoreda is a lecturer in the Department of English Literatures and Cultures at the University of Stuttgart, Germany. His teaching and research interests include contemporary British fiction, Australian literature and Postcolonial Studies. He is the author of *The Mabo Turn in Australian Fiction* (Peter Lang, 2018).

PAPER

Critically Ill: George Orwell, Tragic Biography and the Crisis of Endings

KRISTIN BLUEMEL

This paper compares representations of Orwell's final illness in eight of the most influential Orwell biographies in order to measure the impact of tragic biography upon literary critical accounts of Orwell's most tragic fiction, Nineteen Eighty-Four. *Focusing on the years 1947-1949 when Orwell was on the remote Scottish island of Jura farming and writing, in sanatoria recovering, in hospital marrying and dying, it seeks to encourage a more serious, more critical Orwell Studies by turning away from the heroic appeals of tragic biography and towards the socialist appeals of post-war New Criticism, in particular William Wimsatt and Monroe Beardsley's idea of the intentional fallacy. It offers in conclusion a more socially connected, contingent Orwell, a biographical-critical figure who exceeds and perplexes the forms of tragedy and thus inspires a criticism of* Nineteen Eighty-Four *that is not determined by the crises of critical illness and inevitable death, but by unexamined narrative possibilities and undetermined endings.*

Key words: biography, tragedy, intentional fallacy, *Nineteen Eighty-Four*, George Orwell, Virginia Woolf

Everyone knows that Orwell died tragically young, his literary and political writing brought to an end on 21 January 1950 by the symptoms of tuberculosis. He was only 46 when he died alone in the middle of the night in University College Hospital, London, suffocating on his own blood. Nurses and friends were nearby, but no one was close enough to hear or save him. One of those friends was Sonia Brownell, his new and lovely young wife of three months. She, with the support of Orwell's doctors, had planned a trip for Orwell which would in four days' time have taken him, Sonia and Sonia's ex-lover Lucian Freud to Switzerland. While more recuperative journey than honeymoon, the Swiss reprieve was to include Orwell's favourite pastime of fishing; new fishing rods were in the room, in readiness for departure. Such details – the winter night, the young wife, the fishing rods – are the materials of every good Orwell biography.

KRISTIN BLUEMEL

Here I argue that such good details exert a bad influence upon biographers' literary criticism of Orwell as they tempt readers to turn the story of Orwell and his last story into parallel and interdependent tragedies. In this paper, I focus on those fateful years of 1947, 1948, 1949, when Orwell was on Jura farming, in sanatoria recovering, in hospital marrying and dying. These were the same years during which he was writing, revising, typing and publishing *Nineteen Eighty-Four*. I analyse the rhetorical patterns that turn a life story into a tragedy in order to suggest the effects such tragic biography has upon criticism of Orwell's literature generally and *Nineteen Eighty-Four* specifically. In conclusion, I turn to critical alternatives that reward literary critics who read an author's work in a public sphere freed from that author's illness and his intentions. This is not quite the arbitrary exercise it may at first appear when we recall that in the same post-war period identified with Orwell's critical illness, William Wimsatt and Monroe Beardsley published their immensely influential essay, 'The intentional fallacy'. While the two suited Yale New Critics may seem to have little to do with the down-and-out Orwell, I argue that critical Orwell Studies will do better, be healthier, stronger, more resilient and longer lived, if we affirm the intentional fallacy at the expense of tragic biography.

My advocacy of an Orwell Studies freed from the spectre of tragic death, liberated from speculations about the relation between Orwell's completion of his last great work, his lifetime of critical respiratory illnesses and his death at the moment of marriage and literary success, is a gesture both utopian and contrarian. It aims for a nearly impossible (or at least grandly impractical) ideal, urging a life writing and thus critical knowledge of Orwell that brings us to a place beyond his foretold ending in Sutton Courtenay churchyard. It also runs against the current of biographical practice and theory, both of which depend on the death of the subject in order to make sense of the life and biographers' acts of narrativising it. For example, biographer Hermione Lee begins her collection of essays on biography, *Virginia Woolf's Nose*, with the sentence 'We all want stories' (2005: 1) and finishes it with an essay titled 'How to end it all'.

Biographers are the consummate storytellers, Lee asserts, and no matter whether we think of their works as 'more like history or more like fiction', biographers and their readers are always squinting towards death. She muses:

> Most (though not all) biographies are about the dead. Most biographers, therefore, have to decide how to deal with the death of their subject. But why 'deal with'? Doesn't biography just state the facts? No, because there is a great deal invested,

always, in the death of the subject, in terms of how the death relates to the life, how the subject behaves at their death, and how, if at all, the death can be interpreted (ibid: 95).

Lee's focus on the subject's death as a defining influence upon the biographer's beginnings is nowhere more vividly illustrated than in Dorian Lynskey's *The Ministry of Truth: The Biography of 1984*. It begins: 'December 1948. A man sits at a typewriter, in bed, on a remote island, fighting to complete the book that means more to him than any other. He is terribly ill. The book will be finished and, a year or so later, so will the man' (2020 [2019]: ix). Lynskey spends the rest of his critical study disrupting the plots of tragic biography imposed on a subject who is 'terribly ill', but at the outset he cannot resist the dramatic promise a foretold death brings to his narrative form.

For a critically ill biographical subject, someone like George Orwell who struggled for years with the symptoms of tuberculosis, or Virginia Woolf, who struggled throughout her life with life-threatening mental illness, it seems inevitable that the shadow of death will hover over and shape posthumous stories of their literary lives. Lee argues that the modern biographer's preoccupation with death is perfectly respectable, derived from a long history of medieval writers seeking meaning in the creation of exemplary lives and deaths of saints or, more recently, in the Victorian biographers' penchant for embroidering lives and deaths of great men (op cit: 98). She notes that twentieth-century biographers found themselves writing in cultural conditions that permitted – nay, encouraged – a very different kind of biography, one that paid attention to the 'life of the body' (ibid: 3): 'Masturbation, dental work, body odour, menstruation, gonorrhoea, addictions, and sexual preferences are all permissible subjects' (ibid). The title of John Sutherland's 'pathological biography', *Orwell's Nose* (2016), suggests the morphological bias Lee identifies has only intensified in the twenty-first century.

Virginia Woolf tells us in 'The art of biography' (1939), many years before Lee published her biography *Virginia Woolf*, that it is 'the light of facts won for us by the psychologists' that has recently made the body available for biographical record (ibid: 509). In Woolf's essay, psychologists are gentle heroes who have renamed 'a sin' as 'perhaps a misfortune; perhaps a curiosity; perhaps neither one nor the other' (ibid). Woolf appreciates the potential 'destruction of a great deal of dead matter still obscuring the true features of the human face' that follows upon this twentieth-century shift from sin to psychology, secret to substance (ibid). Her interest in the truth of the human face may have appealed to Orwell given his oft-quoted

KRISTIN
BLUEMEL

comment in his 1940 essay 'Charles Dickens' that 'When one reads any strongly individual piece of writing, one has the impression of seeing a face somewhere behind the page ... the face that the writer *ought* to have' (2000 [1968]: 460). Woolf's 'human face' is, like the ideal writer's face that Orwell imagines, a metaphor signifying not a flesh and blood body part, but rather a secular substitute for the Christian soul, truthfully and variously revealed by aspiring biographers. 'Good biography,' Woolf writes, conveys the reality of a life through material and psychological facts. 'When and where did the real man live; how did he look; did he wear laced boots or elastic-sided ... Whom did he love, and how; and when he came to die did he die in his bed like a Christian, or ...' (op cit: 510).

The last item in the atheist Woolf's light-hearted biographical checklist, which ranges from looks to boots to love, concludes the biographical truth of any 'real man' in his dying body. But her final ellipses obscure and defer the ending of her sentence, inserting into its gaps a productive doubt, a generous, agnostic possibility. She prompts us to contemplate not only the great man's last positions and last rites but also his claim to a Christian death and thus Christian burial and Christian afterlife. We gaze at facts and wonder what it means to ask: 'Did Orwell die in his bed like a Christian?' We know for certain that neither he nor Woolf claimed in life to be a Christian, that at death Orwell was in a bed and after death in a Christian churchyard, and that Virginia Woolf was neither in a bed at her death nor in a churchyard afterwards. Beyond this, we are suspended between ellipses, contemplating – with Woolf – doubts, possibilities, deferred and unknown endings.

Hermione Lee, who alludes to the 'tricky questions' a biographer must confront in recreating a subject's death, asks: 'Why should there still be so much pressure on the biographer to read the whole life of the subject in terms of the death (especially if that death is a suicide)?' (2005: 103-104). She hedges her answer, demurely acknowledging that 'there are conflicting ways of thinking about death, mixed together in biographers' choices about how to end it all' (ibid: 105). Her parenthetical question about the special force of suicide, the writer's decision to kill off their own body, refers us directly to biographers' versions of the mentally disintegrating Woolf of 1941 but also, obliquely, to the physically disintegrating Orwell of 1947, 1948 and 1949. Some biographers and critics would have us regard the final years of Orwell's life as a kind of protracted suicide, Sutherland going so far as to end *Orwell's Nose* with the instructions: 'Write on the unofficial death certificate, "suicide"' (op cit: 230).

Even biographers with more nuanced approaches to measuring relations between Orwell's life and death have found it hard to resist the contours of the story of a great man dying young. Most intensify the tragic impact of their narrative by emphasising Orwell's 'ridiculous', 'mad' decision to live far from doctors and comforts on Jura. Precisely because Orwell and Jura are so far away from Orwell's biographers, the facts they consider sustain and compose 'contradictory versions of the same face' (to quote Woolf), or what Lee would call the 'versionings' of today's biographical theory (2005: 39).

In advising a turn away from tragic biography, I am not only turning away from versions of Orwell as the victim of self-destructive, suicidal responses to bodily illness, but turning away from Orwell himself, from Orwell apprehended *as* a self. I suggest we put in the place of such an isolated, death-tinged character – the doomed, seriously ill Orwell – a more socially connected, contingent figure, an Orwell whose life story may still make us sad, but that exceeds and perplexes the forms of tragedy and thus inspires a criticism of his writing generally and criticism of *Nineteen Eighty-Four* specifically that embraces unpredictable discoveries, unexamined possibilities and undetermined endings.

SERIOUSLY ILL

The terms 'seriously ill' or 'critically ill' that appear in Orwell's biographies to describe his increasingly frequent health crises in the last three years of his life are not scientific terms, but rather vague categories conventionally used by medical experts to communicate with the public. Today in the US, the use of these imprecise, public-facing terms is defined by the American Hospital Association Guidelines. The term 'serious' means that 'vital signs may be unstable and not within normal limits' and that the 'patient is acutely ill; indicators may be questionable'. This sounds bad enough but 'critical' is worse. To be critically ill means that 'vital signs are unstable and not within normal limits. ... Indicators are unfavorable' (Hickman 2014). To speak of a critically ill Orwell thus invokes at least two kinds of discourses and two kinds of publics, both of which are dependent on language intentionally left imprecise; it is the language of the clouded window pane.

On the one hand, the term 'critically ill' signals a medical discourse controlled by an expert who is speaking about a patient, in this case George Orwell, to a general public or audience of non-experts. On the other hand, it signals a literary critical discourse controlled by academics who are speaking to each other about a writer who has been abstracted from medical into literary contexts. Is our study of Orwell in a 'critical' condition thus in decline, doomed to expire? Or is it critical as in valued and important? It appears that Critical Orwell, our disciplinary subject, is spared death by only

KRISTIN BLUEMEL

the narrowest of etymological or algorithmic margins: in the online *Collins Dictionary* (n.d.) this margin is symbolised by a list of terms categorised as 'COBUILD Collocations' that begins with 'critically endangered' and 'critically ill', moves through 'critically successful' and 'critically wounded' and ends with 'examine critically, think critically, write critically'. It turns out that the distance between death and health for those of us who examine critically, think critically and write critically in Critical Orwell Studies is a matter of only twenty words. The stakes of this article suddenly seem much higher than they did when I set out to explore the relation of illness to Critical Orwell.

Each of Orwell's major biographers, Bernard Crick (1980), Michael Shelden (1991), Jeffrey Meyers (2000), D.J. Taylor (2003 and 2023) and Gordon Bowker (2003), deploy to greater or lesser degree a terminology of serious or critical illness and a rhetoric of tragic endings to explain the story of Orwell's life in the years he was writing *Nineteen Eighty-Four*. Taylor's biographies are the most flamboyant, the most prone to adopt the novelist's trick of creating drama through hinting of deathly dangers. Perhaps for this reason, his are the most exciting. Crick and Shelden are the most disciplined of the biographers, abstaining from the rhetoric of the tragic ending, refraining from judgements of Orwell's decisions that typically strike others as at best irresponsible, at worst demented or suicidal. In between these two extremes of colourful Taylor, the novelist-biographer, and restrained Crick and Shelden, the professorial biographers, we have Meyers and Bowker, both of whom are approximately equally invested in reading Orwell's illness in terms of his death.

Taylor's *Orwell: The Life* offers up numerous examples that illustrate his skilful handling of the rhetoric of tragic biography. For example, he is good at tragic titles, with 'Endgame' (2003: 400) heading his chapter describing Orwell's experiences in Cranham Sanatorium and then University College Hospital. Taylor's mordant flair finds expression through well-chosen 'Endgame' epigraphs, the first consisting of Orwell's words in a letter of July 1949 to Jack Common, 'Of course I've had it coming to me all my life' (ibid). The second epigraph comes from Malcolm Muggeridge's diary entry of just over one month later, written in early September 1949 after he learned of Orwell's engagement to Sonia Brownell: 'It will probably be a rather macabre wedding' (ibid). The overdetermined references to death found at the beginning of Taylor's final chapter are exactly the gestures best suited to persuade readers to see Orwell's life in illness as preparation for and anticipation of death. Taylor's Orwell is 'seriously ill' in Jura in 1947 when his first draft of *Nineteen Eighty-Four* is only a few hundred words short of an ending (ibid: 389); again he is said to be 'seriously ill', this time in a citation from a chest specialist who came to Jura from Glasgow to examine him in December 1947. Taylor frames what follows as 'the final phase' of his life and, looking back from the end, calculates that 'of the next twenty-four months, only four would be spent outside a medical ward' (ibid: 390). He asks: 'How much did he know, or suspect?' raising the stakes of Orwell's understanding of his own proximity to death, his own danger. Taylor then, not so subtly, drives home his point by setting up the next scene with the phrase: 'In the dead weeks of late 1947 …' (ibid) before mentioning again in this context: 'Certainly, he was very seriously ill' (ibid).

The same narrative rhythm, the same drum beat or 'tocsin' of ill health also 'clangs' through Taylor's *New Life* (2023: 500). His new biography begins with a wedding rather than a funeral, but we cannot escape the fact that 'the groom had been bed-bound with advanced tuberculosis for the past nine months' or that one witness to the ceremony, David Astor, found it 'very strange' with 'the spectre of approaching death hanging in the air' (ibid: 8). Recreating Orwell's life in London in the bitter winter of 1934-1935, Taylor reminds us of Orwell's 'ever more suspect health' (ibid: 207). By the time we are with Orwell in Barcelona, fighting alongside a Republican militia during the Spanish Civil War in 1937, we are told: 'As ever, there were questions about Orwell's health' (ibid: 296). Spain, so fertile a climate for Orwell's developing political consciousness, 'had ruined what was left of his health' (ibid: 326). The warning tocsin sounds more frequently from this point in Taylor's biography until its end. Orwell is, in the words of his biographer, 'gravely ill' (ibid: 336) and 'seriously ill' (ibid: 349). By the time we get to a chapter titled 'Pain in side very bad' (ibid: 499), we hear Orwell himself using the imprecise language of 'serious illness': Taylor cites a letter to his American publishers in which he describes himself as 'seriously ill' (ibid: 504); another to his agent Leonard Moore in which he is 'seriously ill' (ibid); and one to Julian Symons in which he concedes that he had been 'seriously ill' (ibid: 506). In case we have not caught on to this theme, Taylor summarises, 'Clearly Orwell was seriously ill' (ibid: 505).

Biographer Jeffrey Meyers adopts a fatalistic rhetoric similar to Taylor's but gives the impression of a more stately treatment by setting up a clearer chronology of illness. In April 1947, his Orwell 'resumes his arduous life' on Jura and suffers 'severe attacks' that keep him in bed for weeks at a time. In September and October 1947 he is 'seriously ill' (2000: 275). By the end of December 1947 he had 'lost twenty pounds, seemed to be wasting away and felt deathly sick all the time' (ibid). Just before or after Christmas 1947, Meyers tells us that Orwell was admitted to Hairmyres Hospital, about 20 miles south of Glasgow, where he found himself under the care of the charismatic Dr Bruce Dick. Meyers cites at some length the first precise medical description Orwell ever received about his TB infection, written by Dr Dick's assistant, Dr James Williamson: 'a fibrotic, feverish, wasting disease of a very chronic nature. It was confined to the upper part of both lungs, mostly his left lung. ... There were tubercule bacilli in his sputum, which means he was infectious. ... His lung would have been tough, like leather' (ibid: 275). From this, Meyers judges: 'Orwell had always ignored or denied his condition, but his health was now permanently ruined' (ibid). Serious illness and permanent ruin frame everything that follows. Upon returning to Jura in July 1948 to wander the fields when he was not smoking, coughing, and typing in bed, Orwell managed to finish a legible final draft of *Nineteen Eighty-Four*. By September 1948 he was again 'seriously ill' (ibid: 279). Unable to find a lady stenographer willing to trek out to Jura and type up a revised copy of his full manuscript in October 1948, Meyers tells us that 'the exhausted Orwell, anxious to get on with the work and racing against time, decided to type it himself. ... He'd never admit that he was a permanent invalid, too weak to live on Jura, and that the whole way of life there had been madness' (ibid: 278).

I am entirely in agreement with both Taylor's and Meyers's perspectives and pronouncements but am also aware of the costs we critics pay for building our human judgements out of the rhetorical turns and dramatic plotting of tragic biography. We know very well that Orwell was himself, as he typed and typed, not performing the role of the doomed hero in the final chapter of his biography. Crick may mention Orwell's 'tragically early death' (1980: xiii) at the beginning of his Introduction to *George Orwell: A Life,* but in the final chapters he lets documents tell his story and leaves us room to judge or not judge Orwell's decisions about health and medicine as we see fit. For example, Crick describes Orwell's typing of his draft manuscript of *Nineteen Eighty-Four* late in 1948, admitting that the effort of typing 'brought him near to physical collapse' (ibid: 383), but he does not pursue the implications of this observation to further his own opportunities for moral or medical judgement. Similarly, authorised biographer Michael Shelden does not try to extract causal and, therefore, tragic implications out of the correspondence between Orwell's typing of the fair copy and the fact that 'his health began to decline rapidly' (1991: 425). Instead, Shelden cautions against drawing connections between the endings of Orwell's novel and his life, noting 'His behaviour was irrational and extreme, but it was not part of some death wish. ... [I]n the aftermath of finishing *Nineteen Eighty-Four*, he did not slowly sink toward death without putting up a terrific struggle' (ibid: 437).

We might add: Orwell did not sink slowly towards death at all. Throughout most of 1947, 1948 and 1949, he bobbed up and down on the flows of his writerly life, with bad days and good days, days in medical institutions and days out. We could cite Shelden again as support for this interpretation of Orwell's illness, as Shelden emphasises Richard Rees's report that during part of the 400-mile rail journey south that he made with Orwell from Scotland to Cranham Sanatorium, Orwell was 'very weak, though mentally as active as ever and full of ideas for future work – a novel, and essays on Conrad, Gissing and Evelyn Waugh' (ibid: 425). While Shelden may slip occasionally into the retrospective stance evident in the description of *Nineteen Eighty-Four* as Orwell's 'last great obsession' (ibid: 506), throughout most of his biography he comes closer to the position Crick adopts when Crick reminds us that '*Nineteen Eighty-Four* was no last testament: it was simply the last major book [Orwell] wrote before he happened to die' (op cit: 385). Crick anticipates Orwell's later biographers who apprehend as fact Orwell's intention to complete future projects, although only some of them conclude from this that the critically ill Orwell intended to live. To cite two recent examples: Taylor reminds us that Orwell told others that he was going to write a novel set in 1945 and another 'short novel' based on what he called a 'stunning idea' about a 'young man sent back in disgrace on the boat from Burma in 1927' (Taylor 2023: 516, 533); Lynskey tells us that Orwell planned a 'new collection called *Essays and Sketches*, including an essay about Evelyn Waugh … and another about Joseph Conrad, particularly his political novels *The Secret Agent* and *Under Western Eyes*' (op cit: 171). Evidence of Orwell's early thoughts about these writing projects leads Lynskey to second Crick's view 'that *Nineteen Eighty-Four* was meant to conclude one phase of his work, not his entire career' (ibid: 172).

Gordon Bowker's *Inside George Orwell* is inevitably compared to Taylor's *Orwell: The Life* because both books came out in 2003, intended by their publishers to earn sales and influence celebrations of the 100th anniversary of Orwell's birth. Bowker may lack Taylor's novelist flair, but he shares Taylor's vocabulary of decline and logic of progressive degeneration. *Inside George Orwell* represents Orwell's writing of his last novel and endurance of his last illness as shared, parallel endings. Given Bowker's tragic rhetoric, it seems inevitable that his doomed Orwell, having submitted the 'final typescript' of *Nineteen Eighty-Four* to his publisher on 4 December 1948, joins his sister, Avril, and Bill Dunn in the slaughter of the 'last pig' at Barnhill and consumption of the 'last bottle of wine' in the house (2003: 383). Yet what does it mean to refer from deep inside an Orwell biography to a 'final' novel, 'last' Barnhill

KRISTIN BLUEMEL

pig, or 'last' illness? Of course, we recognise as fact that *Nineteen Eighty-Four* was, indeed, Orwell's last novel. Yet just as surely as the terms 'seriously ill' and 'critically ill' cloud the meaning of a patient's illness in doctors' communications with the public, so too does the phrase 'Orwell's last illness' construct for readers a false coherence and meaning out of biographical desire and strategy rather than historical or medical fact. Bowker himself acknowledges that the 'progress of Orwell's illness is difficult to map' (ibid: 390). He describes in precise medical language, gathered from doctors' private reports and communications, that Orwell:

> … seemed to have inherited bronchiectasis, a condition that would have made him susceptible to lung infection from birth. His recurrent influenza and bronchitis, persistent cough, and his several bouts of pneumonia would be symptoms of that susceptibility. But the condition also made him especially vulnerable to tuberculosis, and he might well have been infected since childhood (ibid: 390).

This description of a mysterious, baffling, multi-dimensional, non-progressive disease history appears immediately after we read: 'Once his book [*Nineteen Eighty-Four*] was finished, his health soon deteriorated' (ibid: 389). In contrast to the medical facts that disrupt a logic of cause and effect, Bowker suggests not only that Orwell's disease followed a steady path of 'deterioration' but also that his disease had a literary cause: we can easily interpret Bowker's sentence to mean '*Because* his book was finished, his health soon deteriorated.' Framed by the chapter title 'The nightmare and the novel', this example of Bowker's narrativisation of serious illness overwhelms the evidence that Orwell suffered from not one progressive, degenerative illness but many illnesses, and that relations of cause, effect, onset and closure between his various illnesses and between his illnesses and his novel are unclear, imprecise and unknowable.

The questionable critical effects of the fondness Orwell's biographers have for tragic narrative structures that culminate in a crisis of endings are most evident in biographers' slippery critical equations between Orwell and *Nineteen Eighty-Four*'s fictional hero, Winston Smith. For example, John Sutherland, in *Orwell's Nose*, repeatedly, insouciantly collapses distance between facts of place or person in Orwell's life and the highly mediated versions of those facts in Orwell's fictions. Since Orwell worked in Booklover's Corner, so too, Sutherland says, does Gordon Comstock, the anti-hero of his 1936 novel *Keep the Aspidistra Flying* (2016: 39); since Gordon works in an 'unnamed' Booklover's Corner, Mr McKechnie, its owner, is really Frank Westrope (ibid: 40); similarly, Orwell's first wife, Eileen, is Rosemary (ibid: 43), and despite all the evidence Sutherland presents to the contrary, Orwell's second wife Sonia 'is' Julia, with whom Winston Smith has a secret affair in *Nineteen Eighty-Four* (ibid). Bowker's similar kinds of conflations of Orwell and Winston exert more tragic distortions upon Critical Orwell Studies than Sutherland's because Bowker's biography is itself a more serious critical study. For example, contemplating Orwell's 'paranoia' that led him during and after the war to fear assassination, Bowker reports that Orwell believed he 'was writing a book which could make him a quarry, just as Winston Smith, in keeping a diary, made himself a target' (2003: 370). Implied here through analogy, Bowker's equation between biographical and fictional subjects, between Orwell and Smith, then becomes explicit. He writes:

> Clearly, in [Orwell's] mind he was living the drama of Winston Smith, so that when he came to write the horror story of *Nineteen Eighty-Four* it was his own horror story that he was setting down. … Undoubtedly the novel was written in the shadow of death. [Orwell] guessed that he might not have long to live and his writing was not untouched by that fact (ibid).

Bowker's adverbs of 'clearly' and 'undoubtedly' and his double negative of 'not untouched' help construct Orwell's novel as an expression of Orwell's critical illness. Simultaneously, the biographer represents the horrors of Orwell's experiences of illness as transparently equivalent to and inseparable from those of *Nineteen Eighty-Four*'s tortured, hopeless, betrayed and abandoned hero. This is tragic biography at its most powerful and most critically dangerous form. We can see Bowker 'clearly' and 'undoubtedly' describing as 'fact' Orwell's hidden mental activity about an unknowable ending: 'He *guessed* that he *might* not have long to live.' Orwell's horrors are Winston's just as surely as Winston's are Orwell's. No critical distance remains between life and art and only the biographer has access to the shared interior motives of both.

We do not need biographical facts about Orwell's critical illnesses nor biographers' suppositions about the possible impacts of these illnesses on the plotting, politics or pessimism of *Nineteen Eighty-Four* to know that Winston Smith's body is an important part of his character. We note in our first encounter with Winston that he has a 'varicose ulcer about his right ankle' and though only thirty-nine, he must ascend Victory Mansions' seven flights of stairs of 'slowly, resting several times on the way' (2003 [1949]: 1). This first image of a young man climbing stairs like an old man prepares us to notice other details that hint of Winston's physical vulnerability. In effect, Orwell prepares us at the outset for his novel's crisis of endings, his

KRISTIN BLUEMEL

biography of Winston benefiting from his adept use of the tragic forms that I am warning Orwell biographers and critics against. Reading *Nineteen Eighty-Four*, in contrast to *Inside George Orwell* and other tragic biographies, we can relish the tocsin warnings of approaching death that clang from the novel's beginning: Winston's thought 'The Thought Police would get him'; Winston's words '… they'll shoot me I don't care they'll shoot me in the back of the neck'; his reflection 'He [Winston] was already dead' (ibid: 19, 20, 29). Tragedy itself is thematised when Winston thinks about his mother's death. Recalling the time when he lost his mother, when she disappeared without a trace, he knows that she somehow sacrificed herself for him although he cannot remember nor recover the nature of her sacrifice. 'The thing that now suddenly stuck Winston was that his mother's death, nearly thirty years ago, had been tragic and sorrowful in a way that was no longer possible. Tragedy, he perceived, belonged to the ancient time, to a time when there were still privacy, love, and friendship' (ibid: 31). The idea of tragedy as a lost art, a series of genres with conventional ways of making narrative sense of loss and death that have themselves died, creates an overdetermined interpretive guide for Orwell's novel. Winston's thoughts about tragedy as a story form whose conventions are only recognisable in an 'ancient time' before the Thought Police and Big Brother have turned England into Airstrip One authorises us to read the novel as a tragedy; it is an imaginative expression of an English writer using Oldspeak, himself fortunate enough to live in the 'ancient time' when privacy, love and friendship are still possible.

Yet the power of Orwell's dystopic vision is, in part, derived from the reader's identification with Winston and the reader's imaginative investment in his world as our world. Orwell's skilful use of third person indirect speech convinces us that we are 'inside Winston Smith' and that 'ancient time', Orwell's time, has run out. According to this interior logic, that of Winston's world rather than Orwell's, Winston's life and the likelihood of his violent and early death cannot be tragic. The narrative's thematic denial of its own structural signs of tragic commitment is confusing, requiring of readers a kind of doublethink. We may begin reading *Nineteen Eighty-Four* as Winston's tragic biography, but we cannot sustain the emotional investments in a doomed hero that tragedy normally invites because that hero has himself denied us his tragedy. To know Winston is to know that tragedy is impossible.

The physical, bodily signs of Winston's disintegration are inseparable from his paradoxical position as the narrative's tragic hero in a world without tragedy. O'Brien, Winston's torturer in Room 101, intones: 'You are the last man,' and then forces Winston to look at his reflection in a three-sided mirror.

A bowed gray-colored, skeleton-like thing was coming towards him. ... The creature's face seemed to be protruded, because of its bent carriage. A forlorn, jailbird's face with a nobby forehead running back into a broad scalp, a crooked nose and battered-looking cheekbones above which the eyes were fierce and watchful. ... Here and there under the dirt there were the red scars of wounds, and near the ankle the varicose ulcer was an inflamed mass with flakes of skin peeling off it. But the truly frightening thing was the emaciation of his body. The barrel of the ribs was as narrow as that of a skeleton: the legs had shrunk so that the knees were thicker than the thighs (ibid: 280-282).

If we somehow have not absorbed the ironies embodied in O'Brien's pronouncement that the tortured form in the mirror reflects the guardian spirit of 'the last man', we have another interpretive opportunity when O'Brien, directing Winston's gaze back to the mirror, spits out: 'That is the last man. If you are human, that is humanity. Now put on your clothes' (ibid: 282). Here, the novel's competing exterior and interior tragic logics unite in Winston's body. That body is both the thing that suggests Winston is human, able to play the part of a tragic hero, and the thing that signifies his inhumanity, an emaciated, rotting body that lives and dies in a time beyond tragedy and tragic biography. Crooked and battered, fierce and watchful, Winston isn't dead, is not even necessarily dying, but he is in a critical position that requires his untimely, unfair death while withholding tragic catharsis from his readers. It turns out that in the end, we should not be thinking about Orwell's nose, but Winston's.

Lynskey's biography of *Nineteen Eighty-Four* offers a model for critical biography that respects the difference between Orwell's and Winston's noses. Avoiding what we might call the biographical fallacy, the error of reading the biographical subject's life as fiction and his fiction as a map of his life, he writes: 'The problem with seeing *Nineteen Eighty-Four* as the anguished last testament of a dying man is that Orwell never really believed he was dying, or at least no more than usual' (2020 [2019]: 160). And he resists what we might call the inventional fallacy, the error of reading the biographical subject, Orwell, as that subject's invented, make-believe character, Winston, by upholding the difference between author and character: 'The crucial difference between Orwell and Winston is that Winston knows, from the moment he first writes in his diary, that he is doomed. But Orwell never gave any indication that he thought he wouldn't recover' (ibid). One might add that another crucial difference between Orwell and Winston is that the

PAPER

former had a flesh and blood face and all too mortal body while the latter's face consists entirely of ink on paper or pixels on a screen. The implications of this obvious material difference are wide-ranging and return us to questions around the crisis of endings with which this paper begins; to the extent that Winston is always Winston, a work of art reproduced millions of times since he first entered the public realm of print in 1949 and to the extent that publishers necessarily and endlessly recreate Winston in whatever diverse modalities they have available to them, he lives on, immortal. He is finished but he cannot die. None of this is to say that Lynskey nor any other Orwell biographer-critic should pretend Orwell's illness did not impact the way he lived his life, the way his friends understood his living and feared his dying, or the way we receive written accounts of all these things. Surveying accounts of Orwell's seemingly fearless confrontation with the treacherous Corryvreckan whirlpool, in August 1947, that capsized his motor boat and stranded him, his niece Lucy, nephew Henry and son Richard on a small stony island, for example, Lynskey asks: 'Was this nonchalance a sign of courage, recklessness or fatalism? Had he grown too used to the possibility of an early death?' (ibid: 159). Lynskey tempts us to answer 'Yes!' but it is important to note that he leaves unresolved his questions about Orwell's attitudes towards death, preferring dry biographical facts to tragic narrative structures: '[This] was the closest Orwell had come to death since Spain' and 'His health worsened in the autumn' (ibid).

Typically, tragic biography treats worsening health as a cause of impending death. Yet Lynskey plays with a different kind of narrative logic, presenting us first with evidence of 'a holiday that nearly ended in tragedy' (ibid) before mentioning Orwell's 'worsening health' (ibid). The reversal or confusion of cause and effect at this moment in Lynskey's narrative – the familiar plot of 'illness, then death' becomes '(near) death, then illness' – opens up new interpretive possibilities for biographers and their readers, modelling how small changes in citation and interpretation of evidence can offset tragedy's distorting influence upon literary criticism of *Nineteen Eighty-Four*.

LITERARY CRITICISM AND ORWELL STUDIES

Another antidote for critics and biographers struggling with the enervating influence of tragedy's forms upon critical studies of Orwell resides in the classic idea of the intentional fallacy. First expounded by Orwell's contemporaries Wimsatt and Beardsley in an article in 1946 that appeared in *The Sewanee Review*, it was revised and republished in 1954 in their co-authored edition of *The Verbal Icon*. This was the time when New Criticism consolidated its theoretical dominance at Yale and elsewhere, and Wimsatt and Beardsley came to define undergraduate and eventually popular reading practices in the US and the UK through the institutionalisation of their core formalist idea that 'the design or intention of the author is neither available nor desirable as a standard for judging the success of a work of literary art' (1946: 468). By the mid-1950s when this idea had become formalist gospel, *Nineteen Eighty-Four* was already a global bestseller, inspiring heated debate between and within the left and right about what Orwell intended with Winston Smith's defeat in Room 101, what Orwell meant with his dark, dark ending. Was it a prediction? A warning? Did Orwell intend to pillory English socialists or was he trying to satirise and undercut totalitarianism more generally? If we bring Wimsatt and Beardsley into this often more political than literary debate, questions about Orwell's intentions, as well as his critical illness and its effect on his fiction, become the wrong questions. Wimsatt and Beardsley explain that:

> The poem [or novel] is not the critic's own and not the author's (it is detached from the author at birth and goes about the world beyond his power to intend about it or control it). The poem [or novel] belongs to the public. It is embodied in language, the peculiar possession of the public, and it is about the human being, an object of public knowledge (ibid: 470).

This passage, like so many passages in Orwell's work, achieves its political power through its faith in the social possibilities for individuals brought and held together through the written word: it inspires hope for a world in which we freely achieve our best meanings and thus our best selves in open partnership with others. In effect, Wimsatt and Beardsley propose a theory of reading that imagines the work of criticism in utopian socialist terms. In prose as clear as a window pane, the professors argue that poems, novels, literature more generally belong to the public, the common people – the proles, if you will. The meanings of literary texts are not waiting to be discovered by experts in the dark corners of an author's mind or even in forgotten letters in university archives, but are available as embodied objects found in the open, common spaces of every community and all human cultures; they are 'the *peculiar* possession of the public'. In contrast to narratives of illness and crises of endings that have shaped approaches to Orwell and *Nineteen Eighty-Four*, Wimsatt and Beardsley offer us a New Critical approach to a Critical Orwell that is capable of challenging the ill effects of the most tragic of biographers.

The academic subject of Orwell Literary Studies is weakened, perhaps even rendered seriously or critically ill, when we mingle medical, biographical and fictional narratives in the interests of

KRISTIN BLUEMEL

creating more compelling, more tragic, biographies. The trouble comes when biography turns too avidly towards the conventions of fiction, adopting the signs, tones and narrative arcs of tragedy. We need to remember that Orwell was first interesting to the reading public as a 'real man' (to quote Woolf again) because he wrote *Nineteen Eighty-Four* and other works of literature. Only secondarily, after the great man had died, did biographers' stories of the living, embodied Orwell consume the public.

To the extent that we read and write Orwell biographies as embodied narratives freed from the writer's death, we are more likely to include good literary criticism within our life stories. The benefit of biography without tragedy is that Orwell's novels, including his last, great, tragic novel, are liberated into a public existence apart from the seriously ill author and his tragic end. My call for a more public, more social understanding of Orwell enlarges the role of literary criticism in Orwell Studies and invites Orwell critics to engage more seriously in allied literary fields. We might seek to influence Virginia Woolf Studies, for example, offering to replace their own tragic biographical confusions with comparative literary critical analysis. What do we learn, what new things do we see, when we read *A Room of One's Own* (1929) in terms of *A Clergyman's Daughter* (1936), *The Voyage Out* (1915) in terms of *Down and Out* (1933), *Between the Acts* (1941) in terms of *Nineteen Eighty-Four*, Orwell's 'last' act?

Nineteen Eighty-Four is 'embodied in language, the peculiar possession of the public' while Orwell the 'real man' was embodied in flesh and blood, the peculiar possession of himself. If critical biography separates the public from private Orwells, the literature from living body, we are more likely to realise a providentially social subject for biography and criticism. This social subject breaks the hold of the tragic ideal that allows Orwell after death to belong to any one person more than another; it resists the biographer's claim that Orwell was 'my' writer the way Norwich City were 'my' football club (Taylor 2023: 11). Creating and sharing a social, public Orwell in our criticism, we are more likely to affirm and thus evade Wimsatt and Beardsley's intentional fallacy, as well as other types of biographical and inventional fallacies that tempt us to imprison literature in personality, confuse biography with fiction, mistake Orwell's tragedy for Winston's.

REFERENCES

Bowker, Gordon (2003) *Inside George Orwell*, New York: Palgrave Macmillan

Collins Dictionary (n.d.) Critically ill. Available online at https://www.collinsdictionary.com/dictionary/english/critically-ill, accessed on 16 September 2023

Crick, Bernard (1980) *George Orwell: A Life*, Boston: Little, Brown and

Company

Hickman, Kris (2014) Patient condition terminology: Do you really know what 'critical' means?, *AHCJ: Association of Health Care Journalists Blog*, 2 October. Available online at https://healthjournalism.org/blog/2014/10/patient-condition-terminology-do-you-really-know-what-stable-means/, accessed on 16 September 2023

Lee, Hermione (1997) *Virginia Woolf*, New York: Alfred A. Knopf

Lee, Hermione (2005) *Virginia Woolf's Nose: Essays on Biography*, Princeton: Princeton University Press

Lynskey, Dorian (2020 [2019]) *The Ministry of Truth: The Biography of George Orwell's* 1984. New York: Anchor Books

Meyers, Jeffrey (2000) *Orwell: Wintry Conscience of a Generation*, New York: W.W. Norton

Orwell, George (2003 [1949]) *Nineteen Eighty-Four*, New York: Plume/Penguin

Orwell, George (2000 [1968]) Charles Dickens, Orwell, Sonia and Angus, Ian (eds) *Collected Essays, Journalism and Letters*: An Age Like This, 1920-1940, Vol. 1, Boston: David R. Godine pp 413-460; first published March 1940

Shelden, Michael (1991) *Orwell: The Authorized Biography*, New York: Harper Collins

Sutherland, John (2016) *Orwell's Nose: A Pathological Biography*, London: Reaktion Books

Taylor, D.J. (2003) *Orwell: The Life*, New York: Henry Holt and Company

Taylor, D.J. (2023) *Orwell: The New Life*, New York: Pegasus Books

Wimsatt, W.K. and Beardsley, M.C. (1946) The intentional fallacy, *The Sewanee Review*, Vol. 54, No. 3 pp 468-488. Available online at https://www.jstor.org/stable/27537676

Woolf, Virginia (1939) The art of biography, *The Atlantic* pp 506-510. Available online at https://www.theatlantic.com/magazine/archive/1939/04/the-art-of-biography/654067/, accessed on 16 September 2023

NOTE ON THE CONTRIBUTOR

Kristin Bluemel is Professor of English and Wayne D. McMurray Endowed Chair in the Humanities at Monmouth University. She is author of *George Orwell and the Radical Eccentrics: Intermodernism in Literary London* (2004) and other studies on modern British literature and culture.

PAPER

John Bull's Other Airstrip: Orwell's Irish Blindspot

MARTIN TYRRELL

Despite Orwell's many Irish connections and the centrality of the Irish Question to British politics during his formative years, he shows little interest in Irish politics. As Kerrane (2007) and Steele (2017) have commented he does not cite the Irish experience even as an instance of decolonisation that might have lessons for a general British decolonisation, a development Orwell hoped to see. Ireland, by the 1930s, was a reluctant dominion of the British Empire that used the freedoms available to it under the Statute of Westminster 1931 – by the letter of which, at least, the dominions of the British Empire were as sovereign as France or Russia – to end its dominion status. Orwell, in his most considered writings on decolonisation – his wartime writings – advocates dominion status for countries such as India but on the understanding that dominion status is less than the full sovereignty sought by the relevant national liberationists. Orwell's idea of dominion status appears outdated – something significantly less than full sovereignty rather than equivalent to it as it had been since 1931. Awareness of the Irish experience of dominion status might have left him better informed. In advocating an outdated version of dominion status, Orwell seeks to keep countries such as India and Burma formally connected to the United Kingdom and its policies, in part because he believes they are unable to survive independently and will remain so for the foreseeable future.

Key words: Orwell, Ireland, Dominion Status, India, Imperialism, National Liberation Movements

Orwell's general silence on Irish matters has been noted by several commentators. Kerrane (2007: 15), for example, asks: 'How could one of the most eloquent critics of British colonialism in Asia sound so tone-deaf about colonialism and its aftermath next door?' while Steele (2017: 150), in the context of a general discussion on Orwell and national liberationists, writes: 'It is odd that … Orwell paid no attention to the example of Ireland, which had been so central to British politics for his entire lifetime.'

It is, indeed, surprising that Orwell did not have more to say on Ireland. The Irish example should in theory have interested so professed an anti-imperialist. In Orwell's lifetime, Ireland – or the larger part of it, anyway – went from being an integral territory of the United Kingdom to full independence. This was not a straightforward process. Nationalist Ireland was granted dominion status in 1922 as the Irish Free State. Full independence was then achieved over the next fifteen years, but gradually and cautiously through a 'policy of pinpricks' whereby dominion status was gradually ended. And an Irish Republic was formally declared only in 1948. Given that Orwell would advocate dominion status for India in 1941, it is puzzling that he did not take note of this, the recent experience of Ireland which tested the extent to which the dominions were genuinely sovereign. Most notable in this respect was Ireland's wartime neutrality, which irked Orwell, as it irked Churchill, but which was entirely consistent with the sovereignty that had been conferred on British dominions via the Statute of Westminster 1931. Orwell, as I shall discuss later, appears not to have appreciated the full import of dominion status and, therefore, how a nationalistically inclined dominion might use it. He appears to regard a dominion as a lesser thing than a fully sovereign state – which was how the dominions had originally been – and with some obligation to follow Britain's lead, at least in wartime.

The Irish experience of dominion status, dominion status in general and Orwell's wartime thoughts on Indian and other national liberationist movements will be the main subject of this paper. However, I also want to look briefly at a number of other reasons why Orwell's relative lack of comment on Irish affairs is curious, namely: the prominence of what was called the 'Irish Question' in British politics during his formative years and its relevance to his political outlook in the late 1930s especially; the fact that several people who were closest to Orwell, including, of course, his first wife Eileen O'Shaughnessy, had strong Irish connections; and Orwell's interest in Irish writers including W.B. Yeats. Orwell reviewed V.K. Narayana Menon's *The Development of W.B. Yeats* in some detail in *Horizon* (Orwell 1998 [1943a]) and more concisely in *Time and Tide* (Orwell 1998 [1943b]).

Yeats frequently addresses Irish politics in his work and was also actively engaged in Irish political life, including as a senator in the early years of the Irish Free State – which Orwell (1998 [1943b]) notes – and later, albeit briefly, as an associate of the Irish fascist movement, the Blueshirts, a connection Orwell mentions in passing in published correspondence arising from his *Horizon* review. However, Orwell's main contention is that Yeats' philosophy is fascist in tendency only and that the poet would be repelled by fascism as it actually is. This, he would soon find out is government not by 'noblemen with Van Dyck faces, but … anonymous millionaires, shiny-bottomed bureaucrats and murdering gangsters' (pp 281-282). O'Brien (1988 [1965]) argues convincingly that Orwell understates the extent of Yeats's contact with real world politics and politicians during both his time as a senator and his Blueshirt period, not to mention his earlier support for the draconian policies of the government side during the Irish Civil War of 1922-1923.

ORWELL'S IRISH CONNECTIONS

Orwell and Yeats had a mutual friend in Ethel Mannin, a member of the Independent Labour Party (ILP), who would live for a time in Ireland, write of the experience in her 1947 memoir *Connemara Journal* and participate in the Irish Women Writers' Club. She is but one of Orwell's many Irish connections. Others include Cyril Connolly, whose mother was Anglo-Irish and his father of distant Irish descent. As a schoolboy, Connolly, who sometimes holidayed with his Anglo-Irish relatives, appears to have been briefly enthused by the Irish cultural revival of the early 1900s. Lewis writes (1997: 21):

> Eager to cultivate his Irish side, and so distance himself from middle-class England with its dispiriting freight of landladies and antimacassars, [Connolly] read up about Irish heroes like Wolfe Tone and Lord Edward Fitzgerald, learned to sing nationalist songs, and struggled in vain to cultivate a brogue and even master the Gaelic.

There was also Michael Sayers, with whom Orwell shared a flat in the 1930s. Sayers was a Dubliner whose father, Philip, had supported Sinn Féin in its breakthrough by-election in 1917 and, during the Irish War of Independence, provided a safe house for IRA volunteers and, on one occasion, Michael Collins himself (Murray 2018). Bowker (2003) quotes Sayers as remembering his relationship with Orwell as 'very close, very tender, even homoerotic' (p. 175). Although Sayers allegedly persuaded Orwell to look again at Yeats (whom Orwell had initially dismissed), he had otherwise little interest in Ireland or, indeed, Britain. Writing to the erstwhile Irish communist Leslie Daiken, Sayers commented: 'I confess I never felt at home on any island. I loathe water. I cannot imagine a country more foreign to me than England and less hospitable to my talents than Ireland. ... I am American by temperament...'[1] (quoted in Goldstone 2021: 66).

Rayner Heppenstall shared the same flat as Orwell and Sayers and, during the Second World War, was stationed in Northern Ireland, a part of the United Kingdom Orwell scarcely mentions. Northern Ireland, which had been created in 1920, was at that time the only part of the United Kingdom with its own devolved government and was, in fact, almost completely autonomous in domestic matters. The main British parties – Conservative, Labour and Liberal – did not engage in the region's political life which was monopolised by the Unionist Party, the party of the Protestant and largely British-identifying majority. Northern Ireland's Unionists would be permanently in government from the creation of the devolved administration in 1920 until its prorogation in 1972 during which time they would gain a reputation for institutional discrimination and heavy-handed internal security directed primarily against the region's large (35 per cent) Catholic and Irish-identifying minority (Farrell 1976, but see also Wilson 1989 and Whyte 1990). Heppenstall, in his semi-autobiographical novel *The Lesser Infortune*, notes some of the peculiarities of Northern Ireland, including its police force: 'The full-skirted, well-tailored black uniform, the holstered revolver and the harp on the black peaked cap contained for the unaccustomed eye a suggestion of the Balkan picturesque and of real violence' (1953: 16).

Heppenstall includes a few other asides regarding the strangeness of where he finds himself. 'It had gone up twice in Battery Orders that the local population must be regarded as 80 per cent hostile and treated with great reserve' (ibid: 27). At the same time, he recalls having been relatively happy during his time in Northern Ireland, particularly his weekends in Belfast which he spent in the company of a circle of local writers and journalists in the Brown Horse, a famous Belfast literary pub, now gone. One of his acquaintances was the poet and art gallery curator John Hewitt with whom he collaborated on a pamphlet, *Socialist Poems*, which was published by the Socialist Party, the Northern Ireland sister party of the ILP, in aid of the Russian Red Cross. Hewitt also recalled having met Orwell at the Adelphi Summer School in Langham in 1936: 'I can remember sharing the potato-peeling with him and listening to some excellent talk … the first man of the left in my acquaintance who could have been fairly called anti-Soviet' (2013: 57).

However, by far Orwell's most important Irish connection was his first wife Eileen O'Shaughnessy, the details of whose life were largely unknown until the pioneering work by Topp (2020). It occurred to me on reading that work how little Orwell himself refers to his wife's background which was, albeit at a remove, Irish Catholic. Eileen's grandmother was a native Irish speaker, her aunt, a nun in Texas, and her grandfather, a member of the Royal Irish Constabulary (RIC). That was a body that may have intrigued Orwell given his own policing background since the RIC had something of the colonial gendarmerie about it – Catholic constables under Protestant officers, deployed anywhere in Ireland except the community they came from.

MARTIN TYRRELL

THE 'IRISH QUESTION' AND THE HOME RULE CRISIS

The 'Irish Question' – whether Ireland should have 'Home Rule', its own parliament to manage its domestic affairs – was a fixture in British politics from the late 1800s. The question split the Liberal Party in 1885 and kept it out of power for most of the next two decades. But the prospects for Irish self-government revived following the great Liberal landslide in 1906 three years after Orwell's birth. What to do about Ireland would be one of the main debates in British politics throughout his schooldays and into his early adulthood. Orwell would have experienced events such as the Home Rule crisis of 1912-1914 and the 1916 Easter Rising as news rather than history and as events in Ireland that had a bearing on British political life. The Home Rule crisis, for example, brought Irish nationalists and their Unionist opponents to the brink of civil war, but also divided British political opinion since the Liberals supported Irish Home Rule and the Conservatives Unionism. This led to a deterioration in political and personal relations between the two parties (Dangerfield 1997 [1935], 1976).

With hindsight, the crisis was perhaps inevitable. Ireland, a century after the Act of Union 1801, had not settled into the United Kingdom. There were many reasons for this including the political exclusion of the Irish Catholic majority until 1829, the famine of 1845-1850, and a fifty-year campaign regarding land ownership that was resolved only at the start of the twentieth century.

That was the state of play in Ireland at the time of Orwell's birth. Central to the 'Irish Question' was that a majority of Irish people considered themselves a different nationality to the British and believed that the best way to move forward was to take at least some of the business of government into their own hands. To the Liberals, Home Rule was a positive and progressive idea, an administrative arrangement that would in the long run strengthen the Union. Conservatives, however, believed Irish nationalists would not remain content with Home Rule. Having secured it, they would sooner or later press for full independence, destabilising the United Kingdom in the process and sending the wrong, subversive message throughout its Empire.

Irish nationalism was largely, though not entirely, a movement of the Irish Catholic majority on the island and Unionism was almost exclusively Protestant. At the risk of over-simplification, Irish Catholics descended from the indigenous Irish and the pre-Reformation Anglo-Norman colonists, while Irish Protestants descended mainly from English and Scottish settlers who came to Ireland in the early seventeenth century. For much of the next century, Irish Catholics were excluded by law from civil, political and economic life with political exclusion, as noted, continuing until 1829. Collective Catholic action to address this exclusion evolved into modern Irish nationalism. In contrast, Protestantism had been culturally important to the creation of a common British identity in England and Scotland (Colley 1992) and, by extension, to the creation of a British identity among Protestants in Ireland. Irish Protestants were generally Unionists because they wished to maintain the territorial integrity of the Protestant United Kingdom. In opposing Home Rule, they made much of the fact that, under any autonomous Irish government, they would be Protestants governed by Catholics. Unionist advocacy played, in part at least, on traditional Protestant views of Catholics and Catholicism – 'Home Rule is Rome Rule', a concern Kipling expresses in his 1912 poem *Ulster*.

> We know the war prepared
>
> On every peaceful home,
>
> We know the hells declared
>
> For such as serve not Rome.

Unionism was initially an island-wide movement opposed to any form of self-government for Ireland. However, its stratagem was to prevent Home Rule by taking over the northern province of Ulster, where Unionists were in the majority, setting up a provisional government in Belfast and defending the arrangement with a volunteer army. The reasoning here was that Ulster was by far the most economically developed part of Ireland to the extent that Home Rule without Ulster would be a non-starter. By taking over Ulster they would, therefore, prevent Home Rule for Ireland in its entirety. In this way, the Unionist minority in Ireland would counter Home Rule legislation even though Irish Home Rule was the preference of the overwhelming majority of Irish voters and, indeed, the agreed policy of the Liberal government in Westminster.

A Unionist paramilitary body – the Ulster Volunteer Force (UVF) – was duly established and then equipped with modern rifles in a well-planned and executed operation (Stewart 1967). The Unionist leadership, which comprised prominent and well-connected people such as Edward Carson and F.E. Smith, then made it clear that in the event of Irish Home Rule being enacted they would resist until such time as they were defeated or Home Rule set aside. In this they were backed, not just by Kipling but other public figures including Sir Edward Elgar, much of the print media and, crucially, the Conservative Party[2] whose leader, Andrew Bonar Law, having reviewed a UVF parade, advised: 'There are things stronger than parliamentary majorities. ... I can imagine no length of resistance

MARTIN TYRRELL

to which Ulster can go in which I should not be prepared to support them and in which, in my belief, they would not be supported by the overwhelming majority of the British people' (see Fanning 2013). Further support came from the army when officers at the Curragh Camp in County Kildare indicated that they would resign their commissions rather than act against the Unionists. This situation, which had the makings of a Conservative and Unionist coup, not to mention a civil war in Ireland (since Irish Nationalists set up their own armed volunteer force) was defused only by the coming of world war in 1914.

Why might this have interested Orwell? Mainly, I think, because it exemplifies how, even in a democracy, a policy that has gone through all of the agreed democratic procedures can yet be threatened by an extra-parliamentary coalition of the powerful. There was a lesson here for democratic socialists. Orwell himself had speculated that any British socialist government that implemented a properly socialist programme would likely provoke counter-revolution from the disaffected right. Two books that interested him in this regard were Ernest Bramah's *The Secret of the League* (1907) and Jack London's *The Iron Heel* (1908), both of which fictionalise such an outcome, London's from a socialist perspective, Bramah's, conservative. In *The Secret of the League*, Bramah's counter-revolutionaries stage what amounts to a Tory coup complete with paramilitarism and economic sabotage. This successfully brings about a patrician restoration – restricted franchise, an end to salaried members of parliament and the removal of trade union immunities. The later and actual Unionist initiative against Home Rule has parallels with Bramah's imaginings – an opposing minority using its superior economic power and establishment connections to thwart a democratic political initiative. It is surprising that Orwell, in speculating a British counter-revolution, looked to fiction for his examples, but not to the one, real-world situation that arguably came closest to it and that had happened in his own lifetime. Newsinger (2018) comments that the behaviour of the army in 1914 is evidence of how it may have behaved in the event of a socialist government.

At around the same time as he was commenting on *The Secret of the League*, Orwell (1998 [1937]) gave Brigadier-General Frank Percy Crozier's *The Men I Killed* a positive review in the *New Statesman*. Crozier had become a pacifist and a regular speaker at pacifist events prompting Orwell to liken him to 'the reformed burglar at a Salvation Army meeting' (p. 74). However, Orwell does not mention the particular conflict that made Crozier a pacifist. This was the Irish War of Independence in which the Brigadier-General had been a serving officer on the British side.

The background to this conflict is as follows. In the UK General Election of 1918, voters in Ireland, then still a part of the United Kingdom, had voted overwhelmingly for Sinn Féin which was committed to establishing an independent Irish state as a *fait accompli* – then having it formally recognised at the peace conference then ongoing at Versailles. The failure of this strategy led ultimately to the war between the Irish Republican Army (IRA) and, on the British side, the RIC supplemented by a paramilitary corps of some 10,000 special constables made up of former servicemen, and the Auxiliary Division, made up of former army officers. The special constables are usually referred to as the 'Black and Tans' on account of the colours of their original uniforms although the name is sometimes extended to include the Auxiliaries as well. Crozier had been an Auxiliary before the work repelled him and, in time, he typified the regime he had been serving as 'fascist'.

> I resigned not so much because I objected to giving the Irish assassins the tit for the tat, but because we were murdering and shooting up innocent people, burning their homes and making new and deadly enemies every day. … I held a camouflaged command as a policeman trying to do a soldier's job without the moral support afforded to soldiers in wartime. I resigned when I discovered the deception, for the Crown regime was nothing more or less than a Fascist dictation cloaked in righteousness (Crozier 2002 [1937]: 136-137).

Orwell reviewed Crozier at a time when he was elsewhere arguing that there was little fundamental difference between liberal democracies like Britain and France with their extensive and often misgoverned colonial empires and fascist states like Italy and Germany. All were in his opinion forms of capitalism and all were capable of atrocity when required. Orwell envisaged that France or Britain, if pushed by, for example, the demands of war, would become more fascistic in their home territories. Crozier alleges that this is exactly what had happened in Ireland, just fifteen years before, and yet Orwell misses it.

Orwell was certainly aware of the Irish War of Independence though he generally refers to it as the Irish Civil War, thereby confusing it with a later, though connected conflict. Whatever the name, he is in no way sympathetic to the manner in which it was conducted on the British side referring to the Black and Tans as 'banditti' (Newsinger 2018) and likening them in *Homage to Catalonia* to the Spanish government's widely hated Assault Guards. In general, in fact, Orwell is strongly sympathetic to Irish nationalism, which he depicts as an understandable response to colonial misgovernment. For example, he considered the British

MARTIN TYRRELL

reaction to the 1916 Easter Rising as 'a crime and a mistake' (Orwell 1998 [1945]: 332).

In general, however, Orwell takes no great interest in Irish history and politics even where it has some relevance to his wider political views. It may be that it was not a priority for him to explore Irish history, perhaps because he found the subject unappetising, or because there were a great many other subjects that appealed to him a great deal more. I do not think that Irish Catholicism put him off. Though Orwell could be crudely anti-Catholic (for instance, his referring to D.B. Wyndham Lewis as 'a stinking RC', see Orwell 1998 [1932]: 268), his main issue is with upper-class English converts of a literary bent rather than people born to Catholicism such as Irish Catholics or the working class Catholics he met in the north of England who could readily tolerate a crucifix on the wall and a *Daily Worker* – the communist paper – on the kitchen table. Nor do I think that he shied from Irish issues because he sensed that this was an area where there might be trouble – when was that ever a concern of Orwell's? It is plausible, however, that he may have thought that the 'Irish Question' had been settled some time in the 1920s and that there was now nothing to see.

IRELAND AND DOMINION STATUS

Topp (2020) writes that Eileen Blair took to calling herself 'Emily' when she worked at the BBC during the war years and had sufficiently established herself there as Emily that some who knew her, like her friend Lettice Cooper, thought of her as Emily not Eileen. Why Emily? I suspect that it may have been to conceal her Irish background at a time when Irish people were sometimes suspect on account of Irish wartime neutrality. Orwell himself shared the general unhappiness regarding neutrality and, in his diary entry of 14 March 1941, he cites with approval Sebastian Haffner, a German refugee, who thought, according to Orwell, that 'the spectacle of our allowing a sham-independent country like Ireland to defy us simply made all Europe laugh at us' (Orwell 1998 [1941b]: 444). Orwell is here paraphrasing Haffner, the author of *Offensive Against Germany*, the second of the Secker & Warburg Searchlight series of books edited by Orwell and Tosco Fyvel. Haffner suggests in that book that Britain should invade neutral Ireland and seize its naval bases, which had been British until a few years before the war. In Haffner's view, this would send a strong signal to Germany and its allies that Britain was taking the business of war seriously. But I think the idea that Ireland is a 'sham' independent state is Orwell's, not Haffner's, in part because 'sham' is a term Orwell uses elsewhere to describe independent states which have no realistic chance of defending their sovereignty against attack and, in part, because Haffner does not, in

Offensive Against Germany, make any comments on the realism or otherwise of Ireland's claim to independence.

The idea that Ireland, in 1941, was a 'sham independent state' has, I think, wider relevance regarding Orwell's views on decolonisation in general. Ireland was the first part of Britain's empire to become independent since the United States in the eighteenth century and it is to date the only part of the United Kingdom proper ever to have, in effect, seceded. The British government had, as noted, refused to recognise the government established by Sinn Féin following its success in the 1918 General Election.

To the British, Ireland remained part of the United Kingdom and the paramilitary actions waged on behalf of its unofficial separatist government were regarded as criminal. Britain, instead, continued to explore Home Rule options culminating, in 1920, in the establishment of two Irish polities, called Northern Ireland and Southern Ireland, that would be autonomous within the United Kingdom and could, in the fullness of bureaucratic time, merge into a single devolved unit. Northern Ireland, of course, remains; Southern Ireland was stillborn, its first and only election delivering a further Sinn Féin majority that was taken (by Sinn Féin) as an endorsement of its unilaterally declared independence. Eventually, formal negotiations were opened between the British government and its unrecognised Irish counterpart. While Westminster would not concede the republic demanded by the Irish, dominion status was offered to the erstwhile Southern Ireland provided that the Royal Navy be allowed to retain its three Irish bases (those mentioned by Haffner) – which now came to be called the 'Treaty ports'. The effect of this latter requirement was that the new Irish dominion would have had considerable difficulty keeping out of any future war involving Britain.[3]

The offer of dominion status divided Sinn Féin but was eventually accepted by a relatively slim majority of its elected deputies mindful that Lloyd George had advised that the alternative to acceptance was an 'immediate and terrible war'. The resultant dominion, the Irish Free State, got off to an uneasy start given that so many of its leading politicians were opposed to its very existence. This division was, as Newsinger notes, encouraged by the British towards civil war, the new Free State versus the old Republicans led by Eamon de Valera a division that would, in less than a decade, provide the basis for the party system that dominated Irish politics into the present century, the Free Staters becoming Fine Gael and the Republicans, Fianna Fáil.[4]

MARTIN TYRRELL

DOMINION STATUS AND SOVEREIGNTY

I want to look at dominion status with particular reference to the Irish experience of it because this was the form of government that Orwell suggested for India in *The Lion and the Unicorn*. Ireland – the Irish Free State – would have been a worthwhile study as a guide to how dominion status may have panned out in India. Orwell is careful in *The Lion and the Unicorn* to propose dominion status for India rather than the less ambiguous independence. I think that he did so because he believed that this was not quite independence since any dominion was still ultimately under Westminster's jurisdiction.

The dominions were, in effect, self-governing sub-kingdoms within the British Empire, linked to the United Kingdom through having the same monarch. The original dominion was Canada, established by the British North America Act 1867. The effect of this Act was to federate the majority of the autonomous British territories in North America under a single government. But no additional powers were conferred on the new polity, which was a purely administrative development. No-one at this stage would have considered Canada a sovereign state.

Following Canada, Australia, New Zealand and Newfoundland acquired dominion status in the early 1900s. All of these were territories of the Empire in which large, sustainable and predominantly British settlements had grown to outnumber by many times the original inhabitants and had established institutions of government on the Westminster model. The next two dominions – South Africa (1910) and the Irish Free State (1922) – were different from these first four: South Africa because a majority of the settler-descended population was not British but Dutch, and because the settler population, Dutch and British combined, was many times *smaller* than the native African population, which was disenfranchised and, in 1913, dispossessed. The Irish Free State was different in that the settler-descended population was very much the minority and because dominion status was less than the full sovereignty aspired to by the majority. That dominion status was less than full sovereignty was tacitly accepted by all on the Irish side. It was only on the understanding that dominion status was less than independence that it had been offered in the first place. ('Dominion Home Rule' was the term used by a number of Conservative politicians, including Churchill.) On the Irish side, those who voted for it did so expecting that it could, in time, be amended and true independence achieved.

As in 1867, few in 1922 would have thought of the dominions of the British Empire as independent states. The British monarch was their head of state, Westminster could still legislate for them and their highest court of appeal remained the House of Lords. In 1914, the then five dominions had had no formal say in whether they entered the war. However, all five attended the Versailles Peace Conference (1919-1920) in their own right[5] and, in the following decade, dominion status began to change further.

Because of pressure from, significantly, the Irish Free State and South Africa, the two anomalous dominions, the Imperial Conference of 1926 declared that the dominions were sovereign states in their own right, equal in status to the United Kingdom. This was subsequently formalised by the Statute of Westminster 1931 from which point the dominions were *de jure* independent, able to legislate inconsistently with Britain and not be legislated for at Westminster.

It is unsurprising that Ireland, the reluctant and most nationalistic dominion, should have led the campaign to develop the Statute. And it is therefore interesting that, when the Statute of Westminster came to be debated in the House of Commons, several speakers advised that it be amended in the case of the Irish Free State precisely in order to keep its sovereignty limited. This was advocated on the grounds that the Free State was on a different footing from the other dominions. It was the only one that was geographically close to Britain (in fact, it had a land border with it) and the one most likely to make full use of the independence now available to it. A particular concern was that a less biddable Irish government might shortly be elected – de Valera's Fianna Fáil party. In the event the Commons voted not to limit the applicability of the Statute to Ireland partly out of concern that to do so risked making a de Valera government more rather than less likely. But, the following year, de Valera won anyway and, for the rest of the decade, used the powers available under the 1931 Statute to enhance his jurisdiction's independence. The oath of allegiance to the monarch was abolished along with the right to appeal to the House of Lords. A new constitution was adopted in 1937 that made the Irish Free State a *de facto* republic (and replaced the name 'Irish Free State' with 'Ireland'). Finally, in 1938, Haffner's naval bases, the three Treaty Ports, were, following negotiations, handed over to Irish control. Their transfer was what enabled de Valera to pursue a policy of neutrality in 1939.

In summary, de Valera in the 1930s used the freedoms available to him under dominion status to end dominion status in Ireland. Other dominions did not do this because they lacked the national liberationist history of Ireland or, in the case of South Africa, the nationalists had insufficient popular support. Had India become a dominion in the 1930s or 1940s, it would probably have used its new status in much the same way as Ireland had used it – to become fully independent and pursue independent policies.

PAPER

The other dominions, or the others aside from the anomalous South Africa, did not use their new freedoms in this way. They were states in which there was widespread popular affinity with Britain, reflected in a shared foreign policy, not so much imperial subjects as partners with Britain in a Commonwealth, a term that was by then gaining currency. When Ireland atypically used the 1931 Statute to phase out its status as a dominion, it did so cautiously. The 1937 Constitution is carefully worded so as not to spell out the new polity's status[6] and in the war years, de Valera's 'neutral island' risked invasion, not by Germany but by Britain.

> '[I]f it had not been for the loyalty and friendship of Northern Ireland,' said Churchill in his VE Day broadcast, 'we should have been forced to come to close quarters with Mr de Valera or perish forever from the earth. However, with a restraint and a poise to which, I say, history will find few parallels, His Majesty's Government never laid a violent hand upon them though at times it would have been quite easy and quite natural... (quoted in Carroll 1975: 163).

Churchill, for one, did not accept that Ireland was sovereign. He alleged that the Statute of Westminster applied to dominions which could not, therefore, use the Statute to renounce their status – to do so would be to create some kind of legal paradox. In his opinion Ireland, the dominion that had used its powers to renounce its dominion status, had placed itself in a kind of constitutional limbo.

ORWELL'S IDEA OF DOMINION STATUS

Orwell did not equate dominion status with independence. Either he still thought of the dominions in pre-Statute of Westminster terms or he thought that, regardless of the Statute of Westminster, there were still some limits on what a dominion could do in practice and some links to Empire that could not be broken. That is what I take from his proposal, in *The Lion and the Unicorn*, that India, when it became a dominion, should have an eventual and conditional, but not an immediate, 'power to secede' (Orwell 1998 [1941a]: 422).

A genuinely sovereign state that becomes part of some wider body voluntarily can secede from it. If India had become a dominion in, say, 1941, it could, based on the letter of the Statute of Westminster, have withdrawn or seceded from the Empire/Commonwealth and/ or declared itself neutral. But Orwell does not envisage his proposed dominion of India as having these rights or, at least, not while the war is in progress and not until the credible threat of further warfare has receded. Either Orwell has not kept up with developments in the law governing dominions and still thinks of dominion status in 1914 terms, or he thinks India should have less than full dominion status, the 1914 version rather than the current. Either way, the Indian dominion proposed in *The Lion and the Unicorn* will not be the sovereign, independent state aspired to by the Indian National Congress. Congress wanted India to be both independent and neutral. But Orwell thought that neither independence nor neutrality were realistic options. Should the British move out, he argues in *The Lion and the Unicorn*, and India declared independent, the Japanese or some other Axis power would move in, mismanage the sub-continent to a still greater extent than it has been in his view mismanaged to date and create a wave of famines resulting in many millions of deaths. Better, then, the British stay, he says, and India remain in the war and on the Allied side.

Orwell further qualifies what he is suggesting for India so that what is on offer seems more like a kind of managed transition towards dominion status than dominion status itself. Rather, there will be a process during which British experts and officials will work with Indians to create representative institutions and constitutional government and deliver a programme of economic development. Orwell stresses that this will be a partnership based on equality, not some kind of benevolent dictatorship. Implicit in what he proposes is, I think, a sincerely held belief that India is not ready for dominion status because it has been neglected and exploited for so long that it needs to be made ready. He comments that only a socialist government could offer such an arrangement.

Orwell, in *The Lion and the Unicorn*, is not, then, proposing Indian independence or even some form of dominion status but a process that will move towards dominion status as he sees it. And the right to renounce dominion status and to secede will come later still and only if unlikely conditions are met – a world no longer dominated by governments with ample supplies of state of the art military equipment. Orwell writes (1998 [1941a]: 415):

> In the age of the tank and the bombing plane, backward agricultural countries like India and the African colonies can no more be independent than a cat or a dog. Had any Labour Government come into office and then proceeded to grant India anything that could truly be called independence, India would simply have been absorbed by Japan, or divided between Japan and Russia.

In the event, Westminster did, in 1942, offer India full, dominion status albeit post-war and in return for full support while the war was in progress. This was the plan discussed with Congress by Labour front-bencher Sir Stafford Cripps and which Gandhi famously likened to 'a post-dated cheque on a failing bank'.

MARTIN TYRRELL

BURMA AND ELSEWHERE

The following year Orwell became involved in a debate on Burmese independence in which he was as sceptical of that country's chances of going it alone as he had been of those of India. *Tribune* had published an article by a Robert Duval, 'Whitehall's Road to Mandalay', which questioned the sincerity of Britain's commitment to eventual Burmese independence and argued that this now needed to be stated unambiguously. Burma had by then been invaded by the Japanese who had established a Burmese state. Discussions in parliament and elsewhere generally looked forward to what was sometimes termed the 'reconquest' of Burma and, by implication, a return to the *status quo ante*. This type of language unsettled both the Americans and those Burmese nationalists who supported Britain over Japan (Orwell 1998c [1943]).

In view of Orwell's time in Burma and the fact that he had written about the country, *Tribune* invited him to comment on what Duval had said, particularly the latter's recommendation that Britain should now commit unambiguously to Burmese independence. Orwell wrote: 'Burma is a small, backward country … it will never be independent' (ibid: 48). Many Burmese, he said, did not want independence but even if a majority were to want it, they would and could never have it. 'It is impossible,' he said, 'for a country like Burma to be fully independent, with its own private army, tariff barriers, etc' (ibid: 50). Talk of Burmese independence was 'nonsense' even if it were sometimes promised in the heat of wartime propaganda. It would be irresponsible for any British politician to say that there would ever be a Burmese state.

'Small nationalities,' Orwell claimed, '*cannot* be independent because they cannot defend themselves' (ibid: 49, italics in the original). In his view, a national state that cannot defend itself has to form some kind of arrangement with a bigger, more powerful state, but if it does that, then its independence is reliant on the protection of that state and is thereby, in Orwell's opinion, a 'sham'. In the whole world, Orwell reckoned, only five or six countries could be truly independent and, as a result, it was essential to discourage 'petty nationalism all over the place' and the creation, in Asia, Europe and elsewhere of a 'patchwork of comic opera states' (ibid: 48). Rather than an independent Burmese state, Orwell advocated a federation of South-East Asian states under Chinese (i.e. Nationalist Chinese) hegemony.

Orwell's views on what could be described as national liberation movements were critical and not especially supportive, at least during the war years. In his opinion, Ireland, India and Burma were strategic assets that could become enemy assets and would certainly become so if not defended by Britain or the Allies. Orwell was keen to prevent this. Just as he abandoned his revolutionary socialist/quasi-pacifist position in 1939, so he amended his commitment to national independence for colonial possessions. Ireland's neutrality was problematic enough for wartime Britain, but India's, in Orwell's view, would have created a much greater headache. In his subsequent comments on Burma, Orwell goes further and suggests that independence is a non-starter for almost all of the small nation nationalist movements that currently aspire to it. The future he envisages is one of large, federations of interdependent states, a prospect he would, of course, soon consider sinister and unsettling.

CONCLUSION

The superstates of *Nineteen Eighty-Four* are non-national – they are not based on any particular national community, traditions or institutions. These latter are, in fact, among the things Oceania at least is aiming to destroy. In contrast, Orwell's idea of socialism, most enthusiastically and explicitly set out in *The Lion and the Unicorn*, is one that draws on the cohesion and shared identity of the English/British national community. The war has impressed on him the unifying power of nationhood and the corresponding weakness of class identity as a transnational unifier. If Britain is to win the war, Orwell argues, it must become socialist but must also build that socialism on the existing British national collective. And in that context, he imagines a truly revolutionary transformation of British society.

Orwell does not envisage extending to India or Burma the same freedom to build an entirely self-determined future. In Orwell's proposals, India will have a continuing relationship with the former colonial power pending its eventual autonomy while Burma will be reassigned. True, some two years after he had said that Burma would never be independent, Orwell relented, proposing, in a letter to his friend, the *Observer* editor, David Astor, while on a war reporting assignment in Paris, that Burma become a dominion (Keeble 2022). It was, however, a suggestion made with the needs of Britain rather than Burma aforethought. 'If we keep Burma on as a colony a fresh quisling movement [sic] will spring up and as soon as we are in difficulties again Burma will drop off into the orbit of China, the USA, or whoever it may be' (ibid: 6).

'He never thought it worthwhile to imagine seriously what it would be like to belong to a people with a quite different historical experience from that of the English,' writes O'Brien (1976 [1965]). 'As far as he considered such matters at all, I think he felt that not to be a product of English history was a sort of moral lapse' (ibid: 61). Indeed, Orwell senses the depth and power of English national feeling, but not the national feelings of others and, therefore, cannot allow India nor Burma to take the same, self-determinist path he allows Britain by default.

Orwell's opinions in *The Lion and the Unicorn*, the Duval controversy and the Paris letter to David Astor were expressed in the heat of a war in progress, when the shape of the post-war world was uncertain. He did not live to see the great decolonisation of the 1950s and 1960s. We can only guess how he may have reacted. Some two years into the post-war era and a more empathetic Orwell advocated increased government support for the preservation of Scottish Gaelic (Orwell 1998 [1947]). If this is, in part, motivated by a desire to pre-empt the development of an antagonistic Scottish nationalism, it is also, and by his own admission, a rejection of views previously held, the result of his having lived in Scotland and listened to and been affected by the concerns of the people he has come to know there.

NOTES

[1] Ironically, Sayers, having relocated to the United States and there propagandised against nazism, would be deemed un-American in the late 1940s and duly blacklisted. Thereafter, he wrote for the Irish theatre and pseudonymously (as 'Michael Collins') for ITV in Britain until rehabilitated in the 1960s when he co-scripted a spoof version of *Casino Royale*

[2] The Conservative Party was, at this time, sometimes referred to as the Conservative and Unionist Party or, indeed, the Unionist Party. This was principally in recognition of Liberal Unionists such as Joseph Chamberlain who had left the Liberal Party on account of its endorsement of Home Rule and joined the Conservatives. There was no formal or organic connection between Ulster Unionism and the Conservative Party although Ulster Unionists elected to the Westminster parliament took the Conservative whip until the early 1970s and occasionally held junior Cabinet posts

[3] De Valera, on a 1920 tour of the United States to gather political and financial support for the unrecognised Irish state, briefly considered Cuba as a potential model for future British-Irish relations. However, he was quickly advised that Cuba was largely subordinate to the United States to the extent that the Americans could intervene directly and militarily in Cuban affairs, and that the US Navy retained a base at Guantanamo Bay the effect of which was to make the island republic an automatic American ally or, less kindly, strategic asset

[4] From 1932 to 2011, Fianna Fáil was the dominant party in Irish politics, in power for most of that 80-year period. Its decline resulted, in part, from its response to the global economic crisis of 2008 and, ironically, the revival of Sinn Féin

[5] India was also represented although Macmillan (2001: 56) comments: 'It was always "the dominions and India" in the official documents …[India's] delegation did not look like that of an Indian nation. It was headed by the Secretary of State for India, Edwin Montagu, and the two Indian members, Lord Sinha and the Maharaja of Bikaner, were chosen for their loyalty'

[6] That it was the constitution of a republic in all but name is evidenced by the fact that it remained the constitution of Ireland after the country became a republic officially in 1948

REFERENCES

Bowker, George (2003) *George Orwell*, London: Little, Brown

Carroll, Joseph T. (1975) *Ireland in the War Years, 1939-45*, New York: Crane, Russak and Company

Colley, Linda (1992) *Britons: Forging the nation, 1707-1837*, New Haven: Yale University Press

Crozier, F.P. (2002 [1937]) *The Men I Killed: A Selection from the Writings of F.P. Crozier*, Belfast: Athol

Dangerfield, George (1997 [1935]) *The Strange Death of Liberal England*, London: Serif

Dangerfield, George (1976) *The Damnable Question: A history of Anglo-Irish Relations*, New York: Barnes and Noble

Fanning, Ronan (2013) *The Fatal Path: British Government and Irish Revolution*, London: Faber

Farrell, Michael (1976) *Northern Ireland: The Orange State*, London: Pluto

Goldstone, Katrina (2021) *Irish Writers and the Thirties: Art, Exile and War*, London: Routledge

Heppenstall, Rayner (1953) *The Lesser Infortune*, London: Jonathan Cape

Hewitt, John (2013) *A North Light: Twenty-Five Years in a Municipal Art Gallery*, Dublin: Four Courts Press

Keeble, Richard Lance (2022) Letters from Paris throw new insights on Orwell, *George Orwell Studies*, Vol. 6, No. 2 pp 3-8

Kerrane, Kevin (2007) Orwell's Ireland, *The Irish Review*, Vols 36 and 37 pp 14-32

Lewis, Jeremy (1997) *Cyril Connolly: A Life*, London: Jonathan Cape

Macmillan, Margaret (2001) *Peacemakers: The Paris Conference of 1919 and its Attempt to End the War*, London: John Murray

Murray, Peter (2018) Big causes and small nations: Michael Sayers, writing, fascism, communism, and Jewish-Irishness, *Irish Studies Review*, Vol. 26, No. 4 pp 531-548

Newsinger, John (2013) 'This poor wailer among the rebels': Orwell, O'Casey and Ireland, *George Orwell Studies*, Vol. 2, No. 2 pp 20-38

O'Brien, Conor Cruise (1976 [1965] Orwell looks at the world, *Writers and Politics: Essays and Criticism*, Penguin: Harmondsworth pp 57-62

O'Brien, Conor Cruise (1988 [1965]) An essay on the politics of W.B. Yeats, *Passion and Cunning and Other Essays*, New York: Simon & Schuster pp 8-61

Orwell, George (1998 [1932]) Letter to Brenda Salkeld, September 1932, Davison, Peter (ed.) *The Complete Works of George Orwell, Vol. X*, London: Secker & Warburg p. 268

Orwell, George (1998 [1937]) Review of *The Men I Killed* by Brigadier-General F.P. Crozier, CB, CMB, DSO, Davison, Peter (ed.) *The Complete Works of George Orwell, Vol. XI*, London: Secker & Warburg pp 74-76

Orwell, George (1998 [1941a]) *The Lion and the Unicorn: Socialism and the English Genius*, Davison, Peter (ed.) *The Complete Works of George Orwell, Vol. XII*, London: Secker & Warburg pp 391-434

Orwell, George (1998 [1941b]) Diary entry, 14 March, Davison, Peter (ed.) *The Complete Works of George Orwell, Vol. XII*, London: Secker & Warburg pp 444-446

Orwell, George (1998 [1943a]) Review of *The Development of William Butler Yeats* by V.K. Narayana Menon, Davison, Peter (ed.) *The Complete Works of George Orwell, Vol. XIV,* London: Secker & Warburg pp 279-283

Orwell, George (1998 [1943b]) Review of *The Development of William Butler Yeats* by V.K. Narayana Menon, Davison, Peter (ed.) *The Complete Works of George Orwell, Vol. XIV*, London: Secker & Warburg pp 69-71

Orwell, George (1998 [1943c]) Comment on Robert Duval's 'Whitehall's road to Mandalay' and Correspondence on Nationalism, Davison, Peter (ed.) *The Complete Works of George Orwell, Vol. XV*, London: Secker & Warburg pp 47-55

Orwell, George (1998 [1945]) Review of *Drums Under the Window* by Sean O'Casey, Davison, Peter (ed.) *The Complete Works of George Orwell, Vol. XVII*, London: Secker & Warburg pp 331-332

Orwell, George (1998 [1947]) As I Please, 14 February, Peter Davison (ed.) *The Complete Works of George Orwell, Vol. XIX*, London: Secker & Warburg pp 43-46

Steele, David Ramsay (2017) *Orwell Your Orwell: A Worldview on the Slab*, South Bend, Indiana: St Augustine's Press

Stewart, A.T.Q. (1967) *The Ulster Crisis: Resistance to Home Rule, 1912-1914*, London: Faber

Topp, Sylvia (2020) *Eileen: The Making of George Orwell*, London: Unbound

Whyte, John (1991) *Interpreting Northern Ireland*, Oxford: Clarendon

Wilson, Thomas (1989) *Ulster: Conflict and Consent*, Blackwell: Oxford

NOTE ON THE CONTRIBUTOR

Martin Tyrrell teaches literature and creative writing at Open Learning, Queen's University, Belfast. He writes regularly on literature, history and psychology and is currently under contract to Athabasca University Press to complete a book on Orwell's wars, from class war to Cold War.

George Orwell, Ayer and Russell and the Battle for the Soul of Philosophy

PETER BRIAN BARRY

Bertrand Russell and A.J. Ayer, two giants of Anglophone philosophy, were not simply friends of George Orwell: they endorsed competing conceptions of philosophy that disagree over how involved philosophers should be with practical and political matters. Philosophy has for some time been concerned with just how detached philosophers should be, but this concern manifested in a comparatively minor affair involving Orwell, Ayer and Russell – all contributors to the journal, Polemic. *Correspondence about this* Polemic *affair buried in the Orwell Archive reveals that Ayer distinguished and preferred abstract and academic philosophy to the practical and political philosophy that interested Russell. This, in turn, suggests that a popular interpretation of Ayer's remarks about Orwell has been seriously misunderstood. Remarkably, a disagreement about the soul of philosophy is relevant to correcting a mistaken interpretation of Orwell as uninterested in or hostile to philosophy.*

Key words: Orwell, philosophy, A.J. Ayer, Bertrand Russell, *Polemic*

Bertrand Russell and A.J. (Freddy or Freddie) Ayer were giants of Anglophone philosophy in the first half of the twentieth century who were also well-respected friends of George Orwell. The philosophical achievements of each are considerable: Russell revolutionised logic and philosophy of language and some of his early essays, such as 'On denoting' (Russell 1905), are still mandatory reading in many philosophy departments; Ayer's *Language, Truth and Logic* (1936) was a canonical statement of the tenets of logical positivism and among twentieth-century British philosophers he arguably ranks second only to Russell (Foster 1985: ix). Orwell seems to have agreed with this ranking: in a 1946 letter to Andrew Gow, Orwell described Ayer as 'a great friend of mine' but named Russell 'the chief star in the constellation' (*CWGO* XVIII: 242).

Russell's influence on Orwell is considerable and acknowledged (Barry 2023b; Dwan 2018). Ayer, by contrast, is occasionally invoked

PETER BRIAN BARRY

to help make sense of Orwell (Shklar 1985; Thompson 1992) but usually thought to have had only a limited influence: biographer Bernard Crick suggests that Orwell may 'have picked something up from Freddy Ayer in Paris or London about "the verification principle"… his sole criterion of meaning in his *Language, Truth and Logic*' (Crick 1980: 361). While Orwell is sometimes thought to be in the tradition of British empiricism,[1] few have been so bold as to claim that Orwell learned much philosophy from perhaps the most influential British empiricist of his day. Sutherland, for instance, while discussing Orwell's invention of Newspeak in *Nineteen Eighty-Four*, stresses he is not 'in any way suggesting that Orwell was influenced by Ayer's book' (Sutherland 1992: 78-79).

While I am not arguing that Orwell studied philosophy at Ayer's knee, I do intend to continue my challenge to what I call *the inerudite interpretation* of Orwell; that is, the reading of Orwell that understands him as indifferent to philosophy at best and outright hostile to it at worst. At present, I aim to consider – really: *re*consider – what Ayer had to say about Orwell and philosophy. My contention is that Ayer's remarks about Orwell and philosophy have been chronically misunderstood and that the misunderstanding dissolves once an important distinction, implicit in Ayer's remarks, is recognised.

The distinction is salient to a centuries-old disagreement about what philosophy, at its best, can be and what philosophers should be doing, a disagreement that Ayer and Russell shared: Russell exemplified one conception of what philosophy ought to be, Ayer exemplified a rival conception. My evidence that Ayer clearly understood the distinction and took a side in the disagreement comes from correspondence about an otherwise minor event involving *Polemic* which involved Orwell if only tangentially. Perhaps it is not that surprising that philosophers as eminent as Ayer and Russell took sides in a 'battle' for the soul of philosophy, but it is perhaps surprising that Orwell played a minor role in that 'battle'.

In what follows, I first consider the case for the inerudite interpretation and Ayer's supposed characterisation of Orwell. Then, I discuss the crucial distinction implicit in Ayer's characterisation of Orwell with Ayer implicitly distinguishing academic and abstract philosophy from applied and practical philosophy. My contention is that defenders of the inerudite interpretation have not been sensitive to this distinction, wrongly understanding Ayer as having described Orwell as uninterested in philosophy generally rather than as uninterested in academic and abstract philosophy in particular. I then discuss some correspondence between Humphrey Slater and Arthur Koestler about the *Polemic* affair that demonstrates, first, that Ayer understood the crucial distinction, and second, put it into practice. The fallout of all this is that Ayer's remarks about Orwell are wrongly understood to constitute evidence for the inerudite interpretation.

ON THE INERUDITE INTERPRETATION

Orwell's reading list for 1949 indicates that he 'tried & failed' to complete Russell's *Human Knowledge: Its Scope and Its Limits* (*CWGO* XX: 219), a book about epistemology, a core area of philosophy, that clearly frustrated him. Orwell's remarks about philosophy included in a letter to Richard Rees deserve to be reproduced in full:

> If the antithesis to a 'some' statement is always an 'all' statement, then it seems to me that the antithesis of 'some men are tailless' is not 'all men have tails' but 'all men are tailless.' Russell seems, in that paragraph, to be citing only pairs of statements of which one is untrue, but clearly there must be many cases when both 'some' and 'all' are true, except that 'some' is an understatement. Thus, 'some men are tailless' is true, unless you are implying by it that some men have tails. But I can never follow that kind of thing. It is the sort of thing that makes me feel that philosophy should be forbidden by law (ibid: 52).

This is not the place to sort out the subtleties of predicate logic, but it may be useful to note that this passage is not the first or only place in which Orwell seems to disparage philosophy or suggest that he is philosophically inerudite. Orwell was prone to denying that the English were philosophical, his friendships with Russell and Ayer notwithstanding. In *The Lion and the Unicorn*, Orwell announced that the English 'feel no need for any philosophy or systematic "world-view"' (*CWGO* XII: 393) and recorded 'the lack of philosophical faculty, the absence in nearly all Englishmen of any need for an ordered system of thought or even for the use of logic' (ibid: 399). Similarly, in a BBC broadcast, reproduced in *The Listener*, about Tolstoy and Shakespeare he explained that 'most Englishmen' have 'no philosophical faculty' (ibid:: 492) while in *The English People* he explains that 'England has produced poets and scientists rather than philosophers' and that 'an inability to think logically' is one of the 'abiding features of the English character' (*CWGO* XVI: 204). 'The English,' he thinks, 'will never develop into a nation of philosophers' (ibid: 227).

Orwell's remarks about philosophy should be taken only so seriously: his remark that philosophy should be forbidden by law was surely a throwaway line, on a par with some of his other better-known generalisations such as 'all scoutmasters are homosexuals'.

PETER BRIAN BARRY

Still, no less an authority than Bernard Crick concluded that Orwell 'would … have been incapable of writing a contemporary philosophical monograph, scarcely of understanding one' (Crick 1980: xx-xxi) and that Orwell simply lacked the 'philosophical ability to resolve' philosophical problems (2007: 157). Crick even convinced some philosophers that Orwell read no philosophy (Rorty 1989: 173). Yet at the time of his death, Orwell's library seems to have included Russell's *The History of Western Philosophy*, multiple editions of *Mysticism and Logic and Other Essays*, *Philosophy and Politics*, *The Practice and Theory of Bolshevism*, and *Roads to Freedom* (*CWGO* XX: 296). His review of Russell's *Power: A New Social Analysis* praised Russell's 'essentially decent intellect' and intimated that Russell's *Freedom and Organisation* was even better (*CWGO* XI: 312). He recommended Russell's *The Practice and Theory of Bolshevism* to Dwight Macdonald, editor of the American leftist journal, *Partisan Review*, as an 'interesting' book since Russell was able to foretell 'in general terms a good deal that happened later' (*CWGO* XIX: 128).[2] Orwell also sometimes quoted or at least paraphrased Russell: for example, in 'Toward European Unity', he identified the greatest obstacle to European unity with, 'as Bertrand Russell put it recently, the unwillingness of the human race to acquiesce in its own survival' (ibid: 164).[3] And arguably – at least, as I have previously argued in this journal (Barry 2022) – Orwell did Russell a great honour by subtly referencing him during Winston's futile argument with O'Brien in *Nineteen Eighty-Four* when the former struggles to recall the fallacy in the latter's wild suggestion that everything exists only because it is perceived by the Party: 'The belief that nothing exists outside your own mind – surely there must be some way of demonstrating that it was false? Had it not been exposed long ago as a fallacy? There was even a name for it, which he had forgotten' (*CWGO* IX: 279).[4] Russell had identified the relevant fallacy in his critique of idealism in *The History of Western Philosophy* but did not name it: no surprise, then, that Winston could not recall it.

In sum, Crick's suggestion that Orwell was scarcely capable of understanding a philosophical monograph is imperilled by the fact that Orwell was so keen on reading Russell. But the defender of the inerudite interpretation has other cards to play.

AYER ON ORWELL ON PHILOSOPHY

Orwell and Ayer first met at the Hôtel Scribe in Paris in 1945 while he was on a reporting assignment for David Astor's *Observer*. Crick suggests that the two 'were … vastly different men of near genius who each recognized the quality in the other without being quite sure what it was' (Crick 1980: 325). In his autobiography,

Ayer explains that he had first heard of Orwell in 1937 after the publication of *The Road to Wigan Pier* and that he subsequently read *Homage to Catalonia* and *Down and Out in Paris and London*, books that he 'greatly admired' (Ayer 1977: 287) before their first meeting. Ayer indicated that Orwell 'was not very communicative to me about himself,' yet Ayer came to understand that Orwell was motivated by a desire to expiate his guilt for having served in the Imperial Police, that he had no religious belief and that his socialism was the product of his sympathy with the tradition of English Nonconformity and not Marxist theory. He was also proud of *Animal Farm* but did not anticipate its success and was dismayed that it gave any pleasure to the enemies of socialism. He said he had become more pessimistic by the time he wrote *Nineteen Eighty-Four*, that he enjoyed good food and drink and gossip, and that he was very good company when not oppressed by ill-health. Ayer's warmest remarks about Orwell suggest that the latter's 'moral integrity made him hard upon himself and sometimes harsh in his judgment of other people' and that he was 'another one of those whose liking for me made me think better of myself' (Ayer 1977: 286-287).

In his account of their relationship, Crick explained that 'Ayer noted that Orwell had no interest whatsoever in philosophy and Orwell seemed to indicate that it would be better for Ayer to interest himself in the future of humanity' (Crick 1980: 325). Biographer Gordon Bowker understands Ayer to have thought that Orwell 'gave no impression of caring much for philosophy' (Bowker 2003: 324); Michael Shelden explains that 'Orwell showed nothing more than a polite interest in Ayer's work' and 'had too much faith in common sense to make any philosophical system the object of serious study' (Shelden 1991: 411). John Rodden explains that Orwell 'evidently never discussed any philosophical topics with the founder of logical positivism' and 'had little patience with ... high-flown philosophical speculation' (Rodden 2011: 253). In other words, if Orwell had (as these writers suggest) no interest in philosophy then we surely have good reason to conclude that Orwell was philosophically inerudite.

However, Ayer's assessment is more nuanced than has been appreciated. Presently, I reconsider what Ayer says about Orwell. In the next section, I discuss the crucial distinction necessary to understand Ayer's assessment of Orwell.

Nowhere in either of Ayer's two autobiographies (Ayer 1977, 1986) does he suggest that he and Orwell had lengthy discussions about metaphysics and epistemology, but neither does he say that Orwell had no interest in philosophy. If Ayer says anything favouring the inerudite interpretation, it is in his interviews with Stephen Wadhams where he says:

PETER BRIAN BARRY

> Orwell and I shared a common outlook – politically, for one thing. We were both radicals, but he wasn't interested in academic philosophy in the very least. I think he thought it was rather a waste of time, that if people were going to philosophize they ought to apply their philosophy to political and social questions. I think the kind of abstract philosophy I went in for didn't appeal to him, and we didn't much talk about it. And he didn't hold it against me that I indulged in it! (Wadhams 1984: 168).

On the face of it, Ayer could not be clearer: Orwell was not interested in philosophy, it did not appeal to him at all, he never discussed it with Ayer, he thought it rather a waste of time. But the attentive reader will notice that is *not* what Ayer says: Ayer indicated it was *academic* philosophy that Orwell was uninterested in and *abstract* philosophy that did not appeal to him, not philosophy generally, a distinction that bears some comment.

A PHILOSOPHER ON PHILOSOPHY

It's easy to make jokes about philosophers. David Dwan points out that 'philosophy-bashing' is 'an ancient and very British sport in which many philosophers themselves gamely partook' (Dwan 2018: 5). So did Orwell. But while a casual reader could be forgiven for thinking otherwise, not all philosophy is well described as academic or abstract, the product of ivory tower philosophers writing tomes that only other isolated philosophers can make sense of. Some philosophical research is empirically informed, suitable for public consumption and intended to promote collaboration between philosophers and civic and professional communities. To be sure, many philosophers communicate poorly with the general public. Timothy Williamson, the Wykeham Professor of Logic at the University of Oxford (a position once held by Ayer), argues: 'A civilized society has popular philosophy just as it has popular physics, popular psychology, popular history.' He continues: 'Recent philosophical research has produced lots of fascinating new ideas, which deserve to be better known. Now there's a task for popular philosophy' (Williamson 2020). The philosophical tent is a large one and includes more than just the dry, stuffy abstract and academic writing that was apparently of little interest to Orwell.

We philosophers have known for some time that some of our work product is less than accessible to the general public and for some time we have debated whether philosophers should aspire to remain in the ivory tower like Kant or immerse ourselves in the public square like Socrates. At the risk of being dramatic, there is a debate about as old as philosophy itself about what philosophy at its very best amounts to. In his *Philosophy and Politics*, one of the books in Orwell's possession at the time of his death, Russell notes that 'The word "philosophy" is one of which the meaning is by no means fixed' and he distinguishes two different ways that it has been understood. On the one hand, 'Philosophy, as pursued in the universities of the Western democratic world, is, at least in intention, part of the pursuit of knowledge, aiming at the same kind of detachment as is sought in science.' But understood in its 'historically usual sense', philosophy 'was distinguished from science by the fact that an essential part of its purpose was to tell men how to live' (Russell 1947: 9). For his part, Russell's early work in logic and philosophy of language exemplifies philosophy in this first sense, but his later work was hardly detached and aimed explicitly at speaking to how we ought to live. David Dwan calls Russell's *The Conquest of Happiness* a 'self-help book for a troubled age' (Dwan 2018: 169), one in which Russell outlined 'a cure for the ordinary day-to-day unhappiness from which most people in civilised countries suffer' (Russell 2012: 5). In a similar vein, many of Russell's texts that Orwell read were aimed at introducing philosophy to a general audience. Russell is widely regarded, at least among professional philosophers, as a public intellectual who endeavoured to speak to professional philosophers and the general public alike. The eminent Harvard philosopher, W.V.O. Quine, suggested that Russell 'wrote a spectrum of books for a graduated public, layman to specialist' (1966: 657).

If Russell's later work exemplifies philosophy in the second sense, one that speaks directly to how life should be lived, Ayer's work exemplifies philosophy in the first sense which commends detachment from practical matters. Ayer's preference for detached and abstract academic philosophy is clearest in the record of an otherwise small matter involving *Polemic*, a matter in which Orwell played some small role.[5]

THE *POLEMIC* AFFAIR

In his letter to Gow, Orwell explained that *Polemic*, Ayer's 'new magazine', had only published a few issues yet Orwell had 'great hopes that it will develop into something good' (*CWGO* XVIII: 242). *Polemic*, subtitled 'A Magazine of Philosophy, Psychology, and Aesthetics', was intended to be a bi-monthly publication. But it ran at a more irregular pace, ultimately appearing in eight issues between 1946 and 1947, and favoured 'a cool, liberal rationalism, sympathetic to science, hostile to the intellectual manifestations of romanticism, and markedly anti-communist' (Collini 2006: 396). Five of the eight issues included essays written by Orwell, including 'Notes on Nationalism,' 'The Prevention of Literature,' 'Second Thoughts on James Burnham,' 'Politics vs Literature: An

PETER BRIAN BARRY

Examination of *Gulliver's Travels*,' and 'Lear, Tolstoy, and the fool'. Orwell also authored an unsigned editorial in May 1946 in which he makes the case that *Polemic* aimed at '*defending* a conception of right and wrong, and of intellectual decency, which has been responsible for all true progress for centuries past, and without which the very continuance of civilized life is by no means certain' (*CWGO* XVIII:: 268, italics in the original). Ayer and Russell were also frequent contributors, each publishing four essays. The especially memorable second issue, published in January 1946, began with Orwell's 'The prevention of literature', concluded with Ayer's discussion of Jean-Paul Sartre, and included Russell's contribution, the longest essay in the issue, on the problem of universals in philosophy.

While Orwell suggested that *Polemic* was Ayer's new magazine, Ayer merely served on the editorial board along with Russell and Orwell himself; Ayer suspected that he joined the editorial board because of his friendship with Orwell (Ayer 1977: 299). *Polemic*'s editor, Humphrey Slater, was described by Ayer as a former commissar for the International Brigade in Spain who turned against the communists 'because of what he saw in Spain, very much in the same way as Orwell had'. Ayer credited Slater for getting 'some money out of a rich Australian, a man called Rodney Phillips, who didn't mind what his money was used for'. Ultimately, Ayer explained, 'our angel decided that he could lose his money in more amusing ways and decided to back musical comedies, where at least he could get to know some chorus girls, and so *Polemic* folded'. It was, apparently, 'fun to write for while it lasted' (Wadhams 1984: 167).

The events that make up 'the *Polemic* affair' involved several eminent thinkers in Orwell's orbit and is recorded in correspondence between Slater and Arthur Koestler: the former in his capacity as editor of *Polemic*, the latter in his capacity as a public intellectual endeavouring to create a successor to the old League for the Rights of Man. Some account of the events leading up to the *Polemic* affair will be helpful (Burgess 2023: 200-203; Scammell 2009: 266-267).

Around Christmas of 1945, Orwell with his baby son, Richard, visited Koestler in Wales where Koestler pitched the idea of a new league to replace the French and British iterations which had come under communist control and gone dormant, respectively. They were joined by Mamaine Paget, Koestler's future second wife, and her twin sister, Celia, who would later work for Slater at *Polemic*. Orwell quickly produced a draft of a manifesto for the new league which ultimately promised both 'theoretical classification and … practical action' to 're-define the term "democracy" which is being interpreted in diametrically opposed ways in East and West, and thus loses all concrete meaning' and 'to make itself the advocate of [resistance to] infringements against the Rights and Dignity of Men' (Smith 2018: 231-233). Koestler and Orwell solicited others to join their cause, including Russell who was sympathetic but worried that world events had already progressed to the point where nuclear war was imminent. Russell recommended a conference organised around the topic of preventing atomic war that would feature about a dozen influential persons, including himself. If this was not quite the project that he originally envisaged, Koestler worked to bring it about: he booked accommodations, identified speakers and guests, including Orwell, with the hope that the event would be paid for by Phillips and that *Polemic* could supply a place for the league's future secretary to work. Things, in the end, did not go as Koestler hoped.

Two letters – one written by Slater to Koestler, the other written by Koestler to Celia – document aspects of the *Polemic* affair.[6] Slater's letter, dated 19 March 1946, clarifies that 'in a political sense I am in favour of the project' – he calls it 'a league against tyranny' – but insists on distancing *Polemic* from it. Here is a crucial passage:

> At the same time I feel that I was not emphatic enough at lunch the other day about my conviction … that there is a necessity in England for a theoretical magazine dealing with ideas on a more general level than that of politics and the particular sciences, and therefore that it is most necessary for *Polemic* not to be associated in the minds of the public with a practical organization for very directly and immediately political purposes.

Slater expresses concern about the reputation and perception of *Polemic* if it were to be seen as a tool for Koestler's league: 'You know how quickly people jump to over-simplified conclusions, and it is certain that if Rodney or I are associated closely with the formation of the league the whole future direction of *Polemic* will be changed in a direction to which neither of us can agree'. Even if its offices were used only temporarily, Slater worries, *Polemic* would 'be inextricably and permanently connected in people's minds with the league'. In this vein, Slater worries about a conversation with Francis Henson, an American in Europe to gather support for the International Rescue and Relief Committee, who indicated that he 'understood that it was intended that *Polemic* would become the official organ of the league to be initiated at the Easter conference in Wales': not for nothing, 'It may well have been from Orwell that Henson got the idea that *Polemic* would be the "official organ" of the League' (Burgess 2023: 202). Since, Slater thought, 'this idea is already all around the town and spreading not only throughout Europe but also America, it is clear that one must be firm about it'. And since 'all sorts of other people' who might have written for

Polemic or lent their names to advertisements could be put off if they came 'to feel that we had swung a quick one over them, and had got them associated with something about which they had not been consulted', Slater is clear that he and Phillips feel 'that we ought not to be involved in the initial stages of your project'. Slater adds that, after many years, wars and marriages, he is sure that 'the most interesting and useful thing that I personally can do is not to engage in practical politics, but to work in the theoretical field towards the consolidation of a humane world outlook synthesizing the aesthetic and scientific discoveries of the day'.

Upon learning of Slater's striking insistence on keeping *Polemic* 'theoretical' and detached from politics, Koestler was predictably put out: in his 21 March 1946 letter to Celia written 'in a mixture of anger and relief', he informs her that 'Humphrey is an ass', denies knowing the worrisome American, wonders where anyone 'got the notion from that anybody wanted *Polemic* as an official organ,' and expresses his frustration at having to cancel the conference and the accommodations for a dozen people that were already booked. The intended conference never materialised, nor did Koestler's league. But while Koestler's ire is focused on Slater and Phillips, Slater's letter makes clear that Ayer had a role in all this too. Another extended passage from Slater's letter:

> The other thing that has brought the matter to a head for us is a conversation with Freddy Ayer, who as you know is an important foundation member of *Polemic*, and who would consider, quite definitely, that he had been misled if *Polemic* were to get the reputation of being anything other than the independently theoretical magazine he and I originally projected and he might not want to go on being associated with it.

Ayer recalled Slater as having 'developed a greater interest in philosophy than in politics and sought to make *Polemic* as much a philosophical as a political or literary magazine' (Ayer 1977: 300). But Slater points to Ayer's threat to quit *Polemic* if it acquired a reputation as anything but a theoretical magazine as an especially weighty reason to keep some distance from Koestler's efforts. Ayer has nothing to say about the *Polemic* affair in his autobiographies but, if Slater is taken at his word, Ayer's apparent commitment to keeping *Polemic* focused on theoretical matters surely indicates that he understood the distinction between academic and abstract philosophy on the one hand and practical and applied philosophy on the other. The *Polemic* affair thus raises a serious challenge to the inerudite interpretation.

CONCLUSION: REVISITING AYER'S ASSESSMENT OF ORWELL

One bit of evidence supporting the inerudite interpretation is allegedly supplied by Ayer who, as the argument goes, recorded that Orwell had no interest in philosophy whatsoever. However, Ayer's actual remarks make clear that he thought Orwell had no interest in academic and abstract philosophy in particular. The record of the *Polemic* affair supplies evidence that Ayer distinguished academic and abstract philosophy from public and applied philosophy and that he preferred the former to the latter. But Ayer's preference creates a problem for the defender of the inerudite interpretation: insofar as Ayer did not equate academic and abstract philosophy with philosophy generally, his explicit suggestion that Orwell had no interest in abstract and academic philosophy provides no support for thinking that Orwell was uninterested in philosophy generally. At least, there can be no quick inference from Orwell's disinterest in a subclass of philosophy to the conclusion that he was uninterested in philosophy writ large, the conclusion that the defender of the inerudite interpretation needs. It would be closer to the mark to suggest that Orwell 'was not philosophically inclined, at least not in an academic sense' (Woodcock 1984: 285) or that he was 'suspicious of metaphysics' (Bowker 2003: 202), that especially abstract and academic branch of philosophy. But here too, suspicion of one branch of philosophy does not entail suspicion of it generally.

What is most surprising to me, a philosopher, is just how trenchant the inerudite interpretation seems even though Orwell so often expressed familiarity with and interest in philosophical concepts and problems. I offer a longer discussion of Orwell's thoughts on these matters elsewhere (Barry 2023a), but I close by noting my hope that Orwellians become more open to the idea that philosophy can contribute fruitfully to Orwell Studies. Indeed, a bit of philosophy helps to demonstrate that a seemingly minor skirmish involving Orwell only at the margins promises a better understanding of the man and his work.

NOTES

[1] '[I]t is reasonable to say that empiricism was a religious belief for Orwell; it gave meaning to the universe, the only meaning it could have after the failure of religion' (Wykes 1987: 97)

[2] Orwell gets the title wrong, reversing 'Theory' and 'Practice' (*CWGO* XIX: 128), although his ordering appears more natural

[3] Russell claimed that 'the difficulty is to persuade the human race to acquiesce in its own survival' (1946: 21). A similar quotation attributed to Russell is included in the communications of the League for the Dignity and Rights of Man, although Russell's last name is misspelled 'Russel', is contained in the Orwell Archive. The reference number is uncertain: Burgess notes one copy is filed as UCL Orwell/I/4/14; another copy is filed as Orwell/I/4/1 (Burgess 2023: 203)

[4] Robert Colls notes that Ayer, having made the case for 'common-sense empiricism' would find O'Brien's metaphysics 'absurd' (2013: 211)

[5] Whether it was a small matter is disputable: Burgess suggests that the *Polemic* affair was 'the second major reason' that a successor to the League for the Rights of Man failed to materialise (2003: 200)

[6] Both letters are housed in the Orwell Archive at University College London, included in a subfolder titled 'Papers relating to the League for the Dignity and Rights of Man (copies)': Humphrey Slater to Arthur Koestler, 19 March 1946, UCL Orwell/I/4/12; Arthur Koestler to Celia Kirwan, 21 March 1946, UCL Orwell/I/4/13

REFERENCES

Ayer, Alfred Jules (1936) *Language, Truth and Logic*, London: Gollancz, second edition

Ayer, Alfred Jules (1977) *Part of My Life*, London: Collins

Ayer, Alfred Jules (1986) *More of My Life*, Oxford: Oxford University Press

Barry, Peter Brian (2022) Bertrand Russell and the forgotten fallacy in *Nineteen Eighty-Four*, George Orwell Studies, Vol. 6, No. 1 pp 121-129

Barry, Peter Brian (2023a) *George Orwell: The Ethics of Equality*, Oxford: Oxford University Press

Barry, Peter Brian (2023b forthcoming) Orwell and Bertrand Russell, Waddell, Nathan (ed.) *Oxford Handbook of George Orwell*, Oxford: Oxford University Press

Bowker, Gordon (2003) *Inside George Orwell: A Biography*, New York: Palgrave Macmillan

Burgess, Glenn (2023) *George Orwell's Perverse Humanity: Socialism and Free Speech*, New York: Bloomsbury

Collini, Stefan (2006) *Absent Minds: Intellectuals in Britain*, Oxford: Oxford University Press

Colls, Robert (2013) *George Orwell: English Rebel*, Oxford: Oxford University Press

Crick, Bernard (2007) *Nineteen Eighty-Four*: Context and controversy, Rodden, John (ed.) *The Cambridge Companion to George Orwell*, Cambridge: Cambridge University Press pp 146-159

Crick, Bernard (1980) *Orwell: A Life*, Boston: Little, Brown & Company

Dwan, David (2018) *Liberty, Equality, and Humbug: Orwell's Political Ideals*, Oxford: Oxford University Press

CWGO (1998) *Complete Works of George Orwell*, Davison, Peter (ed.) London: Secker & Warburg

Foster, John (1985) *A.J. Ayer*, London: Routledge

Quine, Willard V.O. (1966) Russell's ontological development, *Journal of Philosophy*, Vol. 63, No. 21 pp 657-667

Rodden, John (2011) *The Unexamined Orwell*, Austin, Texas: University of Austin Press

Rorty, Richard (1989) *Contingency, Irony, and Solidarity*, Cambridge: Cambridge University Press

Russell, Bertrand (1905) On denoting, *Mind*, Vol. 14, No. 56 pp 479-493

Russell, Bertrand (1946) The atomic bomb and the prevention of war, *Bulletin of the Atomic Scientists*, Vol. 2, Nos 7 and 8 pp 19-21

Russell, Bertrand (1947) *Philosophy and Politics*, London: Cambridge University Press

Russell, Bertrand (2012) *The Conquest of Happiness*, London: Routledge

Scammell, Michael (2009) *Koestler: The Literary and Political Odyssey of a Twentieth-Century Skeptic*, New York: Random House

Shelden, Michael (1991) *Orwell: The Authorised Biography*, London: William Heinemann

Shklar, Judith (1985) *Nineteen Eighty-Four*: Should political theory care?, *Political Theory*, Vol. 13, No. 1 pp 5-18

Smith, David (2018) *George Orwell Illustrated*, illustrated by Mike Mosher, Chicago: Haymarket Books

Sutherland, Stewart (1992) Language, Newspeak, and logic, Phillips Griffiths, A. (ed.) *A.J. Ayer: Memorial Essays*, Cambridge: Cambridge University Press pp 77-88

Thompson, Caleb (1992) Philosophy and the corruption of language, *Philosophy*, Vol. 67, No. 259 pp 19-31

Wadhams, Stephen (1984) *Remembering Orwell*, New York: Penguin

Williamson, Timothy (2020) Popular philosophy and populist philosophy, *Daily Nous*, 8 June. Available online at https://dailynous.com/2020/06/08/popular-philosophy-populist-philosophy-guest-post-timothy-williamson/, accessed on 11 April 2023

Woodcock, George (1984) *The Crystal Spirit: A Study of George Orwell*, New York: Schocken

Wykes, David (1987) *A Preface to Orwell*, London: Longman

NOTE ON THE CONTRIBUTOR

Peter Brian Barry is the Finkbeiner Endowed Professor in Philosophy at Saginaw Valley State University. He has authored dozens of papers in ethics and social and political philosophy and contributed to the *Cambridge Companion to George Orwell's* Nineteen Eighty-Four (Cambridge University Press, 2021) and the *Oxford Handbook to George Orwell* (forthcoming), both edited by Nathan Waddell, as well as the *Routledge Companion to George Orwell*, edited by Richard Lance Keeble and Tim Crook (forthcoming) and *Orwell in Context* (Cambridge University Press, forthcoming), edited by Nathan Waddell. His most recent book is *George Orwell: The Ethics of Equality* (Oxford University Press, 2023).

ARTICLE

Orwell in Cornwall

While holidaying in Cornwall with his family during the summer of 1927, Eric Blair announced his intention to quit a well-paid job with the Indian Imperial Police to become a writer. Six years later he published his first book under his famous pseudonym. **Darcy Moore** speculates on the formative significance of Orwell's Anglo-Indian family connection to Polperro.

1927 was not the first time the Blair family had holidayed in Cornwall. Scant attention has been given to these summer months by biographers except for an anecdote about his resignation and a 'first adventure as an amateur tramp' recounted in a letter with a Polperro address (Crick 1992 [1980]: 176-177; Orwell 1998 [1903-1936]: 76). On closer examination, there is evidence that Orwell may have learnt a great deal about the natural world, science, art, literature and politics during these long summer holidays.

One biography offers a tantalising glimpse of carefree summers, as recalled by Orwell's youngest sister, Avril Dunn (1908-1978):

> Before 1914 and the Great War, the summer holidays were spent in Cornwall, either at Looe or at Polperro. An old Mrs Perrycoste of Polperro had been brought up by Richard Blair's mother, Eric's grandmother, who survived her husband by many years. ... Mrs Perrycoste's children, Honor and Bernard, played with Marjorie, Avril and Eric. 'We used to have a lovely time down there, bathing,' Avril reminisced in a BBC programme in 1960, 'we had some friends down there with children who were almost cousins really, and we used to go rock-climbing and all the sort of usual pursuits and he always seemed perfectly happy.' She remembered Eric, the Perrycoste children and herself going down a lane at Polperro where a headless ghost was said to lurk; and as a precaution they carried sprigs of rowan and a leaf from the Prayer Book. Eric was always interested in ghost stories (Crick 1992 [1980]: 83-84).

Who was Mrs Perrycoste? She was only 'old' in the sense that to Avril, who was a little girl at the time, all adults probably seemed that way. Maud Perrycoste (1864-1938) was a little over 40, active, creative, educated and intelligent. An artist and botanist, she had resided in Polperro with her husband since 1898.

The story of Maud's childhood illustrates a complex web of Anglo-Indian family connections and class consciousness. Born Mary Maud Hastings, she was the illegitimate daughter of Colonel Samuel Hugh James Davies (1820-1869) and a clergyman's servant, Mary Ann Hastings (1842-c.1888). Davies was superintending engineer on the Bengal Staff Corps when he died of fever in Shillong, India (Hewson 2005). From a large Anglo-Indian military family, he had never met his daughter but was wealthy, clearly worried about her wellbeing and made provision for ongoing care and significant financial support. Unusually, his will names the man her mother had subsequently married insisting that his daughter was not raised in the household of this 'reprobate' and 'fugitive' from the law (Davies 1869).

On Davies's death in 1869, five-year-old Maud was living with her mother (ibid). By 1871, she is residing in the household of Orwell's paternal grandmother, Frances 'Fanny' Blair (1823-1908), near Bath (Tovey 2021: 104). Maud must have ended up here as Fanny's younger sister, Laura Elizabeth Hare (1835-1919) was married to Samuel's brother, General James Snow Davies (1823-1903).

Orwell's father, Richard W. Blair (1857-1939), was Fanny's tenth child and one imagines the wealthy Davies family provided much-needed funds to the recently widowed woman ensuring Maud was raised in a genteel home as her father had willed. In 1875, the teenage Richard Blair began his Indian Civil Service career in the Opium Department. He remained in this department until 1911.

By 1881, Maud is being educated at a boarding school in Clapham. A decade later she is studying painting in London. By 1896, Maud is exhibiting her work at Birmingham Art Gallery (Tovey 2021: 105). Around about this time Maud attended botany classes at Chelsea Polytechnic (Derriman 1994a: 176). The lecturer was Frank Hill Coste (1865-1929) who shortly afterwards changed his name to Perry-Coste (written variously as Perry Coste or Perrycoste) to reflect his mother's maiden name (ibid). They married in 1898 and moved to Cornwall where Maud owned a fisherman's cottage in Polperro (ibid).

POLPERRO

> … there were few artists who were not bewitched by its twin harbours, its three old stone piers, one of which had properties built on it, its quaint, haphazard housing, the bubbling River Pol, which ran through the village under intriguingly named old stone bridges, and the jagged crags of Peak Rock at the mouth of the harbour (Tovey 2021: 6).

Frank and Maud Perrycoste c.1900 (courtesy of Jeremy Rowett Johns)

Polperro, an enchanting Cornish seaside village with the requisite history of smuggling, was quite isolated and a popular destination for artists. Maud passionately pursued botanical research. She maintained a significant private herbarium and was a member of *The Botanical Society and Exchange Club of the British Isles*. She continued to paint, exhibiting work at galleries in Falmouth, Exeter, Birmingham and Plymouth between 1898-1901 (ibid: 105).

Frank was 'a gentleman' but appears to have been without considerable means; Maud was wealthy (Derriman 1994a: 176). The couple built a spacious new home, 'Higher Shute', in a prime position on Talland Hill overlooking the harbour and village (Tovey 2021: 104). One local recollected that it was always 'the gentry' back in those days who lived on 'the hill' but felt (a little ungenerously perhaps) they had 'built a very ugly house' (Jerram nd: 19). Today, online advertising describes the place as an 'unusually spacious arts and crafts-style house' with 'wood beams, open fireplaces' and 'oozing character' (Holiday Cottages 2022).

The current owners of Higher Shute are aware that Frank and Maud Perrycoste lived at their property discovering that the newlyweds set about a substantial project to extend and modernise the house:

> The original building was quite a large a 18th century cottage on the hill. The Perrycostes extended the building in all directions and built a south wing over two floors to provide a large drawing room and a studio above for Maud with fine views over the harbour. There is a nice commemorative plaque over the new front door, F&M P-C 1899 (Childs 2023).

Commemorative plaque 1899 (courtesy of Nick Childs)

The Blairs must have enjoyed memorable summers at this residence (which is listed as vacant on the 1921 census suggesting it was available for friends and family). They also stayed at a guest house named 'Grove Terrace' and possibly Maud's other local residence, 'Warren Cottage' (Tovey 2021: 104).

Maud appears to have ceased painting (or at least exhibiting) when her children were born (ibid: 105). Fanny Blair died in 1908 but her son's children developed a fun relationship with her ward's family in the coming years. The 'cousins' Avril mentioned playing with in Polperro before the war were Wykeham Bernard Cuthbert Perrycoste (1902-1972) and Honor Maud Mary Perrycoste (1903-1987) (Derriman 1994b: 210).

ARTICLE

Maud Perrycoste, *A Corner of the Harbour: Polperro*, 1901
(courtesy of David Tovey)

The same contemporary, who did not like the new house much, reminisced in her old age about Maud and Frank. She thought her a 'good artist and botanist, but inclined to be affected and, at times,

DARCY MOORE

hysterical' (Jerram nd: 19). She was 'very kind' and others 'liked her' even if 'they laughed at her' (ibid). She noted an aunt was genuinely 'shocked' by Maud's 'modern ideas on religion, especially on Sunday observances...' (ibid). Frank, although he had a 'reputation for cleverness' she 'never heard of anything he did or said that confirmed this' (ibid).

One newspaper report, 'Alleged damage to corn', from the *West Briton and Cornwall Advertiser*, of 1916, offers an insight into Maud's personality and one can imagine how much a young Orwell would have relished traipsing all over the district looking for botanical specimens with this unconventional woman, Avril and her children.

ALLEGED DAMAGE TO CORN.

Mrs. Perry-Coste wife of Mr. F. H. Perry-Coste, J.P., of Polperro, was summoned at Liskeard on Wednesday, by Mr. Clarence Tuckett, of Killigarth Farm, for doing damage to corn on August 9th.—Mr. Perry-Coste asked for an adjournment, seeing that the summons was only served on Monday, but was quite prepared to go on with the case if prosecutor did not object to being cross-examined.—Prosecutor had no objection, and said he had had considerable trouble through people damaging the corn growing on his farm. On the day referred to he met Mrs. Perry-Coste with two children in one of his fields, through which a road runs, and each was carrying corn. He told Mrs. Perry-Coste that she ought to know better than to pluck the corn if the children did not. She became very insolent, and said she should do what she pleased. He told her that if she did it again he should proceed against her. She then deliberately went amongst the corn and picked more.—During Mr. Perry-Coste's cross-examination of prosecutor the statements as to what actually occurred were so contradictory that Mr. Perry-Coste asked for an adjournment in order that his wife might give evidence, and this was granted.

(*West Briton and Cornwall Advertiser* 1916)

THE POLPERRO FINGERPRINT MAN

Mr Perry-Coste was born at Tottenham, London, in 1865, and had an interesting ancestry being descended paternally from Huguenot refugees, a French protestant community, who were subjected to much persecution in the 16th and 17th centuries, and through his maternal grandmother, from a sister of William of Wykeham! His maternal grandfather was Sampson Ferry, who lived from 1745 to 1823, a physician, journalist, patriot and political martyr and at one time prosecuted by the Pitt Ministry (*Cornish Guardian*, 1929).

Frank Perrycoste (1865-1929) was a polymath. He won a scholarship to St. Paul's School and subsequently completed a Bachelor of Science at London University (studying Mental and Moral Science, with Honours in Chemistry and Botany) which led to employment as an analytical chemist (*Cornish Guardian* 1929; Derriman 1994a: 176). He soon abandoned this job for a literary career, often writing about scientific topics. He published prolifically from the early 1890s, often employing the pseudonym 'Free Lance' (ibid). Titles included: *The Cry of the Children: An Essay in Tyranny and Ignorance* (1892); *Towards Utopia: Being Speculations in Social Evolution* (1894); *The Ethics of Suicide* (1898); and *Ritual, Faith and Morals: Being Two Chapters from an Historical Enquiry into the Influence of Religion Upon Moral Civilisation* (1910). He was a frequent contributor to journals such as *Natural Science*, *Nature* and *The Etymologist* (ibid).

Perrycoste's obituary posited that 'his life's work was a treatise on *Comparative Religion and Morals*, of which he published about five volumes' (*Cornish Guardian* 1929). However, he is now mostly remembered as the 'Polperro Fingerprint Man' (Derriman 1994a: 174). In 1903, Perrycoste corresponded with Francis Galton – a eugenicist deeply influenced by his cousin, Charles Darwin – volunteering to conduct research into inherited characteristics by fingerprinting the entire population of the village (Pearson 1930: 522-524). Galton agreed and their correspondence, discussing fingerprinting Frank's son, poor handwriting and the resulting need for a typewriter, is mildly amusing (ibid).

Perrycoste would spend most of the next 25 years combing parish records, graveyards and conducting oral research which continues to be an invaluable local genealogical and scientific resource. *Pedigrees of Polperro* was published by the *Cornish Times* in 1925 (and other similar studies followed). A posthumously published book, *Gleanings from the Records of Zephaniah Job of Polperro*, is a comprehensive look at smuggling during the Napoleonic Wars (Perrycoste 1930).

HAVELOCK ELLIS

Francis Galton was not the only eugenicist with whom Frank Perrycoste corresponded. Havelock Ellis (1859-1939), who spent winters in Cornwall, was a radical intellectual who wrote extensively on human sexuality. Ellis and Perrycoste had many shared interests, became friends and corresponded hundreds of times from 1893 until Frank's death in 1929. Their initial exchange was in relation to Ellis's first book, *The Criminal* (1890). Perrycoste challenged aspects of Ellis's critical summary of the new science of criminal anthropology. Ellis replied, on 4 June 1893:

> Many thanks for your notes on *The Criminal*. The book was written four years ago, and I should now be more cautious concerning some of the points you mention – especially the question of inheritance of acquired characters (Grosskurth 1980: 117).

The first two volumes of Ellis's seminal work, *Studies in the Psychology of Sex*, were published in the aftermath of Oscar Wilde's incarceration in Reading Gaol for 'acts of gross indecency with another male person' (Old Bailey 1895). This pioneering scientific study of homosexuality soon ran afoul of censorship and morality laws.

The publishing history of these studies is quite complex and beyond the scope of this essay so a summary will have to suffice. Perrycoste had written to Ellis endeavouring to assist in finding a publisher for his controversial research. The first edition was co-authored by the poet, John Addington Symonds,[1] who had assisted with interviewing gay men in an effort to remove the stigma of degeneracy associated with homosexuality. Subsequent editions only listed Havelock Ellis. Watford University Press published the first volume, *Sexual Inversion* (1897), which was almost immediately withdrawn from sale after George Bedborough (who was considerably more than just a bookseller) sold a copy to a police officer, the subsequent trial impacting significantly on Ellis (Nash 2020: 116-136). Ellis thanked Perrycoste in his Preface and included Frank's research in the appendices (Ellis 1927 [1897]: 5, 191-197). It is also noteworthy that Ellis had an appendix on a topic Orwell was to write about in 1933, 'Homosexuality among tramps' (Ellis 1927: 348-353).

What did Orwell know (considering *Studies in the Psychology of Sex* was re-published in 1927)? Did he understand that Perrycoste and Ellis were friends and corresponded? In 1935, Orwell wrote to his friend Brenda Salkeld (who was collector of signatures) indicating he knew Ellis's work:

> Dear Brenda,
>
> Thanks for your letter. No, I cannot say that Havelock Ellis's signature, as I remember it, struck me as being at all like what I expected. I should have expected him to write a very fine hand and use a thinner nib. We bought recently a lot of books with the authors' signatures in, and some of them containing autograph letters as well, but they were all sold almost at once (1998 [1903-1936]: 368-369).

More significantly, the year after Ellis died, Orwell reviewed *My Life: The Autobiography of Havelock Ellis* (1939) in his familiar, vastly amused, trenchant style:

> As the surviving writers of the nineteenth century drop away, one has the feeling that they are dying just in time. Ten years more, even five years, and they might recoil in horror from the world they have helped to create. When Havelock Ellis was born, the *Origin of Species* was a brand-new scandal; when he died, the Germans were in Prague. In between there lay eighty years of 'progress' and 'enlightenment', of patient, courageous effort by men like Ellis himself to chip away the bases of Christian civilisation. It had to be done, but the result was totally different from what had been intended. In every line that Havelock Ellis wrote – and for that matter even in the photograph of him that forms the frontispiece of this book – you can see what he was after: a sane, clean, friendly world, without fear and without injustice. What fun it must have been, in those hopeful days back in the 'eighties, working

away for the best of all possible causes – and there were so many causes to choose from. Who could have foreseen where it would all end? In his autobiography Havelock Ellis does not say much about his work. He is simply telling the story of his life, a studious, physically unadventurous life… (Orwell 1998 [1940-1941]: 154-155).

Orwell includes a trope, familiar to anyone who has read *The Road to Wigan Pier* (Orwell 1997 [1937]: 150-151), in the review, saying: '… a time when Socialism, vegetarianism, New Thought, feminism, homespun garments and the wearing of beards were all vaguely interconnected' (Orwell 1998 [1940-1941]: 155). Ellis and Perrycoste were both the kinds of socialists whom Orwell loved to lampoon.

Havelock Ellis (1913) Public Domain

Did Orwell's aunt, Nellie Limouzin, who also holidayed in Polperro, know Perrycoste – or Ellis? Writing to her nephew in June 1933, Nellie mentions a book that suggests she and Orwell discussed topics that also fascinated Ellis and Perrycoste:

> I am also reading an interesting work on *Les Dogmes Sexuels*; it is a refutation of the generally accepted ideas on sex as regards the contrast between the male and female and is based on biology of which the first long chapter consists, beginning with the single cell etc. Evidently the authoress is a serious scientist (Orwell 1998 [1903-1936]: 314).

A LOVE OF KNOWLEDGE AND NATURE

Orwell's enduring love of rambling in the countryside and his surprisingly detailed knowledge of the natural world is scattered through his letters, diaries and published work (and was mentioned by numerous friends, lovers and even pupils):

> Flowers now in bloom in the garden: polyanthus, aubretia, scilla, grape hyacinth, oxalis, a few narcissi. Many daffodils in the field. These are very double & evidently not real wild daffodil but bulbs dropped there by accident. Bullaces & plums coming into blossom. Apple trees budding but no blossom

yet. Pears in full blossom. Roses sprouting fairly strongly. I note that one of the standards which died is sprouting from the root, so evidently the stock can live when the scion is dead. Peonies sprouting strongly. Crocuses are just over. A few tulips in bud. A few leeks & parsnips in the garden (the latter have survived the winter without covering up & tops are still green), otherwise no vegetables. It appears that owing to severe frosts there are no winter greens locally (Orwell 1998 [1937-1939]: 430).

Geoffrey Stevens, one of the children he taught in the early 1930s, described Orwell as 'a great nature lover' who took delight in showing the class 'Puss Moth caterpillars eggs on the Black Poplar' and how to 'collect marsh gas from some stagnant pond' outside of school hours (Crick 1992 [1980]: 222).

Where did Orwell gain such detailed knowledge? In his youth he rambled extensively around Ticklerton in Shropshire with his friends, accompanied by knowledgeable adults like Lilian Buddicom. The Perrycoste family were not only well-educated and scientifically literate but committed to practical, sophisticated research. In 1920, Frank and his teenage daughter, Honor, co-authored a paper, 'Cornish phenology, 1912-19', which was published in *Science Progress in the Twentieth Century*. Based on data collected over a period of eight consecutive years (in association with the *Wild Flower Society*) they 'emphasise the importance of systematised phenological records as indices to what one may perhaps call resultant climate, or to point out that the net effect of temperature, rainfall, latitude, elevation, exposure, etc., is summed up in, e.g., the dates of flowering of plants without any ambiguity or possibility of error' (Perrycoste 1920: 60).

A text search through the 1922 supplement to *Flora of Cornwall* (1909) reveals just how active Maud and Frank were in identifying local species and correcting errors. The name 'Perrycoste' appears 183 times in the 200-page supplement (Thurston 1922). Honor was awarded a PhD in Botany from Bristol University in 1924 (*Western Daily Press* 1924).

What impact did the Perrycoste family have on Orwell, who was a well-known lover of flowers? Did his experiences with this family form the genesis of his knowledge of nature, especially botany? What else would the young Orwell do in Polperro over the lengthy summer holidays other than ramble with the Perrycostes who had children the same age? Honor and Eric considered each other to be "cousins" (Carter 2023). They were "close when they were young" according to Honor's granddaughter due to Ida Blair's relationship with Maud (ibid).

SOME FURTHER SPECULATION

Orwell and his family visited Polperro during August-September 1920. One imagines that Orwell, his parents, Maud and Frank discussed a range of topical family issues. This letter, to the editor of *Science Progress* from Perrycoste in October 1920, about 'Starvation pay of brain-workers' is an interesting one:

> Dear Sir, I believe that I am correct in stating that a raw youth of about eighteen, if possessing a good physique and a fair character, and if normally 'intelligent', is started, even whilst under training, in the police force at pay of £182 per year; and he may rise to the rank of superintendent at a minimum annual pay of £450: and every rank in the police force carries a substantial pension. Incidentally, I have seen it stated that the average annual pay of university professors is about £400; and the provision for pensioning them is, I believe, negligible.
>
> It was recently decided that dockers – who, I suppose, are at the lowest level of unskilled physical labour – ought to receive £250 per year; and a scheme is under consideration for guaranteeing them, whilst unemployed, pay at the rate of £200 per year at the expense of the industry.
>
> Let it be remembered that those who become policemen and dockers have been earning wages – in these days possibly or probably more than their cost of living – since they were fourteen.
>
> Now we will turn to the other side of the picture. In a recent issue of *Nature* the University of London advertises for two demonstrators in chemistry at a salary each of £200 – equivalent in purchasing power to about £76 in 1913. I presume that such demonstrators will be graduates – i.e. that, instead of having earned their living during seven or eight years previously, they have been kept at school and university at very heavy expense to their parents.
>
> I brush aside at once the myth that only rich men send their sons to the universities. In numberless cases the lads are sent there at the cost of grievous self-denial to the parents, and not even as a good pecuniary investment for the lads themselves (Perrycoste 1921: 478).

Mr and Mrs Blair were certainly considering what their son was going to do post-Eton this summer. Jacintha Buddicom recalled conversations about Oxford University suggesting Mr Blair was against and that Mrs Blair disagreed with him (Buddicom 2006 [1974]: 77).

DARCY MOORE

Orwell joined the Indian Imperial Police in 1922 rather than attend university. Frank was long dead but it is interesting that Orwell noted twenty years later, in *Tribune*, 3 January 1947, the experience of seeing one of the quartermasters on the voyage to Burma:

> ... scurrying like a rat along the side of the deck-houses, with something partially concealed between his monstrous hands. I had just time to see what it was before he shot past me and vanished into a doorway. It was a pie dish containing a half-eaten baked custard pudding.
>
> At one glance I took in the situation – indeed, the man's air of guilt made it unmistakable. The pudding was a left-over from one of the passengers' tables. It had been illicitly given to him by a steward, and he was carrying it off to the seamen's quarters to devour it at leisure.
>
> Across more than twenty years I can still faintly feel the shock of astonishment that I felt at that moment. It took me some time to see the incident in all its bearings: but do I seem to exaggerate when I say that this sudden revelation of the gap between function and reward – the revelation that a highly-skilled craftsman, who might literally hold all our lives in his hands, was glad to steal scraps of food from our table – taught me more than I could have learned from half a dozen Socialist pamphlets? (Orwell 1998 [1947-1948]: 6).

Frank would have appreciated the anecdote.

MORE ON FRANK AND MAUDE

> ... there is one phrase in it that is as individual as a fingerprint (Orwell 1998 [1940-1941]: 48).

Frank Perrycoste was always a progressive thinker and by the end of his life, politically a supporter of the Labour Party (Derriman 1994b: 209). He was eulogised as the 'fisherman's champion' (*Cornish Guardian* 1929). Another view of Frank, and a description of Maud, was provided by Geoffrey Grigson (1905-1985) in *The Crest On The Silver: An Autobiography* (1950). Maud, who knew his mother, encouraged Grigson in his love of plants (ibid: 40-41). A poet, magazine editor and naturalist, Grigson worked during World War Two in the editorial department of the BBC Monitoring Service and was a talks producer. He knew Orwell at this time (and they had many mutual friends) and there is speculation (from a Grigson biographer) that he may have played with Orwell, Bernard and Honor in Polperro before the war (Healey 2023). Julian Symons described him as:

... tall, handsome, and enthusiastic, with an attractive blend of sophistication and innocence. The fierceness of his writing was belied by a gentle, sometimes elaborately polite manner. He distrusted all official bodies dealing with the arts, and served on no committees (Symons 2009).

Grigson founded *New Verse* (1933-1939), described the journal as a 'malignant egg', regretting the 'savage use of the billhook' in his own 'unsparing and at times ferocious' criticism of his contemporaries (ibid). This vitriol is evident in his reviews written for *The Observer*, *The Manchester Guardian* and *The New Statesman* (ibid). Grigson made literary enemies with insouciant ease and his jibes towards the 'X-Ys' (the unnamed Perrycostes in his autobiography) sees him in full-flight, although he does qualify his commentary (Grigson 1950: 40-41). There is some useful information about political associations and personal predilections and Frank appears not to be as popular with the fishermen as his obituary suggested:

> A fairly close friend ('fairly close' is enough because the friendship dwindled during the years) was a woman of intelligence who lived in Polperro. She sketched, and gave oil-sketches of the rocks meeting the rocks to my mother who managed to conceal another bit of the drawing-room wall with them. She was also a botanist, in the commoner sense of one who knew her plants, had adventures in search of them, and contributed to the country flora. She was small and active, a fluffy red-cheeked little woman, not far from the untidiness into which she fell, who tricycled round the district, a thing, so far as I know, my mother never achieved. She married a strange man, who was a bogey. I must once have touched his velvet coat, which I always disliked. He was a scientist – perhaps a chemist – but either he or his wife came into money enough to build themselves a house, and live, and meditate at Polperro. He was also a rationalist, an atheist, and a Radical Wellsian figure, self-educated to some degree, and uncertainty in command of standard English pronunciation, a fault on which my mother would sharpen her claws.
>
> There was an air of failure about this man, with his long face, his distant manner, his habit of disappearing in his house, his wispy moustache, which I felt. He always pronounced my name wrongly, 'Well, Juffrey', if I came to the house; and then disappeared. He was *ungemütlich* and a little pompous, and winter and summer he always bathed, nude or with a minimum of triangle, from a rock pool just round from the harbour. Genetics was one of his pursuits. He studied in-breeding in Polperro fishermen. His unreadable books were

ARTICLE

published privately, but he had friends in the more positive and less amateur world, among them Havelock Ellis; and I was surprised to find a few years ago that he had contributed an appendix to Havelock Ellis's *Studies in the Psychology of Sex*. It was just as well no one knew that in Polperro, or in the vicarage. Polperro did not altogether appreciate him. At election time – he was friendly with the Foots, I believe, as well as being one of their supporters – Tory fishermen would take their trousers down on his doorstep and leave a token of their goodwill to be discovered there in the morning.

I wish now that we had known this family better than we did. There was an earnestness in the household, an activity outside the mere routine of staying alive, and a contact with professional artists and writers and men of science altogether lacking in the vicarage three miles away. But perhaps appearances interfered again. X-Y, hyphened, was not, well, not a gentleman, 'and he was plain Y', said my mother, 'when his old father was alive'. My mother had a justifiable scorn for the creation of double-barrelled names as an easy way of assuming gentility and distinction. As children, we always heard criticism of the Polperro household, which the wife's eccentricities did not diminish; we looked for oddity there and found it, and there was family hostility towards going to parties in the house. My mother was not interested in the husband, in the identification of plants, in tricycling, in bathing, in picnics, and eventually it became the habit in the family, though she was godmother to one of my brothers (in spite of her husband's atheism) and though my father actually stood sponsor to her son, to speak of my mother's old friend with contempt. Still that did not prevent kindnesses and encouragement from her, in one instance, for which I suddenly realise I must be grateful. She discovered my interest in plants, lent me floras, and helped me with identifications; and it was through her that I believed at one time I would make my living as a professional botanist or a forester (ibid: 40-41).

Grigson published many books about flowers, including *Wild Flowers in Britain* (1943), *Flowers of the Meadow* (1950), *The Shell Guide to Flowers of the Countryside* (1957) and *The Englishman's Flora* (1958).

FUTURE DIRECTIONS

It does not seem fanciful to suggest that the Perrycoste family was an important formative influence on the young George Orwell. They are not mentioned in any of his letters or diaries but Orwell rarely wrote about his family and there are so few letters to or from his relatives that one senses they were destroyed on purpose – or possibly the itinerant lives of Anglo-Indian families make for a better explanation. Significant supporters of his professional life as a writer, such as his Aunt Nellie and his first wife Eileen O'Shaughnessy, are barely discernible in his letters or diaries.

Frank and Maud Perrycoste were extraordinary people by any standard. Their combined talents extended into many fields: literary, artistic, scientific, genealogical, legal and botanical. They were politically engaged in progressive, liberal ideas. Throughout his life Frank Perrycoste was always interested in politics and 'as a young man was a frequent debater in the North London "local Parliament"' (*Cornish Guardian* 1929). In 1903, he founded the Polperro branch of the Liberal Association and was their delegate to the South-East Cornwall Division. He was a member of the Moral Instruction League and Rationalist Press Association for many years (ibid).

Frank was intellectually engaged with his world, wrote on an incredibly diverse range of topics and one can easily imagine Orwell, who always took 'great pleasure in … scraps of useless information', enjoying Frank's essays about insect colours, the salts in natural waters, sexual periodicity and colour-blindness (Orwell 1998 [1946]: 320; Derriman 1994b: 210-211). Orwell's eclectic 'As I Please' column in *Tribune* has many examples of random ruminations about nature. And his essay 'Some thoughts on the common toad' is another fitting example:

> I think that by retaining one's childhood love of such things as trees, fishes, butterflies and – to return to my first instance – toads, one makes a peaceful and decent future a little more probable … (Orwell 1998 [1940-1941]: 239-240).

Before resigning from his job with the Indian Imperial Police, it seems that Frank Perrycoste, along with the poet Ruth Pitter, were two of the only writers he could have possibly spent any significant amount of time with besides schoolteachers. Even a cursory read through Perrycoste's bibliography suggests that his themes and preoccupations would have interested Orwell.

Considering the Perrycoste family's presence in Orwell's life has been forgotten for many decades, they are worthy of further research and consideration.

- Special thanks to Stephen Buckley who provided the impetus for this research into Orwell's Cornish holidays and excellent leads about Geoffrey Grigson. David Tovey's intellectual generosity has been greatly appreciated as has research conducted by Kathryn Le Gay Brereton. The support of Jeremy Rowett Johns, Nick Childs and the Polperro Family History Society has been invaluable. Carolyn Boon has also been very generous with her knowledge about Frank and Maude Perrycoste. An earlier version of this research can be found at https://www.darcymoore.net/2023/07/29/orwell-in-cornwall/.

NOTE

[1] Symonds was certainly not the only poet whom Ellis associated with at this time. In 1898, he wrote about his experimentation with psychedelic drugs. He believed the aesthetic experience would be appreciated by W.B. Yeats so he supplied him with peyote (Ellis 1898; Rudgley 1993: 104)

REFERENCES

Ancestry.com. England & Wales, National Probate Calendar (Index of Wills and Administrations), 1858-1995 [database online]. Provo, UT, USA: Ancestry.com Operations, Inc., 2010

Barfoot, C. M. and Healey, R. M. (2002) My rebellious and imperfect eye, *DQR Studies in Literature*, Vol. 33, Amsterdam: Brill Rodope

Brome, Vincent (1979) *Havelock Ellis: Philosopher of Sex: A Biography*, London and Boston: Routledge & Kegan Paul

Buddicom, Jacintha (2006 [1974]) *Eric & Us*, Chichester: Finlay Publishers, postscript edition edited by Dione Venables

Carter, Gina (2023) Email correspondence, 30 August

Childs, Nick (2023) Email correspondence, 2 August

Cornish Guardian, (1929) 24 October

Crick, Bernard (1992 [1980]) *George Orwell: A Life*, Harmondsworth, Middlesex: Penguin, second edition

Davies, Colonel Samuel Hugh James, British India Office Wills & Probate – 1869, Wills – Bengal 1780-1938

Derriman, James (1994a) Frank Hill Perrycoste: The Polperro Fingerprint Man, *Devon & Cornwall Notes & Queries,* Vol. XXXVII, Part V, Spring pp 175-179

Derriman, James (1994b) Frank Hill Perrycoste: The Polperro Fingerprint Man Part II, *Devon & Cornwall Notes & Queries*, Vol. XXXVII, Part VI, Autumn pp 207-211

Ellis, Havelock (1898) Mescal: A new artificial paradise, *The Contemporary Review*, LXXIII

Ellis, Havelock (1890) *The Criminal*, New York: Scribner & Welford

Ellis, Havelock (1927 [1897]) *Studies in the Psychology of Sex, Vol. I: The Evolution of Modesty, the Phenomena of Sexual Periodicity, Auto-Erotism*. Third Edition, Revised and Enlarged

Ellis, Havelock (1927 [1897]) *Studies in the Psychology of Sex, Vol. II: Sexual Inversion*. Third Edition, Revised and Enlarged

Ellis, Havelock (1939) *My Life: Autobiography of Havelock Ellis*, Boston: Houghton Mifflin

Grigson, Geoffrey (1950) *The Crest On The Silver: An Autobiography*, London: Cresset

Grigson, Geoffrey (1960 [1958]) *The Englishman's Flora*, London: Phoenix House Ltd

Grosskurth, Phyllis (1980) *Havelock Ellis: A Biography*, New York: Knopf

Healey, R. M. (2023) Email correspondence, 31 July

Hewson, Eileen (2005) *Assam and North-East India: Christian Cemeteries and Memorials*, BACSA

Holiday Cottages in Devon and Cornwall (2022) *Higher Shute: Holiday Homes in Looe & Polperro*. Available online at https://holidaycottagesindevonandcornwall.co.uk/cornwall/looe-polperro/higher-shute, accessed on 6 August 2023

Jerram, Muriel (nd) *Recollections of a Talland Childhood in the Late 19th and Early 20th Centuries*, The estate of Muriel Jerram

Johns, Jeremy Rowett (2008) *The Smugglers' Banker: The Story of Zephaniah Job of Polperro*, Polperro: Polperro Heritage Press

Nash, David and Kilday, Anne-Marie (eds) (2020) *Fair and Unfair Trials in the British Isles, 1800-1940*, London: Bloomsbury Publishing, Kindle Edition

Old Bailey Proceedings Online (1895) Central Criminal Court. Available online at https://www.oldbaileyonline.org/browse.jsp?div=t18950520-425, accessed on 6 August 2023

Orwell, George (1997 [1937]) *The Road to Wigan Pier, The Complete Works of George Orwell, Vol. V*, Davison, Peter (ed.) London: Secker & Warburg

Orwell, George (1998 [1903-1936]) *A Kind of Compulsion: The Complete Works of George Orwell, Vol. X*, Davison, Peter (ed.) London: Secker & Warburg

Orwell, George (1998 [1937-1939]) *Facing Unpleasant Facts: The Complete Works of George Orwell, Vol. XI*, Davison, Peter (ed.) London: Secker & Warburg

Orwell, George (1998 [1940-1941]) *A Patriot After All: The Complete Works of George Orwell, Vol. XII*, Davison, Peter (ed.) London: Secker & Warburg

Orwell, George (1998 [1943-1944]) *I Have Tried to Tell the Truth: The Complete Works of George Orwell, Vol. XVI*, Davison, Peter (ed.) London: Secker & Warburg

Orwell, George (1998 [1946]) *Smothered Under Journalism: The Complete Works of George Orwell, Vol. XVIII*, Davison, Peter (ed.) London: Secker & Warburg

Orwell, George (1998 [1947-1948]) *It Is What I Think: The Complete Works of George Orwell, Vol. XIX*, Davison, Peter (ed.) London: Secker & Warburg

Orwell, George (1998 [1949-1950]) *Our Job Is to Make Life Worth Living: The Complete Works of George Orwell, Vol. XX*, Davison, Peter (ed.) London: Secker & Warburg

Pearson, Karl (1930) *The Life, Letters and Labours of Francis Galton*, London: Cambridge University Press

Perrycoste, Frank Hill (1892) *The Cry of the Children: An Essay in Tyranny and Ignorance*, Edinburgh: Williams & Norgate

Perrycoste, Frank Hill (1894) *Towards Utopia: Being Speculations in Social Evolution*, New York: D. Appleton and Company

Perrycoste, Frank Hill (1910) *Ritual, Faith and Morals: Being Two Chapters from an Historical Enquiry into the Influence of Religion Upon Moral Civilisation*, London: Watts and Co.

Perrycoste, Frank Hill (1915) *Religion and Moral Civilisation: Being the Prolegomena to an Enquiry into the Influence of Religion upon Moral Civilisation*, London: Watts & Co.

Perrycoste, Frank H. and Honor M. M. (1920) Cornish phrenology, 1912-1919, *Science Progress in the Twentieth Century (1919-1933)*, Vol. 15, No. 57 pp 60-69. Available online at http://www.jstor.org/stable/43769320, accessed on 22 July 2023

Perrycoste, Frank H. (1921) Starvation pay of brain-workers, *Science Progress in the Twentieth Century (1919-1933)*, Vol. 15, No. 59 pp 478-479. Available online at http://www.jstor.org/stable/43768961, accessed on 22 July 2023

Perrycoste, Frank H. (1920) Politics and science, *Science Progress in the Twentieth Century (1919-1933)*, Vol. 14, No. 55 pp. 486-496. Available online at http://www.jstor.org/stable/43431608, accessed on 22 July 2023

DARCY MOORE

Perrycoste, Frank Hill (2007 [1930]) *Gleanings from the Records of Zephaniah Job of Polperro*, Polperro: Polperro Heritage Press

Rudgley, Richard (1993) *The Alchemy of Culture: Intoxicants in Society*, London: British Museum Press

Summers, Anne (1991) The correspondents of Havelock Ellis, *History Workshop*, Vol. 32 pp 167-183. Available online at http://www.jstor.org/stable/4289109, accessed on 29 July 2023

Symons, Julian (2009) Grigson, Geoffrey Edward Harvey (1905-1985), poet and writer, *Oxford Dictionary of National Biography*. Available online at https://www-oxforddnb-com.ezproxy.sl.nsw.gov.au/view/10.1093/ref:odnb/9780198614128.001.0001/odnb-9780198614128-e-31176, accessed 5 August 2023

Thurston, Edgar and Vigurs, Chambré C. (1922) A supplement to F. Hamilton Davey's Flora of Cornwall, *Journal of the Royal Institution of Cornwall, Vol. 21*, Royal Institution of Cornwall

Tovey, David (2021) *Polperro: Cornwall's Forgotten Art Centre: Vol. 1: Pre-1920*, Wilson Books

Tovey, David (2021) *Polperro: Cornwall's Forgotten Art Centre: Vol. 2: Post-1920*, Wilson Books

West Briton and Cornwall Advertiser (1916) 14 September

Western Daily Press (1924) 3 July

NOTE ON THE CONTRIBUTOR

Darcy Moore is a deputy principal at a secondary school in New South Wales. He blogs at *darcymoore.net* and his Twitter handle is @Darcy1968. His Orwell Studies Library can be accessed at darcymoore.net/orwell-collection/.

The Achievement of Ian Angus

The passing of Ian Angus (1926-2022) – little noticed in the wider culture – represented a landmark for those interested in the life and legacy of George Orwell, coming as it did last year on 30 October, just a dozen weeks after the death of Peter Davison at the age of 95. As John Rodden observes, both of them served the life and work of George Orwell devotedly and unstintingly – surely Eric Blair would have found a place for them in Booklovers' Corner. Those of us who stand in their lengthy shadows mourn their departure and salute their memory.

The deaths of Peter and Ian – good friends and close colleagues even before their work together on Peter's edition of the *Complete Works of George Orwell* (*CWGO*) – suddenly reduces the quintet of venerable and distinguished nonagenarian elders in Orwell Studies to a redoubtable duo: Ian Willison and Peter Stansky, Dione Venables having passed away in September 2023. The deaths of Peter, Ian and Dione also serve as a sad and bracing reminder that what I might dub 'the Greatest Generation' of Orwell scholars is fast dwindling, regrettably so.

The loss is incalculable. The debt can only be repaid by honouring their memory and extending their legacy. This essay aspires to do just that, in a spirit kindred to my memoirs of Peter Davison and Peter Stansky in previous issues of this journal.

THE MAN BEHIND THE COLLECTED ORWELL

When I think about Ian Angus, recalling his behind-the-scenes role as co-editor of the four-volume *Collected Essays, Journalism and Letters of George Orwell* (*CEJL* 1968) – as well as his decades-long fierce loyalty to and affection for Sonia Orwell – I am especially reminded of his modesty and diffidence. Sonia was flamboyant, impulsive and mercurial; Ian was reserved, steady and 'collected'. They were a perfect complementary duo when it came to guiding *CEJL* into print. Sonia was the driving force and ultimate decision-maker; Ian was the quiet, indefatigable researcher and 'collector' of invaluable material – letters, little-known publications, copies of foreign translations and more. Ian's dual roles as *CEJL* co-editor

JOHN RODDEN and first director of the George Orwell Archive are too-seldom honoured.

Or to put it differently, just as there was an 'unknown Orwell', there was an 'unknown Angus'. I was privileged to become acquainted with Ian, a painfully shy and wonderfully decent human being whom Sonia Orwell cherished dearly and Peter Davison esteemed highly. Justly so. On three occasions, beginning in July 2009, I enjoyed several days of hospitality with Ian and his wife, Ann Mellis Stokes, in their Hampstead home, where I also met Ian's stepson Philip Stokes. Ian and Ann were wonderful and generous hosts, and Philip looked in on them regularly and handled all sorts of technical tasks, ranging from household appliance breakdowns to computer mysteries and malfunctions. Philip also handled much of Ian's correspondence, which extended to sending me various documents, such as Ian's five-page transcript summarising his telephone conversation with Inez Holden in 1967, after he and I had discussed her deep friendship (and decade-long affair) with Orwell. (Philip was also unfailingly helpful to me personally, even booking my Belfast flight from London to visit my Irish clan in Donegal.) He continued magnanimously to provide filial assistance to Ian after Ann's passing in April 2014.

It was during these visits to Church Row that I got to know Ian, the man behind the dual monuments of *CEJL* and *CWGO*. Ian was then in his mid-80s. Nonetheless, we sat up on several occasions until well past midnight as he reminisced about Sonia and mused about scholars as well as literary Londoners who had flitted in and out of his lives as a librarian and editor. (How I wish today that I had recorded those conversations with him!)

The 'public' Ian was a consummate professional; his indispensable role, first as archivist and later as co-editor of *CEJL*, warrant our thanks and our tribute. Let me share, however, a side of him that he disclosed, I believe, seldom and hesitantly; perhaps he permitted me a glimpse on account of his view that we were literary siblings whose relationship to our 'intellectual big brother' represented a filial bond across the generations.

Rather surprising to those who encountered the professional librarian 'Angus', a formal and even rather withdrawn figure, the 'private' Ian could be witty, unbuttoned and even vehement. I found him to be an engaging conversationalist who laughed and joked readily in a relaxed setting. A *leitmotif* of our exchanges was his anguish about the enormous gap between Sonia's public reputation and the caring, impassioned and often self-tortured friend whom he had known well. When I suggested that he write an article about her (to be titled 'Unfair to Sonia'), he was aghast: he would never put himself forward that way. Even when I merely suggested that we conduct and publish an interview that would present 'the Sonia I knew', he was equally adamant. It was unthinkable.

Ian did, however, relent once, briefly. During a London visit in 2014, when I was attending a conference at University College London (UCL) and lunching with 'the other Ian' of Orwell Studies, the scholar and erstwhile librarian Ian Willison, I persuaded Ian Angus to co-operate in a venture that I had previously discussed with him and which, in principle, he applauded in his capacity as former head of the George Orwell Archive. That is, I proposed that we add Ian Angus's own testimony to the holdings of the Archive in the form of an oral history project. I had arranged with a colleague to do a video of the interview. Unfortunately, when I phoned Ian that morning to confirm the arrangements, he abruptly changed his mind. Clearly, he felt he had committed to the interview rashly and prematurely; it now seemed overwhelming. He may have also had a bad night's sleep and a cold. He would not, however, consider rescheduling it.[1]

GALLANT DEFENDER OF SONIA

I mention Ian's extreme reticence to speak out publicly because the 'private' Ian had no qualms about expressing his views openly and candidly. When it came to Sonia, Ian possessed strong views and did not hesitate to speak his mind forcefully – albeit in private. He generally endorsed the sympathetic image of Sonia in Hilary Spurling's biography, *The Girl in the Fiction Department* (2002), a title that alludes to Winston Smith's initial characterisation of Julia in *Nineteen Eighty-Four*. (Several of Orwell's biographers, along with Spurling, believed that Sonia served as the inspiration for and model of Julia.) Ian admired Spurling as a biographer and found her credible as an intimate of Sonia; he believed that she – like him – had glimpsed 'the real Sonia' and had depicted the woman whom he remembered. Spurling's friendship with Sonia was, indeed, very close, above all during the last two decades of Sonia's life. Spurling handled the funeral arrangements of Sonia, who had been a regular guest in Spurling's home and was also the godmother of Spurling's daughter. Subtitled '*A Portrait*', Spurling's *The Girl in the Fiction Department* is, unsurprisingly, more an affectionate personal memoir *cum* apologia than a biography.

By contrast, Orwell's biographers had been 'less than fair' to Sonia, insisted Ian. He had sharp words about the comments on Sonia by two of the biographers (Michael Shelden and Jeffrey Meyers). She was no 'gold-digger' who had finally and reluctantly agreed to marry Orwell 'on his deathbed'. She had no designs to become a wealthy widow; nor did she figure that her 'literary invalid' husband would quickly pop off, leaving her free to pursue her own life.

JOHN RODDEN

Ian readily admitted, of course, that he had not known Sonia in the 1940s, let alone Orwell. Sonia and Ian became acquainted in the course of his selection as the director of the Orwell Archive, which Sonia set up in 1960 at UCL when she began to deposit Orwell's manuscripts and some personal artifacts there. Responding to the accounts of Sonia by various biographers, Ian based his views on her conversations with him while compiling and editing *CEJL* throughout the 1960s, as well as in the dozen years of contact that they had after its publication.

Like Sonia and many of Orwell's personal friends and literary colleagues, Ian was also no fan of the first biography of Orwell, Bernard Crick's *George Orwell: A Life*. Ian's reservations had nothing to do with its treatment of Sonia, who is merely mentioned in passing in the closing chapter. Rather, Ian shared Sonia's view that it is a skewed account which presents Orwell too one-sidedly as a political figure and scants his literary side. Crick, an admirer of *CEJL*, had been personally selected in 1972 as Orwell's biographer, but as Sonia read drafts of the early chapters throughout the 1970s, the relationship deteriorated.

Whatever his reservations about the Crick biography, Ian concurred with Crick's defence of Sonia against the contentions of Mary McCarthy, Conor Cruise O'Brien and others regarding *CEJL*'s paucity of politically-oriented letters and/or publications by Orwell during the war years. The so-called 'suppression' of Orwell's political pieces, as the scholar Robert Klitzke has characterised the exclusions, was not politically motivated, said Crick, though he acknowledged the validity of Klitzke's claim that the omissions for the period 1941-1949 *in toto* tended to 'suppress Orwell's political commitments to the English Socialist tradition' and give his 'revolutionary period – as it emerged from *The Lion and the Unicorn* (1941) – the character of a momentary mood'. Instead, Crick believed that Sonia's conviction was that Orwell's 'real character' was not at all political, and that in his desire to marry her he was 'showing the dominance of his literary over his political self'.[2]

Whether or not Sonia was correct on this point, observed Ian, that was indeed exactly what Sonia herself believed. Her Orwell was, above all, a literary man. Ian noted that Sonia held that *CEJL* need not incorporate Orwell's 'ephemeral' political journalism and, instead, should honour his 'achievement as a great writer'-to which his wartime contributions in *The Betrayal of the Left* (1941) and *Victory or Vested Interest* (1942), among other occasional pieces, such as his *Manchester Evening Review* articles in 1945, did not contribute.

Among our other topics of conversation was Michael Sayers, with whom Ian had corresponded. Sayers, a left-wing Irish-Jewish poet-playwright-screenwriter, had roomed with Orwell and Rayner Heppenstall in the early 1930s as a 23-year-old. He and Orwell both reviewed regularly for the *New English Weekly*. They developed a genuine friendship, and Sayers stayed in touch through the years and expressed keen esteem for *Animal Farm* on a visit to England after the Second World War ended. Peripatetic and averse to publicity – he was blacklisted during the McCarthy era in the US and spent most of the 1950s in Europe writing scripts under various pen names – he has been little-discussed since Rayner Heppenstall's portrait of Orwell in *Four Absentees* (1960). Only one biographer, Gordon Bowker, had ever interviewed Sayers personally. Ian had shrewdly spotted this oversight as a notable omission in the record. For Sayers had known Orwell quite well and shared his overall political and literary stance, as a fellow anti-fascist with a (chiefly) literary bent, until the mid-1930s. After that, despite widening ideological differences, they continued to feel warmly towards each other. (Sayers once jokingly confessed an 'almost homoerotic affection' for Orwell. He also claimed that he had introduced Orwell to Sonia.)

This cordial, enduring relationship was exceptional for Orwell, given Sayers's outspoken support for Stalin's Russia by the late 1930s and Orwell's deep hostility towards it. (Sayers co-authored a non-fiction book, *The Great Conspiracy Against Russia*, which became an international bestseller comparable to *Animal Farm* in 1946.) Sayers was 97 at the time of my conversations with Ian in 2009. As it turned out, Sayers (1911-2010) died just months later in the following May. Although neither Bowker nor anyone else has reported it, I may add that Ian agreed with me that Orwell and Sayers probably exchanged heated words not only about Stalinism but also about Ireland, for Sayers was a staunch Irish Republican and admirer of the Irish revolutionist Michael Collins, a personal friend of Sayers' father.[3]

IAN AND ANN

This memoir is about Ian Angus, not his wife Ann Stokes (1922-2014). Nevertheless, it would be remiss not to mention the importance of Ann to his sense of purpose and well-being. Given the central role that Ann played in Ian's life during a fulfilling marriage of 38 years, a further word about her is apposite here.

Surely Ann's radiant charm and lightness of heart had much to do with inducing Ian, who had heretofore exhibited the Larkinesque librarian's makings of a lifelong bachelor, to marry at the relatively advanced age of fifty. (Julia Strachey had introduced him to Ann.) Utterly casual and informal, Ann paid little heed to housekeeping; that was the domain of Ian (and ultimately Philip). The historic

JOHN RODDEN

three-storey Georgian residence at 20 Church Row, just three doors down from H.G. Wells's pre-First World War home and a five-minute walk from Hampstead Heath, was crammed with knick-knacks and stray objects. Indeed, I suspect that Eric Blair may have learned as a result of insatiable curiosity – perhaps from his teacher Aldous Huxley at Eton – that Wells was residing at number 17, for it was there that his boyhood literary hero reached his creative peak and wrote the greatest work of his career, composing *Tono-Bungay, The History of Mr Polly, Ann Veronica, The Sleeper Awakes, The New Machiavelli* and *Marriage* in a spectacular three-year stretch between 1909 and 1912, among other books. In his essay 'Wells, Hitler, and the World State' (1941), Orwell recalled that the Wells of these years 'up to 1914' was 'a true prophet': 'This wonderful man who could tell you about the inhabitants of the planets and the bottom of the sea, and who knew that the future was not going to be what respectable people imagined.'

Occasionally when I was in London, Ian and Ann were abroad, or preparing to leave and spend time at Ann's studio in Cortona, Italy, where Ann drew inspiration for many of her artistic projects while Ian enjoyed the Tuscan sunshine, lovingly tending an olive grove on the property and interacted with locals. 'So Ian puttered while Ann pottered,' I once joked to Ian, a shameless pun that he merrily repeated to her with delight. By all accounts, they were 'supremely happy' together, as a memoirist of Ann wrote. For my part, as a household guest who shared morning breakfast and had numerous opportunities to observe them together, I saw nothing to contradict that judgement; they enjoyed each other's company immensely in a harmonious, loving marriage.

It also warrants emphasis that Ann, the widow of the distinguished art critic Adrian Stokes, was in the process of establishing herself as a nationally recognised decorative artist by the time of her marriage to Ian in 1976. Even before he married Ann and moving to the Stokes family home at Church Row, Ian supported her fully. I believe that her ultimate flourishing as an artist by the mid-1980s was partly due to Ian, who tended her late-blooming artistic career with the same devotion that he had given to the development of the Orwell Archive. Praised by generations of art critics, Ann's artwork was bold in conception, broad in scope and ingenious in its treatment of both the history of art and the natural world. It ranged from small decorative art objects (jugs and pots) in the tradition of Etruscan pottery to fountains mounted with dancing birds, fearsome rhinoceroses modelled on the famous Albrecht Dürer woodcut and 'flashing' ten-foot crocodiles (illuminated from within, thanks to the technological skills of her son, Philip, an electronics whiz and excellent sound engineer). Ann ultimately turned out to be a 'Grandma Moses' of ceramics; she did not even pursue her art seriously until her late 40s. The crocodiles were not created until she neared eighty. Among Ann's legions of admirers in her later years were art critics and historians such as Ernst Gombrich, Richard Wollheim and David Sylvester.[4]

Ian and I had extensive conversations about Ann's late husband Adrian Stokes (1902-1972), an art critic-theorist of stature in the middle decades of the last century and an innovative thinker on psychoanalysis, aesthetics and Renaissance sculpture who co-founded the pioneering psychoanalytical collective known as the Imago Group. I felt honoured when, during my stay at Church Row in 2011, Ian asked me to read an unpublished biography of Adrian in typescript that had been sent to the family for constructive criticism. He wondered if the biography were publishable in its extant form. (Gracefully written by Michael Sayers' daughter-in-law, Janet Sayers, the biography reached print a few years after I read it.)

I should add that, given that Orwell's (future) wife Eileen O'Shaughnessy was pursuing a Master's degree in Educational Psychology at University College London in 1935 when she met Eric Blair at a party in his Hampstead flat – he was then living at 77 Parliament Hill – I consider it quite possible that either or both of them knew of Adrian's work (and may have even met him before or after their marriage in June 1936). The London literary and bohemian circle was small and the intellectual community of psychology even smaller; often the two worlds overlapped. For instance, Blair's landlady Rosalind Obermeyer was a UCL classmate of Eileen; a half-dozen fellow students and UCL faculty attended his February 1935 party. Eileen was studying for her advanced degree under Cyril Burt, whose research interests extended to psychoanalysis as a member (and later president) of the British Psychoanalytical Society and Tavistock Clinic.[5]

Beginning in the mid-1930s, Adrian underwent six years of psychoanalysis (with Melanie Klein) and developed his intellectual interest in British psychoanalysis; far better known than Orwell, he was the author of six books by 1935 devoted to the arts (painting, sculpture and ballet), including *The Quattro Cento* (1932) and *The Stones of Rimini* (1934), and had established himself as a nationally prominent critic and younger associate of several Modernist masters (e.g., Ezra Pound).[6]

THE UNKNOWN ANGUS

In co-operation with Sonia as co-editor of the four-volume *CEJL*, published in 1968, Ian was the single most crucial figure for shepherding Orwell's reputation in the early 1960s from a modest

JOHN RODDEN

standing within international cultural circles and the literary academy to a worldwide public reputation of enormous proportions by the mid-1980s. Ian handed off the editorial baton, as it were, to Peter by the early 1980s, who thereupon carried Orwell's fame to historic proportions in the next two decades with his edition of the *Complete Works* in twenty volumes.

Meanwhile, Ian continued to superintend the George Orwell Archive at UCL. It became a jewel in the crown of the UCL holdings, as other scholars will attest, and the Archive was the source from which the riches of *CEJL* came. Obscured in the reception history of Orwell is the indispensable role that *CEJL* played in reviving Orwell's reputation in the 1970s. *CEJL* set the stage for Orwell's 'take-off' in the media during the 'countdown to 1984' in 1983-1984 – and for his critical and scholarly launch immediately thereafter with the publication of the first nine volumes of the *Complete Works* in 1986-1987.

Put differently, *CEJL* and *CWGO* operated in hindsight as a double-booster shot to Orwell's posthumous reputation. Before *CEJL*'s appearance, Orwell was known in the mid-1960s as the anti-communist author of a pair of early Cold War fantasias; he was also respected, chiefly in literary London and among English professors, as an important writer of the 1930s and 1940s who wrote excellent reportage (e.g., *Homage to Catalonia*). *CEJL* brought him to the attention of a new generation of readers, just as he was starting to seem a stale and dated relic belonging to the receding Stalinist era. The four volumes served to broaden Orwell's audience beyond his Cold War allies as well as raise his standing in the intellectual world as an essayist of the first rank, reminding everyone that he was far more than merely a two-book writer, let alone the millions of readers who vaguely still regarded him as just an author of fiction for pupils in high school (or 'O-levels') – where most people had their only encounter of him. Similarly, two decades later, *CWGO* transformed Orwell – now an author with a worldwide public reputation – into a figure whom scholars, equipped with twenty volumes of meticulously edited and annotated work, were induced to study and scrutinise – and squabble over anew.

The title chosen for the four volumes was straightforward and well chosen: the collection showcased the three main strands of Orwell's accomplishment as a non-fiction writer. Starting with the 'E' of *CEJL*, critics honoured him as a magnificent essayist, perhaps the greatest in at least a century. Critics and readers respectfully placed him on the same plane as a successor to Edmund Burke and William Hazlitt.

Meanwhile, other readers and critics responded chiefly to the next letter in the collection's title, the 'J', by saluting Orwell as a gifted political columnist and literary/cultural journalist. Never before had his journalism, much of it hitherto uncollected, appeared in bulk. *CEJL* included dozens of hitherto unpublished book reviews and occasional articles as well as all of his 'London Letters' during 1941-46 for *Partisan Review*, the New York literary-intellectual journal, and his 'As I Please' columns for *Tribune* during 1943-1947, among other additional material.

Finally, the 'L' – Orwell's letters, not only public (as in the case of the *Partisan Review* columns but also his personal correspondence), enriched the biographical record. No biography yet existed. Appreciation of the man and of his literary achievement grew enormously. Thanks above all to the letters, which established how embedded he was within the London literary scene, he became recognised as far more than merely a two-book author of the late 1940s.

OUT OF THE SHADOWS

It has often been remarked that the 'foundation' of Orwell's thinking abides in one of his favourite words – a character trait of his own that Orwell in turn applied to one of his own favourite writers, Charles Dickens: 'decency'.[7] And I would apply the same word to Ian himself, along with 'humility' and 'selflessness'. One might also add 'stoicism'. I hope that Ian's ghost will not object to my citing an example that he confided to me. On one of my visits, in 2011, Ian was in terrible pain, undergoing treatment for prostate and bladder difficulties, which required that he obtain a catheter. Unfortunately, the 'treatment' ultimately proved more taxing than the pain of urination, and he eventually chose to have the catheter removed. Unless you had asked him explicitly about this or any other health challenge, however, you would not have ever known about it, uncomplaining and forbearing as he always was.

Ian had no drive to put himself forward. Was there ever a twinge of envy upon seeing others get all the credit? The question is understandable, and so too would have been the impulse. If so, I never detected a trace of it. And I very much doubt it. I do not believe such thoughts ever crossed Ian's mind. Envy was just not part of Ian Angus's nature.

Ian was content to remain in the shadows, always offstage, joining in the audience's applause. That is to say, Ian was always comfortable as a deputy – deputy librarian, deputy *CEJL* 'co'-editor, editorial 'assistant' of *CWGO* and ever-supportive husband of Ann.

Today, however, when he is no longer here to remonstrate, we should bring to light the yeoman editorial labours of Ian Angus himself. Although Ian not just willingly but insistently took second billing to Sonia and Peter Davison in the publication of *CEJL* and

JOHN RODDEN *CWGO* respectively – and almost invariably avoided the limelight thereafter – it is high time to honour his historic achievement as archivist and editor. Across a span of several decades, it is time to honour his immense contribution to Orwell Studies and his unfailing help to researchers and readers of Orwell.

NOTES

The author would like to thank Darcy Moore, Philip Stokes, Sylvia Topp, Janet and Michael Sayers, and Jason Crimp for their kind assistance with this article.

[1] In hindsight, I also realise now that the proposed interview was just four or five months after Ann's death. Ian's own health was beginning to decline too; somewhat reclusive by nature, he was virtually housebound by the end of the decade

[2] Klitzke is quoted in Bernard Crick, *George Orwell: A Life*, Middlesex: Penguin, 1980 p. 621. See also Crick's article, Orwell and biography, *Biography*, Vol. 10, No. 4, 1987 p. 292

[3] I have not been able to establish any of these possible connections. Nor have other scholars and biographers whom I have contacted. Neither Adrian Stokes nor the Mellis girls (Ann or her sister Margaret, Adrian's first wife) are mentioned in *CWGO*, nor by Sylvia Topp (in *Eileen: The Making of George Orwell*, of 2020) nor by any of George Orwell's biographers. Neither do Janet Sayers nor three other biographers of Adrian refer to Eileen or George Orwell

[4] See Tanya Harrod, Ann Stokes: Obituary, *Guardian*, 14 May 2014

[5] During his later years Cyril (later Sir Cyril) Burt (1883-1971) aroused controversy over his studies in eugenics linking intelligence (and IQ test scores) with race and genetics. Claims of fraudulent scholarship and falsified research data against him have been well established since the 1980s. Did Eileen, who had abandoned her degree before marrying Eric in June 1936, intend to follow Burt's work in intelligence testing and genetics? She was one of Burt's 'star pupils', as Sylvia Topp, her biographer, noted in our correspondence. Neither letters between Eileen and her UCL friends nor other information regarding her views of Burt have ever surfaced

[6] See Janet Sayers, *Art, Psychoanalysis, and Adrian Stokes: A Biography*, London: Karnac Books, 2015. Professor Sayers is married to Michael's son, Sean, a retired professor of philosophy. Sean holds that Michael's politics were chiefly anti-fascist rather than pro-Stalinist, describing his outlook in our correspondence as 'romantic and poetic rather than doctrinaire'. The blacklisting and travel difficulties arose because US officials believed that Michael had joined the British Communist Party in the 1930s, though Sean 'doubts he ever was'

[7] See the opening chapter of John Atkins's biography, Decency: The foundation, in *George Orwell: A Literary Study*, London: John Calder, 1954

NOTE ON THE CONTRIBUTOR

John Rodden has published memoirs of Orwell scholars and intellectual admirers ranging from Peter Davison and Peter Stansky to Christopher Hitchens and Irving Howe. He is completing a study dealing with ideologically motivated controversies about Orwell's life and work, *George Orwell, Plagiarist?*

ARTICLE

The BBC'S *Nineteen Eighty-Four* remastered for a new generation

Hassan Akram reassesses the BBC 1954 adaptation of Orwell's dystopian masterpiece and argues that it emphasises drama over politics and sensation over satire.

INTRODUCTION

Until quite recently, anybody who wished to view the 1954 TV adaptation of George Orwell's last novel would have been sorely disappointed. The first screen version of *Nineteen Eighty-Four* (not to be confused with the 1956 Hollywood one) existed mainly in bootlegged prints which, even for those lucky enough to track them down, were frankly unwatchable. Fortunately, however, the British Film Institute's remaster of the film in 2022 restored it for a new generation and made clear – literally – several points of interest. For all its production flaws and divergences from the novel, it nonetheless has positives in respect of a first-rate cast and some glimmers of cinematic brilliance, all of which are worth examining.

Firstly, I should note that although it is easier to call it a film, it was, in fact, a teleplay. Most of it was recorded and broadcast live; while only establishing shots, connecting scenes and the most ambitious sequences were filmed in advance. Rudolph Cartier was director and Nigel Kneale wrote the screenplay. Critically it was fairly well-received, though its bleak tone and depiction of torture stirred a moral panic that started in the tabloids and ended in parliament, where five MPs condemned 'the tendency, evident in recent British Broadcasting Corporation television programmes, notably on Sunday evenings, to pander to sexual and sadistic tastes'. One woman reportedly died of horror while watching it.[1]

CAST

Winston Smith is played by a young Peter Cushing – an odd casting choice, for, as appearances go, he has little in common with the character. The literary Winston is fair-haired, rough-faced and has a limp due to his ulcer; Cushing is dark-haired, fresh-faced and moves and acts with vitality. Moreover, he is known to most modern audiences as a classic villain – whether in Hammer Horror, *The Avengers*, or *Star Wars* – so to warm to him as an identifiable hero is initially difficult. Yet, with all this stacked against him, Cushing manages to deliver the first truly great performance of his career. He is perfect as the bookish, relatable 'last man in Europe', and one only has to hear his haunting shrieks in Room 101 to understand why the broadcast so horrified contemporary audiences. 'That's possibly the first time anyone had a real blood-curdling scream on television,' BFI historian Dick Fiddy explains, 'and that's very terrifying for a fifties audience.'[2] Cushing himself also recalled: 'For this piece of emoting … I became known as "The Horror man of the BBC".'[3] His reputation was well-deserved for, on the whole, Cushing is the best thing about the film and holds it together.

Even a glance at Yvonne Mitchell's Julia is enough to see that she, at any rate, is the living image of her fictional counterpart, 'bold-looking'[4] and 'dark-haired'.[5] She perfectly embodies both the rebel and the lover in Julia. Her introduction in the film presents a striking image that reveals Cartier's skill in page-to-screen translation: she is framed in a close-up that spotlights her face against a shadowy background, to mirror the sense of uncertainty and duality that surrounds her in the first part of the book, when she is implied to be agent of the Thought Police.

The quiet power of O'Brien is nicely captured by André Morell, even though he does not completely look the part and lacks the intensity and presence that Richard Burton would later bring to the role in Michael Radford's 1984 feature film. Initially Morell is not given very much to do besides fiddling with his spectacles, but in the Ministry of Love he reaches his peak. Here, towering over Winston, he speaks on power and the Party with the very 'faint, mad gleam of enthusiasm'[6] that Orwell described.

Winston's 'venomously orthodox'[7] colleague Syme is played by Donald Pleasance, who would go on to act as the Bond villain Blofeld in *You Only Live Twice* (1967). There is a foretaste of that villain's fanaticism in evidence here, especially when – with a visible, not metaphorical, glint in his eye – he raves over Newspeak and the beauty of the demolition of English. With this air of menace, 'Pleasance ooze[s] star quality'[8] and if given the chance, he may well have made an even better O'Brien than Morell.

PRODUCTION FLAWS

There are several limitations with the production. First of all, the action is not sufficiently explained. In this respect, the opening of the film is representative of the whole. After the credits there are a few shots of atomic explosions and then of a bombed-out London. From the epic opening we are taken into Winston's office in the

Ministry of Truth and to the first falsification scene (Chapter Four of the novel). It's extraordinarily dry and matter-of-fact. Winston reads out the notes that instruct him to 'correct' a speech of Big Brother's, he scrawls something down – and that is that. There is none of Orwell's horrified fascination at the invention and erasure of truth. In the book, this chapter is, in effect, an essay, elucidating the authoritarian's method of falsification; and this is the kind of thing that visual media simply cannot capture. *Nineteen Eighty-Four* is as much a treatise as it is a novel, so half of it is immediately lost on screen. Any audience members unfamiliar with the source material probably did not have a clue what was going on.

Nor would the audience have found much to enrapture them in the soundtrack which, though effective when played, is for the most part absent. According to the audio commentary on the film, a seventeen-strong orchestra was hired to provide a background score during broadcast, and if better use had been made of these musicians, some of the drier segments would have benefitted from the added tension. The most captivating scenes are the few which do have complementary music, such as in the Ministry of Love, when a chilling score rises parallel to Winston's convulsions and to the dial on the torture machine.

Budget constraints were responsible for both the under-used score and, more broadly, for the narrow scale of the entire piece. At £3,000, the budget was the highest to date in television, but not enough for a project as ambitious as this one. The scope of Orwell's novel is lost. Aside from the tacked-on nuclear montage at the start, there is never a real sense that *the whole world* is under totalitarian oppression. Too much of the action takes place in what is so obviously the same room dressed up in different furniture for each scene: Mr Charrington's shop is a lone shelf of rusty pots; and even the countryside sequence is accommodated only by a plastic tree in the room. The only shot of an actual crowd lasts 1.8 seconds and is clearly stock footage. The only view of London is of the backlot of the BBC studio. The live-filmed sections have so little in the way of cinematography that at times it becomes absurd. For instance, although a real prop Fiction Machine was built for the scene with Julia in the Fiction Department, it can hardly be made out because she positions herself right between it and the camera and completely blocks the view! Overall, from the poor camerawork and cramped sets, the film gives the impression not of a totalitarian empire but of a particularly nasty office block. In other words, it has all the limitations of a play and few of the advantages of the screen.

ADAPTATION FLAWS

Perhaps it is unfair to dwell so long on technical limitations, for which the creative team can after all hardly be blamed. However, there are some more serious flaws with the adaptation itself, which is riddled with simplifications and misinterpretations. Firstly, the film lacks politics: doublethink, for instance, is not even mentioned. Structurally, too – though this is not so much of a major point – the plot has been streamlined and follows a conventional chronological narrative, so avoiding all analepsis. We actually see Jones, Aaronson and Rutherford in the Chestnut Tree Café whereas, in the novel, this is done through flashback. But the biggest mistakes made – each of them minor points, but collectively skewering the source material – are about the story's genre, the role of the proles and the nature of vaporisations. Though it is unreasonable to expect every nuance of the book to be perfectly translated to the screen, these kinds of mistakes betray much larger oversights.

The theme of nuclear Armageddon, which is the root basis for the plot, and which Orwell foresaw as early as 1945,[9] was a cliché by the 1950s, especially in science-fiction. Perhaps that is why Kneale and Cartier dressed up this political satire in the *mise en scène* of a sci-fi show. The Ministry of Truth in particular, with its pads of buttons and metallic design, gleams in the monochrome; each character's vivid costume is emblazoned with his or her name and number while the telescreens, the recurring gimmick of the production, are somewhat overused because they look so flashy. But, crucially, Orwell's dystopia is not, in the strict sense of the term, science-fiction. Science-fiction is based on ideas of rapid technological progress. Indeed, the dystopias of H.G. Wells and Aldous Huxley, on which Orwell wrote an essay,[10] were centred on visions of scientific advancement whereas the most distinctive feature of Oceania is that it 'is more primitive today than it was fifty years ago ... experiment and invention have largely stopped'.[11] *Nineteen Eighty-Four*'s greatest mechanical marvel is the telescreen, and even that was a very logical and foreseeable extension of the television. Other technologies, such as speakwrites and Fiction Machines, are incidental. Therefore, though there are some such elements, science and technology are not as central to Orwell's novel as they are to, say, H.G. Wells's novel *The Sleeper Awakes* (1910). But the BBC's decision to exaggerate those elements and to transform *Nineteen Eighty-Four* into a conventional sci-fi-style dystopia is understandable. This was, after all, the genre in which Kneale and Cartier specialised, and it would likely have gained the programme much more of a mass appeal. The same issues and questions of genre would plague future adaptations, as D.J. Taylor explains: 'How ...

should Orwell's text be approached on film? As a piece of futuristic prophecy, welded to the conventions of contemporary sci-fi? As a realistic satire? As a mixture of the two?'[12] Overall, the sci-fi elements do not detract hugely from the BBC version but do still represent a dilution of the source material.

What this means is that Kneale and Cartier cannot have grasped the essentially *political* core of the novel, and their ignorance of its political message is confirmed by their treatment of the proles. For Orwell the significance of the proles is grounded in Marxist theory and in the concept of the masses being unaware of their own oppression – 'false class consciousness'. His message about them is that they provide hope for the overthrow of the ruling class; but at the same time their lack of political awareness makes them hopeless for such a task. 'If there is hope ... it lies in the proles'[13] but at the same time 'The proletarians will never revolt, not in a thousand years or a million. They cannot.'[14] The Party's power hinges on the essential point that *the proles are ignorant of their own position*. Kneale and Cartier do not appear to have understood this. In the film, the 'Prole Sector' is signposted like a town, and a prole barman actually refers to himself as a 'prole'! If the proles call themselves proles, they are conscious of their own position and understand the social hierarchy, defeating Orwell's whole point about false class consciousness. They cannot be both politically conscious and not rise up against the Party. The BBC not only missed the point but was evidently unaware that there was one, which also seems to be the case with their handling of vaporisation.

'Vaporisation' in the book is a euphemism for the totalitarian's purging. The essential point about it is that it is abrupt and can rarely be seen coming: 'People simply disappeared, always during the night.'[15] In the film, however, this is completely overlooked. There is a painful scene with Syme in the Chestnut Tree, where he explains that he has been 'suspended' from the Party and feverishly begs Winston to help him, before the camera leans into his face and he is ... vaporised. The scene is dramatically effective, but by having Syme know his fate beforehand, it compromises Orwell's point for a few minutes of sensation. After all, who in Stalin's Russia or Hitler's Germany had time to phone a friend? In another scene on the same theme, Winston's line 'He doesn't exist. He never existed', which ought to have been emphasised by a fade-out or by silence, is spoken so dismissively that it is robbed of its power and meaning. The horror of being 'lifted clean out of the stream of history'[16] is completely lost. Nor is this anything to do with the limits on run-time. Many lines in the film *are* emphatic, but these are those which have a dramatic quality rather than a polemical one. The best example of this is O'Brien's statement that 'They got me a long time

ARTICLE

ago' which, though startling both onscreen and on the page, has nothing to do with Orwell's message.

POSITIVES

If, to this point, I have seemed especially harsh or dismissive towards the teleplay *Nineteen Eighty-Four*, it is only because it must live up to such a high standard of source material. Although it fails to deliver in the areas that I have outlined, there are nonetheless several positive elements of the film.

The tone is perfect. The essence of the novel is never lost. At the end of the film, just as at the end of the book, you are left with hopelessness at what the opening disclaimer calls 'man's inhumanity to man'. This is complemented by the cinematography, which in the pre-recorded segments is far better than in the live-filmed ones and which, with its dark and noirish quality, reflects the mood of the novel. A particularly memorable image, redolent of the best shots in Carol Reed's *The Third Man* (1949), comes when, across a darkened London, Winston walks back from Mr Charrington's shop with light streaming past his silhouette. The Two Minutes' Hate scene is equally effective. It has not only that shadowy quality about it but a superb execution to boot. The scene cuts between Goldstein on the telescreen and the rising wild chants of 'Hate!'; the camera pans to Winston as he picks up the chant, until they all descend into frenzy. Cinematically, this is a terrific sequence and does not compromise the point about collective hatred and mass fervour. (Goldstein, by the way, is depicted as a cosplay Trotsky, so at least Kneale understood something of Orwell's intentions). This cinematic quality, which was only made possible by the blend of live and pre-filmed segments, is also what marks the production as 'a transitional moment between the more conservative "filmed theatre" of early TV drama and the new era which was about to dawn'.[17] Another of Cartier's flourishes appears in Winston's flat, where the director performs a clever piece of screen-sound juxtaposition. The audio of the scene is of the telescreen crying 'Big Brother!' while, onscreen, Winston is scrawling 'Down with Big Brother', rendering Orwell's ideas about the clash between conformity and individuality into the language of the cinema. Even aside from that, the very image of Big Brother staring out at the audience paralleled the fictional telescreens and, as Dorian Lynskey suggests, fills 'the viewer's heart [with] the same chill that the characters in the play experienced whenever they heard his voice coming from *their* watching TV screens'.[18]

Aside from these especially vivid moments, the best sections are those which are taken unedited from the novel – usually dialogues – but even a couple of these benefit from some embellishment.

In the canteen, Winston is discussing Newspeak with Syme and unconsciously mutters a line from *Hamlet*. This line is not in the original, but still works because it incorporates that other moment when he 'woke up with the word Shakespeare on his lips'.[19]

The film's final third is its best. By this point, neither the low budget nor the previous mistakes are able to constrain the power of Orwell's vision. The Ministry of Love scenes are exactly as they were originally written. O'Brien's face looms large in the frame as he stands over Winston, who is feeble, greyed, toothless and tied into a coffin-like torture machine. Indeed, Morell's most intensely delivered line, just before the great monologue, is as he looks down and tells Winston: 'If you want a picture of the future imagine a boot stamping into a human face forever.' Eerie music, actual rats in a machine and Cushing's all-too-convincing performance combine to make Room 101 extremely graphic. The tone of the final scene in the Chestnut Tree Café, where grey-looking Winston and Julia sit together, is in tune with the wistfulness and pessimism of Orwell's conclusion. The film ends on the same note as its source: with a sense of the futility of the individual in the face of the Party.

CONCLUSION

Nineteen Eighty-Four is as much a treatise as it is a novel, so half of it is immediately lost on screen. Then, as the inevitable result of being simplified for television, the BBC emphasises drama over politics and sensation over satire, so it is no longer surprising that this production has taken so long to be made publicly available. It was a commendable effort but ultimately the BBC skewered too much of the original for it to rank as one of the great novel adaptations. The under-used cast and cinematic quality may have come through better in a full-on feature film with a higher budget and a willingness to engage with the story's nuances. On the whole, the teleplay *Nineteen Eighty-Four* does have curiosity value and, so long as you treat it as a piece of 1950s sci-fi TV and not as the watered-down version of a masterwork, is worth watching at least once.

- *Nineteen Eighty-Four*, Rudolph Cartier (dir.), BBC, London, 1954 [Teleplay], EAN 5035673014455 (Blu-ray/DVD)

NOTES

[1] Fordy, Tom (2022) How the 'unadulterated horror' of Peter Cushing's *Nineteen Eighty-Four* broke the BBC, *Telegraph*, 4 May. Available online at https://www.telegraph.co.uk/tv/0/unadulterated-horror-peter-cushings-nineteen-eighty-four-broke/, accessed on 31 July 2023

[2] Murray, Andy (2017) *Into the Unknown: The Fantastic Life of Nigel Kneale (Revised and Updated)*, Manchester: Headpress Books p. 285

[3] Cushing, Peter (1986) *An Autobiography*, Oxford: Clio Press p. 154

[4] Orwell, George (2021 [1949]) *Nineteen Eighty-Four*, Hertfordshire: Wordsworth Editions p. 9

[5] Ibid p. 23

[6] Ibid p. 201

[7] Ibid p. 39

[8] Ryan, David (2018) *George Orwell on Screen: Adaptations, Documentaries and Docudramas on Film and Television*, North Carolina: MacFarland and Company p. 59

[9] You and the Atom bomb (1945) *Tribune*, 19 October

[10] Prophecies of fascism (1940) *Tribune*, 12 July

[11] Ibid p. 145

[12] Taylor, D.J. (2019) *On* Nineteen Eighty-Four, New York: Abrams pp 131-132

[13] Ibid p. 54

[14] Ibid p. 200

[15] Ibid p. 16

[16] Ibid p. 126

[17] Cooke, Lez (2003) *British Television Drama: A History*, London: British Film Institute p. 28

[18] Lynskey, Dorian (2021) *The Ministry of Truth: A Biography of George Orwell's 1984*, London: Picador p. 190

[19] Ibid p. 25

NOTE ON THE CONTRIBUTOR

Hassan Akram is a student and a writer of short stories and essays. In 2018, he picked up a worn copy of *Nineteen Eighty-Four* and he has been a devoted Orwell fan ever since. His main research interest is Orwell's connection to other twentieth-century writers, on which he has written for the journal of The Orwell Society. He has written essays on other topics for publications such as *Sherlock Holmes Mystery Magazine*. His fiction has also appeared in publications including *Humour Me Magazine*.

Attwood's Imaginary Interview with Orwell

Richard Lance Keeble assesses Margaret Attwood's imaginary interview with her 'hero'. And while Orwell, in his own imaginary conversation with Jonathan Swift, concentrated entirely on his writings Attwood takes in also his biography. With mixed results.

One of the writers Orwell most admired was Jonathan Swift, author of *Gulliver's Travels* (1726). And the wonderfully inventive and witty imaginary interview he conducted with Swift, broadcast on the BBC African Service on 6 November 1942, displays Orwell in a typically jovial, life-affirmative mood. In all of Orwell's works, it ranks high amongst my favourites.

Orwell begins with words of praise: 'I believe *Gulliver's Travels* has meant more to me than any other book ever written. I can't remember when I first read it. I must have been eight years old at the most, and it's lived with me ever since so that I suppose a year has never passed without my re-reading at least part of it' (*CWGO* XIV: 157).

Not surprisingly, Orwell takes the opportunity to direct a few jibes at the corporate press of his day. Playing the devil's advocate, Orwell asks: 'Don't you find that the mass of the people are more intelligent than they were, or at least better educated? How about the newspapers and the radio. Surely they have opened people's minds a little? There are few people in England now who can't read, for instance.' Swift replies drily: 'That is why they are so easily deceived. Your ancestors two hundred years ago were full of barbarous superstitions but they would not have been so credulous as to believe your daily newspapers' (ibid: 159).

Orwell is also keen to challenge Swift over his pessimistic view of the human predicament. For instance, Swift reads directly from *Gulliver's Travels* about life in England: 'I cannot but conclude the bulk of your natives to be the most pernicious race of little odious vermin that nature ever suffered to crawl upon the surface of the earth.' To which Orwell responds in his concluding remarks: 'His vision of human society is so penetrating, and yet in the last analysis it's false. He couldn't see what the simplest person sees, that life is

RICHARD LANCE KEEBLE

worth living and human beings, even if they're dirty and ridiculous, are mostly decent' (ibid: 161).

Margaret Attwood, the celebrated Canadian author of the feminist dystopian novel, *The Handmaid's Tale* (1985), has always stressed her indebtedness to Orwell's *Nineteen Eighty-Four*.[1] In her latest collection of short stories, *Old Babes in the Wood* (London: Chatto & Windus, 2023), interestingly, she includes an imaginary interview with the spirit of her 'hero' George (with the help of a medium called Mrs Verity).

She repeats her profound admiration for the author of *Animal Farm* and *Nineteen Eighty-Four* in no uncertain terms: 'You were very brave, and not only in Spain, during the Civil War. Much of what you said was unpopular at the time. Your work has really been invaluable and you've been – how can I put this? – an inspiration' (p. 92).

But overall the interview is rather disappointing.

It begins with Orwell somewhat inappropriately slagging off his father. When Attwood reports: 'He said you'd thrown away your advantages,' a disgruntled Orwell replies: 'Class advantages, he meant. The family silver. Schools for junior snobs and so forth. I do not consider those things advantages. Bundle of prejudices based on falsehoods. A muddying of the truth' (p. 82). But before his father died in 1939, Orwell had become much closer to him. Indeed, there is evidence that the reconciliation began earlier – in the early 1930s. Then, joining his family in Southwold, Orwell accompanied his father in one of the old man's favourite pastimes: watching films in the tiny local cinema in Duke of York's Road near the common. Attwood appears unaware of all this.

She next suggests that Orwell's father disapproved of him being a 'sloppy dresser' (ibid). To which Orwell responds: 'I did not have the money to spend on tailors' (p. 83). But this is wrong. Jack Wilkinson Denny, the leading tailor in Southwold, outfitted Eric Blair (as he was known to him) with made-to-measure clothes throughout his life and, in an interview with Stephen Wadhams for CBC in 1983, said that 'he invariably bought the best cloth'. For instance, an overcoat purchased in January 1928 cost him £6 (a lot of money in those days), a three-piece suit in September 1937 cost £9.10 shillings.

Attwood certainly has a few laughs on the way – though the jokes often tend to be somewhat forced. At one point, Orwell (coughing regularly) asks if he can smoke. 'It's very bad for you,' advises Attwood to which Orwell responds: 'Not anymore. You only die once. Wasn't that the name of some shocking book?' (p. 85). Later Attwood, in trying to dissect the name 'George Orwell', focuses on 'well' and links it to the phrase 'All shall be well' of Julian of Norwich. To which Orwell replies: 'That's stretching it my dear. I have no pretensions to holiness. I wanted a river, yes, a natural feature but an ordinary kind of river. Not a holy river and not some damned private trout stream, bunch of aristocrats sticking their fishing rods into it' (p. 88).

Attwood manages to insert some of her preoccupations into the interview: she's clearly not keen on 'anti-vaxxers' (to which Orwell asks predictably: 'Anti-what?'), on the 'invasion of the Capitol' nor on Trump's attempts to overturn the election results. 'Sounds familiar,' says Orwell. 'I lived in an age of coups, of one kind or another. Different slogans but same idea' (p. 85).

She is also a fan of Rebecca Solnit, author of the much-acclaimed *Orwell's Roses*. 'Her book takes as a point of departure your passionate interest in gardening, in growing things. Not many people know that about you. She makes you sound, well, kind of adorable. That photo of you with your adopted son, such a sweet child. …. You weren't Mr Doom and Gloom at all! Enthusiastic about living, full of plans, until …' (p. 93). At which point Orwell chips in: 'Until the end, you mean. Don't worry. There must always be an end. As in novels…' (ibid).

The main problem with the interview is that Attwood has stuck far too closely with what is *known* about Orwell rather than the *unknown*, so failing to use it as an opportunity to fill in some of the gaps imaginatively in his biography. That would have been far more fun. Indeed, while so much is now known about Orwell's life, questions still hang over many of the big events of his life. What did he really think about his slave-owning ancestors? He wrote a long essay – part fiction/part memoir – about his time at his Eastbourne prep school, St Cyprian's, but so little on his years at Eton. Why? After Eton, why did he choose to ignore Oxbridge and become an Imperial Policeman in Burma? How much did guilt about his attempted rape of his childhood friend, Jacintha Buddicom, affect his decision? Did he really shoot an elephant while serving as an Imperial Policeman in Burma? And did he actually see a man hanged? When he returned to England in 1927 why was Andrew Gow (his Classics tutor at Eton and now installed at Trinity College, Cambridge) one of the first people he was keen to meet? *Down and Out in Paris and London* (1933) covers only a few months of his time in Paris. What else did he get up to in the French capital – who were his main friends there? Why did he write so little about his first wife, Eileen O'Shaughnessy? How much did her poem, '1984' actually influence his decision to call his great dystopian novel *Nineteen Eighty-Four*? To what extent did his great friend, David Astor, introduce him to the world of intelligence? And so on.

ARTICLE

RICHARD LANCE KEEBLE

You will all have your own Orwellian preoccupations and special queries you'd like to put to the man. Who knows, in time, with Orwellian scholarship constantly developing in so many remarkable directions all the time, some of my own questions may well be answered.

NOTE

[1] See, for instance, https://www.theguardian.com/books/2013/jan/18/my-hero-george-orwell-atwood

NOTE ON THE CONTRIBUTOR

Richard Lance Keeble was chair of The Orwell Society 2013-2020. His latest publication (with David Swick) is *Literary Journalism Goes Inside Prison: Just Sentences* (London: Routledge, 2023) in which he examines Orwell's attitudes and writings on prisons.

ARTICLE

Pedagogy of the Distressed?: 'Politics and the English language' in and out of the Classroom

John Rodden shares his experience of teaching Orwell's celebrated essay and discusses how and why Orwell's essayists have become mainstays in English-language anthologies and in school and university curricula.

'Politics and the English language' is the most famous and widely-read political essay ever written – and also the most frequently anthologised essay of the twentieth century. Millions of American students have encountered it in college freshman composition courses or in introductory rhetoric classes. A 1999 study by Lynn Z. Bloom found that it was reprinted 118 times in 325 editions of 58 readers published between 1946 and 1996 that were intended for use in college-level composition classes[1] – and I would estimate that the current totals are easily double those figures.[2]

This article chiefly addresses my own pedagogical experience of teaching the essay to diverse student levels across more than four decades. Before sharing my observations about the essay as a classroom staple, however, let me dwell further on the too little-studied empirical evidence pertaining to these matters. For Orwell, like many canonical authors, is often honoured in the breach with vague generalisations, anecdotes and impressionistic 'evidence' cited to bolster contentions about their alleged ubiquity. All too seldom is concrete quantitative supporting evidence, derived from extensive survey research, presented to sustain a claim to 'fame'. So let me briefly attend here to some relevant empirical evidence that illuminates the origins and foundation of Orwell's canonical status, not only of 'Politics and the English language' but also of Orwell's *oeuvre in* general.

CANON FODDER? FROM 'FAME' TO FACTS AND FIGURES

Close examination of Bloom's research yields insight into the role of anthologies and composition readers in establishing Orwell's

JOHN RODDEN

dominant place in the essay canon. With 357 appearances in dozens of anthologies, Orwell tops the list of 174 essayists – and no other essayist is even close. (E.B. White is a distant second, with 268 appearances – and Orwell has more than double the appearances of most authors in the top twenty.) 'Politics and the English language' (118) and (perhaps surprisingly) 'Shooting an elephant' (113) are the second and third most frequently anthologised selections. Jonathan Swift's 'A modest proposal' ranks first with 151 appearances. (No other essay even approaches 100 appearances.) But the popularity of 'A modest proposal' is virtually Swift's only work in the anthologies – unlike the case with Orwell, whose total includes selections from 17 different works of prose nonfiction (such as 'A hanging', 'Why I write', 'England your England', 'My country, right or left', 'Charles Dickens' and 'Reflections on Gandhi'.

As one might expect, the list is heavily weighted towards American authors, given that the vast number of anthologies are American composition readers. Only three British authors are in the top 20, including Virginia Woolf, Swift and Thomas Hardy; merely two other non-Americans are in the top fifty (Plato and D.H. Lawrence). Rounding out the top 10 are E.B. White, Joan Didion, Lewis Thomas, Henry David Thoreau, Swift, Virginia Woolf, James Thurber and Mark Twain.

Given the reliance of Bloom on composition readers, I would emphasise that the title of her article may mislead some readers, for her list does not pertain, properly speaking, to 'the essay canon'. It addresses, rather, 'the *pedagogical* essay canon'. That is a noteworthy qualification because Orwell is virtually the only author in the top fifty whom I would regard as a canonical mainstay of 'the essay canon'. The composition readers seldom include such figures as Montaigne, Edmund Burke, William Hazlitt and Thomas de Quincey – and, I would argue, that policy is based on a sound practical rationale, since their work is heavily rooted in its historical moment and this is liable to be difficult for student writers to gain access.

So Orwell is practically the only 'classic' essayist who has managed to cross the divide between what I might call the 'historical essay canon' and the 'pedagogical essay canon'. Whether he will still do so in the future remains to be seen. As we proceed through the second decade of the twenty-first century, however, Orwell's essays show every sign of continuing to occupy a prominent place in composition and rhetoric courses. According to the extensive data gathered in the Open Syllabus Project (OSP), which contains more than 9 million syllabi from 140 nations, 'Politics and the English language' is the most commonly assigned essay in American (and foreign, English language) classrooms. Among nearly 8 million books and articles that the OSP has listed as tertiary-level course assignments, Orwell's essay is ranked #381, just behind selections from Marx's *Das Kapital* and immediately ahead of Maxine Hong Kingston's *The Woman Warrior: Memoirs of a Girlhood Among Ghosts* (1976).[3]

That ranking may not seem impressive – until one specifies that 'Politics and the English language' is the single most frequently assigned essay in the OSP survey research. It is notable that writing handbooks head the OSP list of assignments in university syllabi. For instance, the first three spots are occupied by William Strunk and E.B. White's *The Elements of Style*, Diana Hacker's *A Writer's Reference* and Kate L. Turban's *A Manual for Writers of Term Papers, Theses, and Dissertations*. (They are immediately followed by Marx's *The Communist Manifesto*.) Three other writing guides also make it into the top 15 assignments. (Further down in the OSP compilation is 'Shooting an elephant', which is listed as #1251.) Significantly, the OSP also shows that, among those university syllabi that assign a standard writing guide such as *The Elements of Style*, 'Politics and the English language' is the single reading most often paired with it.

Readers and scholars who wonder about the frequency of Orwell's other works in university courses will also be interested to learn that *Nineteen Eighty-Four*, with 3007 adoptions in OSP syllabi, ranks in the top 10 per cent of assignments. It ranks #194 in the OSP list, a few places ahead of *The Second Sex*, by Simone de Beauvoir. A few rankings further back is a collection of Twain's *The Adventures of Huckleberry Finn* and several places behind a collection of Hawthorne tales (*Young Goodman Brown and Other Short Stories*) and short stories by Flannery O'Connor (*A Good Man is Hard to Find*).

While this may seem to indicate that *Nineteen Eighty-Four* has become a literary staple – contrary to my research in the late 1980s – a closer look at the OSP data makes clear that this is not at all the case. Unlike the cases of Hawthorne, Twain and O'Connor – and every other novel in the top 200 – only 35 per cent of the appearances of *Nineteen Eighty-Four* are in English literature syllabi. (By contrast, more than 90 per cent – and often close to 100 per cent – of the other fictional works are in literature courses.) Why then does Orwell's novel rank so highly in the OSP list? Because of its extraordinary appeal across numerous disciplines (e.g., hundreds of appearances in history and political science syllabuses alone – as well as in courses in philosophy, education, sociology, law and even business). If Orwell's novel were ranked simply on the basis of its number of syllabus appearances in English literature, it would not even gain a place in the top 1,500 assignments on the OSP list.

JOHN RODDEN

One may, however, argue: 'Well, *Nineteen Eighty-Four* is just as much a canonical work as *Huckleberry Finn*.' Yes, indeed – or better: just as *little* a canonical work as Twain's novel. Just as Orwell's dystopia has long been denigrated as a weak novel (wooden characters, poor plot etc.) according to modernist criteria, Twain's novel has more recently suffered because of its retrograde racial politics.

The fact is that Twain's masterwork is assigned in American literature classes much less often than in the 1980s – chiefly on account of heightened sensitivity to its portrait of the runaway slave Jim and because of Huck's use of the n-word. Many American literature scholars speculate that the day may soon come when *Huckleberry Finn* is no longer a central text of American literature; it may soon be assigned as a reflection of Twain's racist attitudes and white privilege.

And what about Orwell's other works? *Animal Farm* (#1029 in the OSP list) trails distantly behind his essays, followed much later by *Homage to Catalonia* and *The Road to Wigan Pier*. Here again, merely 35 per cent of its syllabus appearances are in English literature. If it were ranked exclusively on that basis, it would fail to make the top 5,000 assignments.

As I first argued in *The Politics of Literary Reputation* (1989), the absence of *Animal Farm* and *Nineteen Eighty-Four* from English literature (and other) courses reflected a phenomenon that may be termed 'tiered canons' whereby purportedly 'simple' (i.e., accessible, non-experimental) works – given the ongoing emphasis of modernist critical values – are largely excluded from the 'high' canon of twentieth- and twenty-first century literature. *Animal Farm* and *Nineteen Eighty-Four* are, thus, relegated to the status of junior and senior high school reading. It is revealing and relevant here that *Animal Farm*'s rank at #1029 in the OSP list places it immediately behind another canonical high school assignment: *The Stranger*, by Albert Camus (and several places behind Jack Kerouac's *On the Road*). Of the top 50 authors taught in universities worldwide, according to OSP data, George Orwell ranks #39, immediately ahead of Jean-Jacques Rousseau, John Milton, and Nathaniel Hawthorne. (Shakespeare and Plato occupy the top two spots, followed by Michel Foucault and Karl Marx.)

'POLITICS AND THE ENGLISH LANGUAGE': HISTORY, RHETORIC, RECEPTION

How was Orwell's essay received by its original audience? And why do teachers and professors assign the essay today?

To answer the latter question first: the motives of classroom educators are diverse. Among the key reasons: to promote cultural literacy, to foster critical thinking, to introduce the plain style, to heighten awareness of euphemism and jargon and to clarify the interconnections between politics and language. One of the great ironies of literary history, however, is that the essay was rejected when it was first submitted to a prominent London editor, George Weidenfeld, at *Contact*, only later to be published by *Horizon*, edited by Orwell's friend, Cyril Connolly. Weidenfeld, seconded by his assistant Philip Toynbee, rejected the essay on the grounds that it did not meet their editorial criteria. Weidenfeld subsequently regretted his 'sacrilegious mistake'. Like *Animal Farm*, therefore, which was turned down by at least four leading London publishers (including T.S. Eliot at Faber), 'Politics and the English language' is paid homage today as a canonical work of enduring distinction despite the 'sacrilege' committed by London editors against it. Irony of ironies, the twin turndowns give Orwell the dubious, bizarre (yet also rather amusing) distinction of being the recipient of the most famous British rejection notices of the century for both nonfiction *and* fiction – and from two of the leading intellectual gatekeepers of his day, Weidenfeld and Eliot.

'Politics and the English language' argues that the English language is deteriorating as a tool of communication as a result of an onslaught of vague and misleading words, dying metaphors and obfuscatory diction and bureaucratese. Political discussion has become corrupted, Orwell contends, and only a serious effort to seek the truth by both writers and readers will reverse the decline. To illustrate the worrisome conditions of language use, Orwell selects five passages written by well-known writers of the early post-Second World War era and examines their shortcomings. Throughout the essay his commitment is to the use of language as an instrument for the clear and accurate expression of thought; his derision is focused on language that serves to distort meaning and hide intentions.

'Political language and writing are largely the defence of the indefensible,' Orwell concedes, citing various euphemisms and jargon aimed at rationalising or justifying jingoist nationalism, ideological purges, nuclear weapons and political imprisonment. Politicians are responsible for much of the abuse, Orwell notes – certainly nothing has changed since his day in that regard. If anything, as the author of *Nineteen Eighty-Four* would readily grant if he surveyed the present political landscape in Washington and London (or virtually any nation's capital), we are ever more engulfed by Newspeak and doublespeak, that is, by language 'designed to make lies sound truthful and murder respectable, and to give an appearance of solidity to pure wind'.

Bleak as the linguistic climate was in the immediate aftermath of Nazi-dominated Europe and in the midst of Soviet-style

JOHN RODDEN

dictatorships arising everywhere on the Continent as the Cold War (Orwell's own coinage) dawned, Orwell did not regard the situation as utterly hopeless. He suggested six simple, practical rules for combatting imprecise and corrupt language, among them a refusal to indulge in hackneyed metaphors, a resistance against tempting long words when short ones suffice, a ruthless pruning of verbiage and unnecessary words and an avoidance of the passive voice and pretentious (largely inaccessible) foreign phrases. (The antinomian sixth rule was typical of the schoolboy gadfly Blair and the heterodox radical Orwell – 'Break any of these rules sooner than say anything outright barbarous.') English could once again 'become a language of meaning and precision', Orwell contended, if we would battle our 'lazy habits of thought', retire 'worn-out phrases', and exert 'a conscious determination to achieve the utmost clarity of statement'.

The English-speaking world has obviously failed, and failed miserably, to do any of these things in the last three-quarters of a century – and in our era of 'fake news' and 'alternative facts'. the need for 'linguistic climate change' is, if anything, far more dire than it was even in the totalitarian Europe of 1946.

Orwell was far from the first writer to worry about how civic society, as a corporate body of living language, suffers when language is abused. Just as Thucydides implicated the crisis of public language in the fall of Athens into anarchy, so too did Cato the Younger during the Catiline Conspiracy (63 BCE) and, a millennium later, Hobbes during England's Civil War (of the 1640s). Today, whether it manifests in the form of buzzwords or pseudo-profundity, or the crudities of twittering tweets or the arcane evasions of legalese and bureaucratese, the pandemic of fraudulent political language obstructs serious thought, fatally degrading political discourse into Orwellian doublespeak.

AN EDUCATOR'S PERSPECTIVE

The scale and complexity of the problem are obviously far greater than a single article by George Orwell can hope to address. Still, one could be forgiven for drawing that conclusion – namely, of the essay's therapeutic magic – as a result of the unique attention that the essay receives, not only from admirers but also detractors of Orwell. Indeed, if any further evidence of the exceptional, outsized influence of 'Politics and the English language' is needed, consider also the following singular distinction. It is remarkable enough that several book-length studies have been devoted each to *Animal Farm* and *Nineteen Eighty-Four,* but how often are entire books by leading scholars devoted to exhaustive analysis and far-ranging application of a single essay?

'Politics and the English language' may be the most widely discussed modern essay ever written, as exemplified by *What Orwell Didn't Know: Propaganda and the New Face of American Politics* (New York: Public Affairs, 2007). Sponsored by the Open Society Institute, which is funded by the politically progressive financier George Soros, this volume attacks what its contributors deem the far-right-wing political agenda of the Republican Party and the Christian Right by drawing on the prestige and intellectual pedigree of Orwell and his celebrated essay. The collection consists of proceedings from a 2007 conference organised by the deans of five prominent journalism schools 'who were worried about what was happening to political language'. Its 18 chapters feature contributions from prominent political philosophers, cognitive scientists, anthropologists, psychologists and journalists, including an epilogue by Soros himself.

Although the thrust of the book is rather presumptuous and even contradictory – the title dismisses Orwell even as the contents acknowledge him as a visionary – the overt gesture of tribute to his essay is obvious: what other essay could possibly attract this range of thinkers, none of whom are English professors or men and women of letters? In an implicit acknowledgement of the imaginative power and inventive genius of Orwell as a political prophet, *What Orwell Didn't Know* addresses topics ranging from the American invasion of Iraq in 2003, nuclear proliferation and global warming to the 'carnivalesque' infotainment industry, the role of metaphor in cognitive linguistics, research in neuroscience and the psychology of emotion, and even the 'Orwellian' Postal Reorganization Act of 1970 (which hiked mailing rates for journals of opinion and 'little magazines'). Several contributors argue that the United States has adopted a permanent 'war' footing like that of the three superstates in *Nineteen Eighty-Four*, attesting to the propagandistic success of the allegedly endless, fraudulent 'War on Terror', which functions (as in Oceania) to keep the masses (i.e., us 'proles') in a fixed state of fear and passivity.

Permit me to mention a further irony connected with this conference collection that may be of special interest to scholars and critics of Orwell's work. I find it tiresome that this group of radical and neo-Marxist critic-theorists – especially given the Marxist Left's long history of deep hostility to Orwell traceable to his battles with the Stalinists of his day – would invoke Orwell's name and pedigree for the very purpose of chastising him for his so-called liberal, empiricist naïveté and allegedly regressive ideological outlook. Such an invocation represents a more subtle and devious way to attack him, which again has a long history (e.g., witness the faint praise of earlier generations of British Marxists such as Raymond Williams).

ARTICLE

JOHN RODDEN Even the conference title ('There You Go Again: Orwell Comes to America') – which draws on a famous Ronald Reagan zinger in a presidential debate against Democratic nominee Walter Mondale (in the year 1984, no less!) – makes it sound as if paleo-Reaganite George Orwell had 'come to America' and was spreading his lies and obfuscations here again. This confusion exemplifies a cultural phenomenon to which I have often called attention: how Orwell and 'Orwell' are regularly blurred and even inverted.

That sort of ideologically motivated criticism from Orwell's detractors is misplaced and unjustifiable. And yet, speaking as an educator and teacher who greatly admires much of Orwell's work also, I regret to say that we have done George Orwell and his essay a grave disservice by turning it into a dusty school assignment for study and imitation by beginning student writers in college classes. Let me emphasise that I am speaking here about the situation in most American college classrooms, which certainly differs from that of British and other Commonwealth university classrooms. (British and Canadian colleagues have informed me, however, that the essay is also sometimes assigned in secondary school courses – and the same is true in the US and elsewhere. To that extent, the difficulties go beyond the situation in introductory US college rhetoric courses.)

Important and relevant though the advice in the essay was and continues to be, I believe that we serve poorly both it and our students by turning it into a prose model for classroom teaching, let alone to a group of beginning (or remedial) English students. Its general excellence as a *political essay* does not mean that it proves valuable as a beginner's guide for learning how to write better.

Those claims may at first appear to be ironic and even implausible. As a professor who has taught the essay in writing courses, however, I regret to report that I have had mixed experiences with it as a teaching tool. I question its suitability as a pedagogical staple. I certainly don't believe it is a good model for beginning students.

Let me explain. First we need to distinguish between a fine *essay* and an exemplary student *prose model*. The fact is that the status of 'Politics and the English language' as one of the most often assigned essays in beginning composition classes has generated an unfortunate halo effect, whereby we teachers fail to admit how poorly the essay serves our beginning and remedial writing students.

I am convinced that the problem lies not so much with Orwell's essay as with the preparation of our students – and with us teachers and the misguided uses we try to make of it.

I should grant immediately that not everyone is likely to agree with me about 'the problem' – an exasperated Stanley Fish, for example, insists with heavy *Weltschmerz* that the problem is, indeed, precisely with Orwell's 'really terrible essay'. As is Fish's wont, he claims to reveal the glaring, always paradoxical truth overlooked by the obviously 'spectacularly empty'-headed butt of criticism – in this case, an obtuse George Orwell. Fish writes:

> Orwell's insistence that we 'let the meaning choose the word and not the other way around' is so silly. ('Politics and the English language' is a really terrible essay.) He says that 'when you think of a concrete object, you think wordlessly,' and the trick is to choose the word that reflects (without adding to or overlaying) the object's concreteness…' First 'think wordlessly' sounds good as an antidote to the tyranny of words; unfortunately, it's not something that any human being can do. 'Active open-mindedness' – standing to one side of our beliefs and assumptions in the service of unbiased observation – is another name for having no mind at all. Open-mindedness, far from being a virtue, is a condition which, if it could be achieved, would result in a mind that was spectacularly empty. An open mind is an empty mind.[4]

With regard to our student population, it warrants emphasis that exemplary prose models should be sufficiently accessible to allow readers to imitate the author's writing strategies and to identify with his or her writing situation. But Orwell did not write this essay for an audience of potential students, let alone as some sort of *vade mecum* for beginning and remedial students. Rather, he originally submitted it to George Weidenfeld's newly-founded highbrow cultural magazine, *Contact*. When Weidenfeld rejected it, Orwell had it published in *Horizon*, the leading intellectual journal in literary London during the 1940s. The point is that his impetus for writing the essay was that it might serve as a reminder to serious readers and fellow journalists about the sorry state of contemporary political discourse and the need for both readers and writers to resist lax literary habits. (The essay was circulated with those aims in mind among the staff of the London *Observer*, a newspaper for which Orwell wrote that was published by his friend David Astor. In fact, Astor went so far as to insist that all his journalists read 'Politics and the English language').[5]

Perhaps that explains why so many journalists, professional writers and lovers of the English language (including many English professors!) cherish this essay. Perhaps it also explains, however, why my own pedagogical experience with it is not so surprising, namely that I find that Orwell's essay offers advice that may undermine, rather than nurture, the developing literary skills of beginners.[6]

Let me re-emphasise here that – the changing trends in literary academe notwithstanding – I see no sign that 'Politics and the

ARTICLE

JOHN RODDEN

English language' is less widely taught today than in the late twentieth century, when I (in *The Politics of Literary Reputation*) and Lynn Z. Bloom (in *College English*, 1999) conducted our research into student composition readers and American pedagogy texts.

Take, for instance, Orwell's advice to avoid clichés. 'Politics and the English language' closes with a plea to 'send some worn-out and useless phrase, some *jackboot, Achilles' heel, hotbed, melting pot, acid test, veritable inferno* or other lump of verbal refuse into the dustbin where it belongs'.

Bravo! I heartily concur. Until I discover, on gazing at the blank looks of my students, that this invaluable counsel does not register at all. Beginning students don't know that these phrases are worn out, or sometimes even what these phrases (or the individual words within them) *mean at all.*

It is not enough to say: 'Well, go ahead and tell them!' Or to say: 'Then let them look it up!' No, the problem runs much deeper. In the case of many beginning students who are just entering the academic environment, we are asking too much all at once. Before we burden these students with anxieties about improper usage or the political dangers posed by invoking dying metaphors, we might first encourage these students to become aware of clichés by freely using them in the first few weeks of class. Let them discover how clichés *become* clichés through overuse. Let them learn for themselves how metaphors tire and die. Let them wear them, as it were – and let them *wear them out.*

The cautionary warning should be clear. If Orwell's advice in 'Politics and the English language' (the 'six rules') is taken too baldly or prescriptively, the exact opposite of his intentions may occur: bad writing.[7]

CONSIDERATIONS, CAUTIONS, CONTEXTS

George Orwell developed a limpid straightforward prose style that has exerted enormous influence on writers and journalists of the last seven decades. This was his famously so-called 'simple style'. Yet as most serious writers will attest, Orwell's 'simple' style is only seemingly so. Or rather: what is *simple* is by no means necessarily *easy*. The plain style masks an intricate art of argumentation. Like an Olympic athlete who makes world-class performances look so natural and easy, Orwell's apparently casual conversational style is notoriously difficult to master. It projects a plain man persona and a populist ethos that enabled an intellectual like Orwell to speak 'for us' – as a common man expressing common sense. His plain style was a writing strategy that he developed and perfected over many years. However natural and effortless it seems when we read it, that style demands consummate mastery of the English language.

Other bits of Orwell's advice in his essay are also unhelpful for beginning students – even though advanced students and professional writers will profit from them. Consider, for instance, his injunction to 'use short words and to cut unnecessary words'. Experienced journalists take such an exhortation as self-evidently, indubitably *right*. Yet what may aid experienced writers, and also assist our more advanced students, may hamper the progress of beginning and remedial students. Many of them have severely limited lexicons and can't even meet word limits. Rather than issue them too many cautions about verbosity and diffuseness, we could foster in them a linguistic exuberance. Let them first discover and exult in 'the joy of mere words', the phrase that Orwell used in 'Why I write' (1946) – another of his great essays, published just two months after 'Politics and the English language'.

We could invite those students with small vocabularies to be wordy, and embolden them to go to the dictionary or the thesaurus and then experiment with the bounty that they discover. Admittedly, 'the joy of mere words' will lead some students for a time down the path of prolixity. That is fine. We should remember that Orwell himself spent long years struggling to be a writer (and destroyed at least two novels and several short stories during his twenties).

Even Orwell's sensible advice to avoid foreign words and idioms should be qualified. An occasional, strategic placement of foreign language usages may add spice and even humour to one's prose, as the masterful personal and literary essays of Joseph Epstein repeatedly demonstrate. Epstein's foreign usages are part of his signature prose style. In fact, he deploys foreign words and idioms in the indirect service of honouring Orwell's counsel to avoid clichés – because Epstein's foreign usages *reinvigorate* worn-out English-language clichés by reverting to a recognisable foreign-language 'translation'. He peppers his essays with foreign phrases that are almost always quite recognisable – given the sentence's context and the reader's familiarity with the English analogue. It usually takes no more than a slight effort on the part of an attentive reader to figure out what Epstein means – thereby avoiding the real intent of Orwell's warning against foreign words, namely that they are inaccessible to many readers. To the contrary, Epstein's clever stylistic innovation adds colour, brio, panache, zest and often hilarity to his prose – and readers will even have the expansive feeling of satisfaction after a momentary pause: a feeling of edification from having expanded their vocabularies and learned new, amusing foreign locutions.

Epstein's penchant for using humorous foreign phrases in order to revive dead metaphors fulfils a different aim in Orwell's essay: bust clichés. So Epstein breaks the 'rule' against foreign words in order to honour the 'rule' against clichés! In each of the examples

ARTICLE

JOHN RODDEN   cited below, use of the English phrase would induce a ho-hum nod by the literate reader, who would hardly register yet another dead metaphor slouching across the page. By invoking a French or Jewish translation of the cliché, however, Epstein provokes the reader to rethink the meaning of the metaphor and thereby brings it to life anew.

Consider, for instance, how Epstein makes use of words or references in Yiddish and Russian, respectively. Note how, in the following pair of examples, he plays on his Jewishness for comic effect and exploits the oddness of an unfamiliar city near the Volga River in central Russia with its alliterative sound.

- Speaking of a deceased friend, the social scientist Edward Shils, Epstein writes that Shils, even in his mid-eighties and in very poor health, would go into a store to buy some kitchen appliance 'knowing full well that he needed it like a *loch in kop*'.

- From 'Why I am not a lawyer': 'Another younger man I know, after going from Southern Illinois University to the Harvard Law School, a trip, measured in academic miles, slightly longer than that from Nizhni Novgorod to Miami Beach – could bear no more than a few years at a high salary at a large Chicago law firm....'

Epstein often makes amusing use of French to give a fancy high-toned turn of phrase to a low or mundane subject.

- Fellow essayist A.J. Liebling is 'always on the *qui vive* for scam artists' and 'has had three marriages, two of them disasters and the third, to the writer Jean Stafford, itself no *déjeuner sur l'herbe*'. In a discussion about his ageing body and its maladies, Epstein observes that 'what the French call my *décomposition générale* ... proceeds roughly on schedule, though at a less than alarming rate'.

- A memoir of his working-class Chicago boyhood mentions a rare family dinner outside home: 'When we went to restaurants it chiefly meant one steakhouse or another, for Chicago in those years was still the site off the stockyards, and beef in all its forms was the *specialité de la ville*.' And on a favourite local Chinese diner: 'Food at The Bird? Mr Moy served nothing goofy, went in for no exhibitionistic exoticism: no cheeks of veal, no head of pork, no *schwantz de boeuf*.'

- Reviewing Sigrid Nunez's memoir of her experience as Susan Sontag's secretary (and her son David Rieff's lover), Epstein reports, mockingly, how Nunez became frustrated with Sontag's invasive, helicopter-mother style of interfering in her son's sex life: 'Her advice to the couple was to desist from fornication and instead practice – I revert to the French to protect the innocent – *soixante-neuf*. ... Let us rest assured that neither replied: "Golly, Mom, thanks."'[8]

Rather than resort to English-language clichés, therefore, such as 'hole in the head', 'on the lookout' and 'picnic in the park', Epstein follows the Horatian call to 'delight and instruct'.

The larger point is that Epstein, a vocal admirer of Orwell, aims to accomplish, albeit by different means, the same goals as Orwell in 'Politics and the English language'. Epstein does not *avoid* but rather *indulges*, quite deliberately, in foreign words in order to vitalise his language – that is, his English sentences as well as his imported usages. Epstein's use of unfamiliar foreign names extends beyond places to people. Consider also this example from the Russian, which invokes a world-famous composer simply because it represents a funny-sounding name to American ears and is near-unimaginable in a conversation about hapless Chicago pro sports teams and their long-suffering fans. By making no attempt to contextualise the reference, Epstein effectively dispenses with its meaning or significance; it is merely the equivalent of a series of exclamation points that amusingly dot the end of his sentence. 'Why do we hang in there,' wails Epstein, cheering on and generally getting worked up over youthful millionaire athletes who have no more real affiliation with the city of Chicago than Dmitri Shostakovich?[9]

CONCLUSION

So my final word as a teacher of English and a scholar of George Orwell's work is this. Fellow teachers, assign Orwell's famous essay on politics and language if your aim is to promote cultural literacy and critical thinking, or to present the plain style, or to discuss the niceties of good versus bad usage.[10] If you are seeking to improve the literary skills of beginning student writers, be sure to emphasise the sophistication and original audience of the essay. Be sure to stress that the sixth rule is the all-important counsel – and such advice ('Break any of these rules sooner than say anything outright barbarous') is merely another way of saying that writing is a craft and an art.

Be sure, that is, to tell your students that good linguistic hygiene means avoiding bad habits – and the rest is diligence and daring and the relentless struggle for *le mot juste*.[11]

In doing so, you will enable them to appreciate better what good prose style and cogent argument require, and thereby assist them in their quest to achieve the same in their own literary endeavours.

JOHN RODDEN

NOTES

[1] See Lynn Z. Bloom, The essay canon, *College English*, Vol. 61, No. 4, March 1999 pp 401-430

[2] During the 1980s, I conducted extensive research on the appearance of the essay in anthologies devoted to rhetoric and composition. See my chapter, Canonization and the curriculum, in *The Politics of Literary Reputation: The Making and Claiming of St. George Orwell*, 1989. For revised and updated versions of the chapter cited above in *The Politics of Literary Reputation*, see Reputation, canon formation, pedagogy: George Orwell in the classroom, *College English*, Vol 53, No. 5 September, 1991 pp 503-530 and Teaching Orwell in the classroom, *Festschrift for Walter Sokel*, Steven Taubenack (ed.) Duke University Press, 1992. For my earlier work on pedagogical issues specifically related to Politics and the English language see John Rodden responds, *College English*, Vol. 54, No. 5, September 1992 pp 608-611; revised and updated in my book *The Unexamined Orwell*, University of Texas Press, 2011

[3] These and other rankings pertain to OSP research dated 2022

[4] See Stanley Fish, The all-spin zone, *New York Times*, 6 May 2007 p. 8

[5] See Gordon Bowker, *Inside George Orwell*, London: Little, Brown, 2003 p. 428

[6] See Rodden 1992

[7] The advice in the next section of the essay elaborates on some of my observations from the 1980s and 1990s on Orwell in the classroom

[8] For the sentence on Shils, see his essay collection *Narcissus Leaves the Pool*, Boston, New York: Harper Perennial p. 316. For the Liebling example, see his *Essays in Biography*, New York: Axios Press pp 272-273. For the passage on Susan Sontag in the review of Sigrid Nunez's *Sempre Susan*, see p. 288. The others are all from *In a Cardboard Belt!*, Boston, New York: Houghton Mifflin Company pp xiii, 60, 70, 79. It warrants mention that the Russian reference also exposes our own American ignorance and provincialism, since the allusion is to a locale that we treat as just as alien as Timbuktu, even though it is the sixth-largest Russian city, with a metropolitan population exceeding two million people

[9] See Joseph Epstein, *Masters of the Games: Essays and Stories on Sport*, Lanham, Maryland: Rowman & Littlefield p. 95

[10] For examples of two teachers who have focused on how Orwell's essay can assist students in classes on argumentation and contemporary politics and media respectively, see George Y. Trail, Teaching argument and the rhetoric of Orwell's 'Politics and the English Language', *College English* Vol. 57, No. 5 , September 1995 pp 570-583; and William Haltom and Hans Ostrom, Teaching George Orwell in Karl Rove's World: 'Politics and the English Language' in the 21st Century Classroom. Delivered at the Western Political Science Association, Vancouver BC 2008, and available online

[11] May I urge you to follow a variation on Orwell's counsel? I propose the following as the ultimate 'Golden Rule' of the essay (a.k.a. Orwell's Great Commandment for Impious Stylists): 'Break any rule' if it serves your purpose!

NOTE ON THE CONTRIBUTOR

John Rodden has published memoirs of Orwell scholars and intellectual admirers ranging from Peter Davison and Peter Stansky to Christopher Hitchens and Irving Howe. He is completing a study dealing with ideologically motivated controversies about Orwell's life and work, *George Orwell, Plagiarist?*

To George Orwell/Eric Blair

Paul Abdul Wadud Sutherland

I often yearn for you to outlast that 1950's death
outwit coughing blood, a remote island's whirlpool,
to return to us, who, minus fame, merely live and die.

To receive your commentary on the cursable events
since 1945, our rebirth year, to listen to your debates.
I want to see how your convictions would have altered.

You might respond, 'that surviving a Franco bullet blast
in Spain, in the late 30s, was enough adding on of days.
Two million words are enough to grieve for a legacy.'

History of the pen comes down to sorrowful intimacy.
I know you fled. You are hazy on this point. I crossed
the Atlantic. With greater legs you ran to the far east.

I trust you as a faithful servant who learned to hone
manners, smashing idols, no matter the personal loss.
Though many idolised your struggles, you kept drafting.

I wish you could have endured another decade or longer
to disrobe more imitations our minds adore, expose again
what being here is about – the love between all mortals.

Paul Abdul Wadud Sutherland immigrated from Canada to the UK in 1973. Since then he has made the British Isles his home. In 2004, he became a freelance writer and converted to being Sufi Muslim. He has eighteen collections of poems to his name. His *New and Selected Poems* (Valley Press, 2017) was selected by the *Morning Star* as one of the best ten books of that year. The University of Lincoln archives his work. His website is www.authorpaulsutherland.com. He lives with his wife in Lincolnshire.

POEM

A Song for Orwell

David Punter

An individual's biography - no such thing
we are all composed of fictions, narratives
a web of words that allow us still to sing

'My father dealt in opium'

perfectly legally, of course,
for the Indian Service, promoting the trade to China
and then there came the world of 'force

and fraud and secrecy', a minor
public school – such, such were the joys
of liberal imperialism's imperatives

'Life was hierarchical and whatever happened was right'

including, as it turned out, in Malaya,
Kenya, Ireland, Palestine, where coercion
provided employment for empire's violent boys

ever conjoining myths of civilisation
with the necessity sprung from failure
to understand the killing fields of Burma

'There were the strong, who deserved to win and always did'

so many years of surveillance by Special Branch
joke or malignity we shall never know
in Paris, London or Southwold, down on the ranch

or in those other killing fields, in Spain
tortured by ill health and fear
Communism's loss, Fascism's brutal gain

POEM

'Free speech is my right to say what you don't want to hear'

wounded in the throat while saying 'No',
but 'however much you deny the truth, the truth goes on existing'
doubling down perennially on doublespeak

but it can't be heard. Otherwise this would stop,
extraction of surplus profit, deep sea mining,
starving even Everest of snow.

'The war is not meant to be won, it is continuous'

burn another village, destroy another crop
in Vietnam, Ukraine; we know it's wicked
but we are the powerless, we know the drop

in sterling will affect our mortgage, so
we buy in to the myth; what else
is there to do under the starkness of the rain?

'He wears a mask, and his face grows to fit it'

in mud-filled trenches all around the world
one so-called 'pig' dissolves another with no memory
of how this played out last time bombs were hurled

and nothing's learned; even how words
drop their freight of meaning, their terrible liberty,
when sewn up, forced into a straitjacket

'In a time of universal deceit – telling the truth is a revolutionary act'

where tyranny equals and outstrips democracy
and even journalists who fail to hack it
end up in a land where there are no birds

on islands where flying narratives are grounded
by force and fraud and secrecy. But our stories,
yours and mine, remain. Impounded.

'*and there were the weak, who deserved to lose and always did lose, everlastingly*'

But this is no ending, no kind of ending.
There will come another day, so he believed (we hope)
when lies will be exposed, the truth unbending

and each true word, each lacerating phrase, each trope
will stand in line, mess-tray in hand, demanding
before a higher court, a larger scope.

David Punter is an academic and poet, attached to the University of Bristol, UK. His most recent book of poems is *Ship's Log* (2023), available from his website david-punter.org.

TRIBUTES TO THE FOUNDER OF THE ORWELL SOCIETY

Dione Venables' Contribution to the Development of Orwell Studies

Quentin Kopp pays tribute to Dione Venables, who overcame much academic and other opposition to the formation of The Orwell Society.

Dione Venables, who launched The Orwell Society in 2011 and who played a major role in the development of Orwell Studies, died peacefully on 12 September, aged 92. Dione had been struggling with a number of debilitating medical conditions over the last 18 months. She faced all these with great fortitude and good humour and departed in the way she had planned with her family around her.

Dione overcame a lot of academic and other opposition to the formation of The Orwell Society. Her persistence and approach to garnering support created a core of committed people including Orwell's son, Richard Blair. She made huge contributions to the success of the society, not least to help it overcome the inevitable early financial difficulties facing any such venture.

Dione made three other very important personal contributions to the development of Orwell Studies. Firstly, in 2006, she republished Jacintha Buddicom's *Eric & Us*, with a revealing and valuable postscript. She then commissioned distinguished Orwell scholars to write pieces which she put on a dedicated website created for them. They are now available on www.orwellsociety.com. Thirdly, Dione compiled and published *The Complete Poetry*, in 2015, which she beautifully annotated with scene-setting and explanatory notes for each poem. Not surprisingly it became a best-seller.

Dione's brainchild, The Orwell Society, has more than doubled in size in the last two years and now has more than 580 members in 29 countries and is a great force for good through its charitable aim to provide bursaries for young journalists and teachers in schools. These are the two professions Dione identified as those which could particularly contribute to highlighting the importance of Orwell to future generations. In addition, the society has an award for student dystopian writers. Dione was very proud of the fact that the atmosphere of co-operation she fostered has led to many excellent collaborations between academic members.

Dione had a very personable and direct style which elicited commitment. I will never forget my first meeting with her at a very early Orwell Society committee meeting. Dione took one look at me and said: 'We all need clear roles. You look like someone who makes things happen. Please will you organise events for members?' I have enjoyed doing that ever since and have retained the task since succeeding Richard Keeble as chair of the society, in 2020.

Dione had many friends in the Orwell world because of the atmosphere and culture she helped cultivate. They will always remember her and continue to value what her warm friendship meant to them.

Quentin Kopp,
Chair of The Orwell Society

Dear Dione

Darcy Moore reflects on the kindness and intellectual generosity of the late Dione Venables, who felt herself to be an 'honorary Australian'.

Dione Venables kindly contacted me six years ago about an article I had written and was generous in her praise:

> I very much enjoyed your piece online about your devotion to Orwell, with which I so agree. His many imperfections have only made him more *real* and acceptable!

She also served up a well-deserved rebuke (and I really did need to proof-read more closely, having misspelt two names). I responded in appreciation (and embarrassment). We corresponded regularly after that.

Dione shared many stories from her life, including, in response to my explanation of why I had been enamoured with the writer since my teens, the challenges she faced endeavouring to establish The Orwell Society:

> I am so glad you highlight intellectual stimulation. I am not an academic, nor am I a journalist, simply a writer, and I really was battered to death by both sections when I was trying to get things started but I so wanted Orwell to be read and understood *by the ordinary man in the street with a modicum of intelligence.* Luckily, Richard Blair is such a man, not academic, nor journalistic but genuinely dedicated to the memory of his father. We hit it off well from the beginning.
>
> I was given support and encouragement by him, by Peter Davison and by Gordon Bowker – and they were the only friends to give me encouragement and approval for over four years. But we got there – and now how wonderful it is to see the way the whole thing is burgeoning, and with such friendship.

Dione certainly was genuinely 'a writer' right until the end of her very long life. Her emails always conveyed vitality, character and a sense of humour. Anyone who read her introduction to Ron Bateman's recent book, *Radio Front: The BBC and the Propaganda War 1939-45*, will know that she continued to write with acuity and flair at 90 years of age. Possibly it will be news to some that Dione

TRIBUTE

birthed seven novels, as D.G. Finlay, between 1978 and 1989. The reviews at *Goodreads* are ones any writer would be proud of:

> ... some books get into your soul, don't they? And this is one of them.

> ... I read this book (borrowed from my local library) and I've never forgotten it! A story about a haunted house that's haunted me for 30 years...

Other topics we discussed over the years included art, books, genealogy, family-trees, adoption (I was adopted as a baby), DNA, travel, *schnauzers* (I have an 'Ollie' and Dione fondly remembered 'Gus') and Australia. Dione discovered that I lived just south of Wollongong, in New South Wales:

> I went to Wollongong because of my great grandmother Mary Gedye who was something of a very good landscape artist in the 1800s. She died in 1876 aged 46 but left work, some of which lie in the Mitchell Gallery in Sydney and another at Wollongong's main Art Gallery. She can be found in the *Dictionary of Australian Artists*: Mary Harriet Gedye.

> My lot lived in Surry Hills, then Darling Point, Double Bay. The four children, of whom my father Alan was the youngest, were born in Darling Point, Brisbane, Newcastle and Turramurra (my Pa). All North of Sydney as they were farmers and import/export people with a Sydney agency called Dangar, Gedye & Co. Our Dangar cousins are all over the same area but they came out to NSW in the 1830s to survey the Hunter River and adjoining lands. They can be found all over Armidale.

Henry Dangar (1796-1861) was a significant surveyor and his surname especially familiar as it graces many a geographical feature in the regions I have lived in NSW.

Dione, as have so many other incredibly friendly members of the society, provided contacts and introductions to people who could assist with my research. She diligently answered a very large number of questions (sent in what feels like hundreds of email exchanges). Dione generously provided access to original, unseen documents and allowed me to publish them on my website. She encouraged me endlessly – and paid me the courtesy of being forthright when she disagreed.

While I did not like to raise questions with Dione about some aspects of the Postscript she wrote in 2006, for *Eric & Us*, when I did ask her to confirm my research into the identity of the father of Jacintha Buddicom's only child and that 'peer of the Realm', she did so believing the time had come for these secrets to be revealed.

During July last year, Dione invited me to visit her home for an afternoon to chat about Orwell and Jacintha while I was staying in London. Having just visited Ticklerton and Church Stretton, in Shropshire, where the Buddicoms and Orwell had roamed in their youth, we had much to discuss. Dione shared her treasures, including letters written by Orwell and art Jacintha had created for Aleister Crowley. She was very twinkle-eyed, sharp as a tack, keen for a laugh and very, very generous with her knowledge and insights which have proven invaluable to my research. I snapped this photo, just before departing with the driver Dione had organised, that summer afternoon.

TRIBUTE

Dione Venables, July 2022

The last correspondence from Dione, just a week or so before she died, was on 2 September. She had read my latest research and sent an encouraging, 'Congratulations on your discovery. ... Keep up the good work.'

I will miss her!

BOOK REVIEWS

Orwell: The New Life

D.J. Taylor

Pegasus Books, New York and London, 2023, pp 598

ISBN: 9781639364510 (hbk)

Orwell enthusiasts and experts will be familiar with the life story D.J. Taylor tells, as we have not only his previous biography to consult, *Orwell: The Life* (2003), but those many others that have appeared since Peter Stansky and William Abrahams published their unauthorised biography, *The Unknown Orwell*, in 1972.[1] Each Orwell biographer has aspired to write a 'new life', discovering hidden sources and offering fresh interpretations of old ones in the hope that they can create a new Orwell for readers to buy or borrow and consume by lamp light. However, the question, 'Is D.J. Taylor's new Orwell truly new?' is much less interesting than the question 'Who is D.J. Taylor's Orwell?'

Taylor's Orwell is, above all, *his* writer, '"my" writer,' just as 'Norwich City were "my" football club' (p. 11). This declaration of loyalty and love reminds us that each Orwell biography is as much about the (male) biographer as it is the (male) biographical subject. To the extent that the biographer's relationship to a literally unknown and unknowable (because deceased) man can be 'personal' – as Taylor claims – it is unique (p. 11). In this *New Life* the relationship between Taylor and his 'mysterious' subject is intense and interesting, revealed in compelling ways, but it has not changed in character since Taylor published his first *Life*.[2] *The New Life* is a one-sided love affair, Taylor pursuing Orwell and Orwell, of course, caring nothing about Taylor.

My description of Taylor's and every biographer's lopsided relation to Orwell might just as well describe many of Orwell's relations with women, he pursuing with impassioned intensity, they remaining just out of reach, 'mysterious'. And it is these mysterious women and Orwell's relations with them, including his first wife, Eileen O'Shaughnessy, who take on new life in Taylor's new biography. In this case, quantitative analysis supports intellectual impression. Taylor's first Orwell biography covered Orwell's life between 1927-1936, the years of his transformation from bachelor to husband, from Eric to George, in 83 pages; his new biography devotes 170 pages to those same years.³ Again, a little quantitative analysis suggests what sources and subjects support this expansion. If we examine the index of the *New Life* closely, we will see that Avril Blair, the youngest of the three Blair siblings, who was mentioned or cited 16 times in *The Life*, has been transformed into a major player with a whole half column of index entries devoted to her. Similarly, Brenda Salkeld, one of Orwell's Southwold sweethearts, has 18 citations in the first biography index, 70 in the new; another Southwold sweetheart, Eleanor Jaques, has 46 citations in the old and 75 in the new; Eileen Orwell (née O'Shaughnessy), who has 46 citations in the first Taylor biography, earns 128 entries in this new one. Most telling of all, Taylor's first biography had an index sub-category 'Women, attitude to', with four entries while his new biography fills half an index column with entries under the autonomous category, 'Orwell, George (GO), WOMEN'. With *Orwell: The New Life*, we finally have an Orwell biography that moves women from the periphery of the life story of this stereotypically man's man – tough, stoic, heroic – to its centre, right where they belong.

The timeliness of Taylor's inclusion of more women's voices in Orwell's story is suggested by the increased presence of women authors and researchers contributing to Orwell studies. Publication in 2020 of Sylvia Topp's biography *Eileen: The Making of George Orwell*, Rebecca Solnit's 2021 study, *Orwell's Roses*, and Anna Funder's 2023 biography-novel *Wifedom*, also about Eileen, has doubled in three years the number of full-length, woman-authored books about or inspired by Orwell.⁴ Concerns about the politics of class, nation, despotism and freedom that have always interested Orwell's readers are now more likely to be attached to the politics of sex and gender. Taylor contributes in important ways to this welcome development in Orwell Studies by recording in more detail than has yet been available in popular biography Orwell's private history of relations with women, including the ways he and other men competed over women, and with Orwell's and others' thoughts and feelings about sexuality, sexual difference and gender. In effect, Taylor's biography offers a rebuttal to John Sutherland's offhand remark in his *Orwell's Nose: A Pathological Biography* that 'The three Blair women [Mrs Ida Blair, eldest sister Marjorie, and Avril] knew Eric best: what they knew, we never shall' (Sutherland 2016: 55). Now, thanks to Taylor, we know more of what these women knew.

Taylor's web of citations from letters and documents by, to and about Orwell from his various women family members and friends throws into question which three women would have known Eric/Orwell best. The new Orwell that emerges from these pages is a young man whose diffident wanderings around and beyond Southwold can only make sense once measured against the record of his attachments to family members and friends who offered him love, shelter and support. Especially in the crisis years following Orwell's return from Burma in 1927, the Blair home in Southwold, whether in Queen Street or the High Street, 'would remain a reliable bolthole for at least the next six years' (p. 141). Refuting Orwell's translation of Southwold into the 'genteel hellhole' of Knype Hill in *The Clergyman's Daughter*, Taylor argues that 'most of the evidence indicates that just as the town was by no means so awful as Orwell painted it, so he himself played a much more conventional part in its activities than the formal record of his stays there might suggest' (p. 142). We conclude with Taylor that while Orwell or Blair may not have been 'a paid-up member of the East Suffolk bourgeoisie', he could 'on occasion, feel perfectly at home' participating in the humdrum routines of East Anglian town life (p. 143).

Taylor's longer, stronger vision of Orwell at home in Southwold matters because so much of our understanding or misunderstanding of Orwell's dissident writing depends on accepting his later performances of solitary rebellion against the conventions and niceties of domestic life. We may in the past have sought the real Orwell in grainy black and white photos of him at Wallington, posed with goats, or in Islington, pushing a baby carriage, but rarely do we follow Orwell into the rooms where women come and go, where he, like Prufrock, yearns for women, tea and kisses. Taylor's decision to listen more carefully to Avril and many other women who knew Orwell deflates the myth of Orwell as the saintly, suffering Last Man in Europe, asocial, abandoned and coughing on his Inner Hebridean island. While Orwell may have divided and kept apart his girlfriends of those Southwold days, and later kept these and other girlfriends apart from his wife, Taylor shows us the extent to which he relied on all these women for the same things he had received from his family when he was young and most vulnerable: socially binding love, shelter and support.

Taylor reinforces this version of Orwell as a connected person, seeking, yearning, even at times begging for social and sexual inclusion, in one of his delightful mini-chapters titled 'Orwell's diaries'. Here he writes that Orwell's diaries, all eleven volumes and 200,000 words, 'confirm – if any confirmation were needed – that ineradicable grounding in the world of his boyhood' (p. 172). This world, like that of his young adulthood, was one of middle class comforts, routine social rounds and plenty of conventional ideas about white imperial masculine superiority. Taylor, always good on literary allusions and language, finds the adult Orwell resurrecting his boyhood in the diaries not only through idealised place images of Edwardian Henley, but through adjectival choices ('frightful', beastly', 'monstrous') that locate his mind in the time of Edwardian Henley. Also keen is Taylor's observation that 'From his upbringing, too, comes that infallible tendency to place people, to generalise about social types and ... to arrive at a judgement based on class or gender divides' (p. 173). Ginger, Orwell's pal on his hop picking expedition in Kent, is 'a fairly typical petty criminal'; the crowd at a political meeting represents 'a fair cross-section of the more revolutionary element in Wigan' (p. 173). Taylor asks: 'What does Orwell know about either of these demographics?' and answers: 'Not a great deal, you suppose, but wherever he fetches up in the world – Wigan, Barcelona or the Kentish hop fields – the taxonomist's urge to classify, segregate and judge goes with him' (p. 173). Indeed!

In Taylor's little breaks from the main narrative, we often find his keenest insights and most amusing assertions. Preserving in this *New Life* several of the most imaginative mini-chapters that appeared in his *Life* (e.g., 'Orwell's voice', 'Orwell and the rats', 'Orwell and the Jews'), he entertains us with new mini-chapters, the best of which, like 'Orwell's diaries', help us enter the main story from unexpected directions and leave it with fresh critical insights. The excellent 'Orwell and the toads', for example, again brings us back to the terrain of Orwell's Edwardian boyhood, 'the high ground above Henley where he spent his school holidays roaming the greensward with [his first girlfriend] Jacintha Buddicom' (p. 202). Taylor speculates that Henley and Jacintha formed the deep spring in memory and experience that fed Orwell's lifelong 'fixation' on the flora and fauna of England. For example, having amused us with his irreverent description of English fish as Orwell's 'spiritual kitemark', Taylor pivots to the more sober observation that 'Orwell's feelings about nature were inextricably bound up with his feelings for women' (p. 202). Other biographers and critics have made this connection, but none with such a perfect combination of diminishing wit and gentle compassion for the foibles of this great writer whose motives and decisions still have the power to energise, anger or dismay those of us who care about Orwell, his literature and his legacy.

It is important to note one failing. Taylor, while giving women in Orwell's life voice and character, discounts the value of women researchers and critics writing about Orwell's life and literature. He mocks Beatrix Campbell, one of the only women who has dared to write a full-length study on Orwell, *Wigan Pier Revisited*, and treats another one of those rare woman-authored, full-length studies about Orwell, Daphne Patai's *The Orwell Mystique: A Study in Male Ideology*, as the last word in feminist scholarship on Orwell (p.

BOOK REVIEW

11). We may as well say there is only one socialist take on Orwell, or only one interpretation of class, race, Jews or imperialism in Orwell's writing, as to imply that one feminist study can account for all time for Orwell's attitudes towards women, sex, gender and sexism. Change, or what Sutherland describes as the 'strange turns in Orwell's life' that have 'stumped' Orwell's previous biographers (p. 37), is the key driver of Taylor's biography, too. Change and strange turns also drive our shifting movements of political and critical inquiry. Feminist criticism, in its multiple, divided, often conflicting twenty-first century forms, has changed as much as any literary critical-political movement. If Taylor's new biography is, indeed, one of our best pieces of evidence that women and related themes of gender, sex and sexism have found their way into the centre of Orwell Studies, it is time for more, not less, feminist engagement with Orwell and time to welcome more, not fewer, women writers into the debates that keep Orwell Studies alive and kicking.

NOTES

[1] D.J. Taylor, *Orwell: The Life* (New York: Henry Holt, 2003) and Peter Stansky and William Abrahams, *The Unknown Orwell* (London: Constable, 1972)

[2] See, for example, pp 90, 96, 102, 122, 159, 220, 223, 511 for descriptions of some aspect of Orwell's life as a 'mystery' or 'mysterious'

[3] *The New Life* devotes 103 pages to Orwell's youthful years, 1903-1927 where *The Life* devotes 85 pages. There are no significant differences of length in Taylor's two biographical treatments of Orwell's life between the years 1936-1939, 1939-1945 or 1945-1950

[4] Before 2020, three women authors had published full-length books on or inspired by Orwell: Jacintha Buddicom's *Eric & Us: A Remembrance of George Orwell* (London: Leslie Frewin, 1974; republished with an Afterword by Dione Venables, Chichester: Finlay Publishers, 2006); Beatrix Campbell's *Wigan Pier Revisited* (London: Virago, 1984); and Daphne Patai's *The Orwell Mystique: A Study in Male Ideology* (Amherst, MA: University of Massachusetts Press, 1984). See also Sylvia Topp, *Eileen: The Making of George Orwell* (London: Unbound, 2020), Rebeca Solnit, *Orwell's Roses* (New York: Penguin, 2021) and Anna Funder, *Wifedom: Mrs Orwell's Invisible Life* (New York: Knopf, 2023)

REFERENCE

Sutherland, John (2016) *Orwell's Nose: A Pathological Biography*, London: Reaktion Books

Kristin Bluemel,
Monmouth University

The Tramp in British Literature, 1850-1950

Luke Lewin Davies

Palgrave Macmillan, Cham, 2021, pp 344

ISBN: 978303073434-3 (pbk); 978303073431-2 (hbk); 9783030734329 (ebk)

BOOK REVIEW

By the time George Orwell wrote *Down and Out in Paris and London* (1933), the tramp – the singular, restless vagabond who travelled across continents on foot, on steam ships and in boxcars – was an enigmatic fixture in the popular imagination. This status was doubtless on Orwell's mind when he first donned the tramp's costume in his own vagabond text, an experience that instantly transforms him. 'I had worn bad enough things before, but nothing at all like these,' he writes, 'they were not merely dirty and shapeless, they had – how is one to express it? – a gracelessness, a patina of antique filth, quite different from mere shabbiness' (1933: 174-175). The difference Orwell foregrounds here already calls to mind the unique history of the tramp at the time of his writing. Emerging from the nineteenth century, tramps quickly became stock figures in fiction, on the stage and in film, where they were alternatively celebrated as roaming dreamers or demonised as senseless criminals. In short, tramps were at once a specific identity group and heavily symbolic figures in culture. Orwell acknowledges the contradictory associations connected to tramping in his text, which celebrates the freedom tramping affords him and, at the same time, marks the 'irrational but very real' sense of feeling 'genuinely degraded' that comes with this freedom (ibid: 176).

The complexity Orwell clearly associates with the figure of the tramp is front and centre in Davies's *The Tramp in British Literature*. A primary interest of the book is to push back against reductive readings of tramps as either victims or heroes of the industrial era. Instead, as Davies remarks, 'real-life and fictional homeless individuals represented in literature on tramping can be seen to have embraced their status as figures on the fringes of society – simultaneously critiquing the causes of their exclusion and celebrating the opportunities this afforded for investigating alternative ways of life beyond the mainstream' (p. 3). This identification of both real-life and fictional tramps is essential to the book's approach, which focuses on textual representations of tramping which often blended first-person reportage with more fanciful artistic licence.

Tramps were, Davies explains, 'a new cultural construct' that appeared in the late nineteenth century in Britain and other industrialised states in Europe and North America. Facilitating this emergence was the concomitant proliferation of two genres of vagrancy literature during the nineteenth century: tramp memoir writing and tramp fiction (p. 14). Drawing heavily from Foucault, Davies foregrounds the imbrication of cultural and governmental institutions, which together facilitated a shift in the reception of homelessness. The result in this shift was clear by the middle of the nineteenth century, when Britain developed 'a new, disciplinary societal model for controlling populations' that demanded that the homeless 'cease being so unproductive' (pp 18, 19). Idleness thus posed a threat to the workings of a healthy, productive society – a formulation that marked tramps, the singular embodiment of idleness, as pressing social problems in more ways than one.

As this last point should indicate, the tramp literature Davies considers touches on a much wider range of cultural and political issues than one might assume. In fact, tramping authors at times signal their resistance against the compulsion to be a productive member of society, not only in the sense of labour and work but also of sexuality and social reproduction (pp 30, 31). Davies further distinguishes between tramping texts that deploy this oppositional stance towards social productivity – which he terms 'reverse discourse tramp literature' (p. 49) – and the wider body of literature surrounding tramping. While the book is careful to acknowledge the various permutations of tramping over the course of the nineteenth and twentieth centuries – including not only memoirs by real-life tramps but also fictional depictions by canonical authors such as Wordsworth and Dickens – it consider sources that adapt this reverse discourse to explore 'the possibility of a world less oriented around productive behaviour' (p. 55). Thus, reverse discourse tramp literature, according to Davies, involves the appropriation of an identity foisted onto a particular population of people – one not fully representative of homelessness in general, to be sure – as well as the rejection of the wider compulsion to be productive that informs the public's fascination with tramping in the first place.

The connection Davies makes between tramping literature and the radical vision of a life without work stands out as a forceful case for rescuing the tramp figure from the margins of academic study. To consider how tramping literature rejects the compulsion to be productive requires a critique not only of capitalism but also, as Davies point out, of an overwhelming majority of left discourse following Marx. In a compelling overview, *The Tramp in British Literature* lays out the high esteem labour continues to receive even in anti-capitalist thinking, which typically offers not so much an escape from labour but the freedom to choose one form of work over another. In contrast, tramp writers from the turn of century, such as Bart Kennedy and Morley Roberts, pursue the possibility of a life without work entirely, a critique of the productive paradigm whose radical credentials have been largely overlooked. Framing his book around this nuanced and consequential debate affirms the relevance of tramping literature not only to the historical context signalled in the title but also to the present day – and to emerging studies of the anti-work imagination. Indeed, Davies points out that examples of tramping literature did relatively heavy lifting with regards to sustaining anti-productivism discourse between 1850 and 1950, an otherwise fallow period when it comes to literature on the subject.

Given this chronology, however, one will be surprised to find relatively little attention paid to Orwell, whose *Down and Out in Paris and London* offered quite extensive observations about the tramp in Britain. As noted here, Davies is particularly attentive to carving out tramp literature as a distinct genre, one which facilitated and reflected on the tramp as a specifically new configuration of homelessness. Orwell is thus assigned to another literary category, the genre of 'social exploration literature' alongside Mary Higgs and Ada Chesterton. Indeed, Luke Seaber in *Incognito Social Investigation*, wrote that Orwell's *Down and Out* was at once the genre's masterpiece as well as its swansong (Seaber 2017: 73). Echoing Seaber, Davies sees Orwell as a writer whose personal investigations into tramping and homelessness blur the lines between fiction and non-fiction as well as displaying 'varying degrees of sympathy' for the people he observed (p. 29). In *Down and Out*, for instance, Orwell calls attention to the harmful impacts of poverty 'physically and spiritually' while also indicating that such harms can be rectified by a 'sound day's work' (pp 276, 279). According to the critical terms laid down by *The Tramp in British Literature*, then, Orwell's preoccupation with the value of hard work shows little of the reverse discourse regarding productivity that Davies foregrounds.

If there is little space dedicated to Orwell in this study, readers will undoubtedly find much to learn about the body of tramp literature that inspired the author and shaped the reflections on work and productivity contained in his works. Given the number of sources that appear in Davies's text, one finds not a comprehensive account of any single writer but, instead, an exhaustive overview of an entire literary genre. If tramp literature has languished in relative obscurity, *The Tramp in British Literature* contributes substantially to bringing the genre, along with its often-radical observations about the nature of work, the renewed attention it warrants.

BOOK REVIEW

REFERENCES

Davies, Luke Lewin (2021) *The Tramp in British Literature, 1850-1950*, London: Palgrave Macmillan

Orwell, George (1933) *Down and Out in Paris and Lonodon*, London: Victor Gollancz

Seaber, Luke (2017) *Incognito Social Investigation in British Literature: Certainties in Degradation*, London: Palgrave Macmillan

Bryan Yazell,
University of Southern Denmark,
Danish Institute for Advanced Study

George Orwell's Perverse Humanity: Socialism and Free Speech

Glenn Burgess

Bloomsbury, New York, 2023, pp 280

ISBN: 9781501394652 (pbk); 9781501394669 (hbk)

The most recent book by the accomplished historian of British thought, Glenn Burgess, begins by noting a debt to Bernard Crick and his pioneering biography of Orwell (p. ix). Burgess finds Crick's biography to be especially useful to someone interested in Orwell as a political thinker. I find Burgess's book especially useful to someone interested in Orwell's philosophical and normative thought. I do confess to experiencing some confusion about the title: *George Orwell's Perverse Humanity: Socialism and Free Speech*. Orwell's democratic socialism should be well known to his readers as should his abiding interest in free speech. But perverse humanity? There is no entry for 'perverse' or 'perverse humanity' in Davison's *The Complete Works of George Orwell*. So why is perverse humanity referenced in the title's lead, a rhetorical move suggesting that it is of central importance? And what does it have to do with either socialism or free speech? Burgess's synthesis of these three topics – perverse humanity, socialism, and free speech – is a novel effort to make the case that Orwell thought socialism and free speech were neither independently valuable nor in conflict. In what follows, I first recount Burgess's synthesis and explain why I regard it as so successful. I then explain why I think Burgess improves our understanding of Orwell's egalitarianism, that is, his commitment to the moral importance of equality. I then turn somewhat critical and note a tension in Burgess's interpretation.

Burgess notes repeatedly that Orwell knew that there is no necessary connection between socialism and free speech: Socialism was 'inevitable, at least in the sense of the emergence of a collectivist society with a planned economy', or so Orwell thought, although what lay in doubt 'was the particular form that this Socialism might take' (p. 114). Accordingly, the question that really concerned Orwell 'was whether the arrival of Socialism would prove compatible with the survival of freedom ... especially the freedom to write and say what you thought' (p. 122). To that end, Burgess explains that the 'heart of Orwell's Socialism' concerned freedom of the intellect (p. 165), that is, 'the freedom to be honest' (p. 154), which is only possible if free speech is secure, and reminds us of Orwell's conviction that 'the only regime which in the long run, will dare to permit freedom of speech is a Socialist regime' (p. 127). So, Orwell's democratic socialism 'didn't just allow for individual freedom; it required it' (pp 38-39).

So far, so good. But all this leaves my earlier question: Why is perverse humanity so central to Orwell's thought? unanswered. Burgess, again, clearly thinks it is given that *Perverse Humanity* opens with a passage from Orwell's essay, 'Books and the people: A New Year's message', that explains: 'We hold that the most perverse human being is more interesting than the most orthodox gramophone record' (Orwell 1998 [1945]: 11). Here, Orwell implicitly juxtaposes orthodoxy and perversity, although he does not explain what perverse humanity is. Burgess explains that expressing his preference for perverse humanity was Orwell's 'way of aligning himself with heresy rather than orthodoxy, with nonconformity rather than conformity, with plain-spokenness not ideological evasiveness, with direct speech not circumlocution, with speaking truth (as you see it) not hiding it in a "good" cause, with fearlessness not timidity, with eccentricity not conventionality' (p. 1). For his part, Orwell was a 'worshipper of perverse humanity' (p. 89) who 'lived his perversity' and thought that the world 'needed to be made safe for perverse people of Orwell's kind' (p. 1). Further:

> It could be made safe by a sort of liberal Socialism, one that both cherished the intellectual freedoms that gave perverse people the space to speak their minds, and ensured an equality that empowered everyone with the resources to exercise their own particular form of perversity (p. 1).

It may be that perverse humanity could be made safe by liberal – that is, democratic – socialism, but the novelty of Burgess's text is better captured by the suggestion that making the world safe for perverse humanity is necessary to bring about democratic socialism, a robust commitment to free speech and the sort of equality

BOOK REVIEW

that interested Orwell. That would help to explain why perverse humanity is valuable: it is instrumentally valuable insofar as it gets us other things that are themselves valuable.

I don't know if Burgess would endorse my reading of his book's central thesis – again, perverse humanity is valuable because it is necessary to facilitate socialism and free speech, justice and liberty as Orwell understood them – but I think that this way of putting things is crucial to understanding the synthesis of concepts that Burgess provides. It is also consistent with Orwell's worry that socialism was going to be terribly difficult to realise and his reasons for fearing that it would be so difficult. Burgess captures the urgency when he writes that, for Orwell, 'the world needed revolutionary transformation to abolish privilege and inequality; it also needed transformation so that free individuals could flourish' (pp 35-36) and that the requisite revolutionary transformation demanded the creation of 'a liberal Socialist culture' (p. 242). These points are worth emphasising. We know from *The Road to Wigan Pier* (1937) that Orwell was convinced both that overcoming class hostilities was necessary to align middle class people with the working class and that this would not be easy. Speaking for himself, Orwell explained that while it 'is easy for me to say that I want to get rid of class-distinctions … nearly everything I think and do is a result of class-distinctions' and all 'my notions – notions of good and evil, of pleasant and unpleasant, of funny and serious, of ugly and beautiful – are essentially *middle-class* notions' (Orwell 1997 [1937]: 149, italics in the original). But there is also an obvious defensiveness in the later chapters of *The Road to Wigan Pier* when Orwell urges his fellow socialists to take things slow and knock off the crankishness that alienated the middle class. So, at least two cultural changes must be brought about on a large scale to realise socialism: first, individuals need to revise those beliefs, values and commitments that may be central to their identity but fatal to solidarity; second, actual social interactions between people needed to become more inclusive, certainly less adversarial.

Implicit in Burgess's discussion of Orwell and free speech is the recognition that similar cultural changes are necessary to secure the protection of the latter: one kind of change implicates social interactions between persons, another implicates individual beliefs, values and commitments. Burgess reminds us of Orwell's warning that 'the relative freedom which we enjoy depends on public opinion' and that the 'law is no protection' (p. 194). Acknowledging John Stuart Mill – more on him below – Burgess explains that public opinion 'must be encouraged to value intellectual liberty, and a body that defended such liberty impartially … was essential' (pp 194-195). As Mill recognised, the legal protection of free speech was no bulwark against 'the moral coercion of public opinion', that is, those informal social pressures exacted to coerce or compel persons to conform to some prevailing belief or practice or norm, which can be just as fatal to the exercise of free speech. So, on the one hand, public opinion needs to be revised so that the general public becomes more tolerant of unpopular opinions, less likely to shame and more prone to encourage the free exchange of ideas. But changing public opinion is not enough. Noting, rightly, that free expression was a matter 'not just of legal rights and the freedom from official censorship', Burgess again invokes the gramophone mind and recalls Orwell's worry that 'Western intellectuals censored themselves and encouraged others to self-censor' (p. 173). Crucial to the gramophone mind is that it suppresses original thought and expression to maintain conformity with some prevailing orthodoxy. So, while public opinion must become more amenable to the free exchange of ideas, individuals must also change for the better. Just as socialism demands a cultural transformation at the level of both public practice and individual personhood, free speech can only be secured if similar cultural changes obtain.

BOOK REVIEW

This is why I suggested above that the order of explanation in Burgess's early summary of *Perverse Humanity* is slightly off. Even if a liberal socialism would make the world safer for cranks and eccentrics, we might have socialism and free speech *only if* we first make the world safe for perverse humanity, and otherwise not. This explains why Orwell's commitments to socialism and free speech are not orthogonal but deeply entwined – the same sort of cultural transformation is necessary to secure both – and speaks to the genius of placing perverse humanity at the forefront of a discussion of Orwell's normative views. But there are, I think, still more reasons to admire *Perverse Humanity*: Burgess's central argument also helps to explain why equality is such a central concept, perhaps the central concept, in Orwell's normative thought.

Orwell valued equality: about this there is no disagreement. But, and I write this as a philosopher with an interest in the concept and practice of egalitarianism, it cannot be understated just how many competing conceptions of equality are available as evidenced by the explosion of philosophical interest in the concept beginning in the last few decades of the twentieth century. The sort of equality that Orwell prized was exemplified and made visible to him in Spain where, by his account, his conversion to socialism was completed, and if it was not perfect equality, it was nonetheless worth fighting for. This near-perfect equality was a function of the classless, casteless and anti-hierarchical nature of Spanish society, one in which all the trappings of rank and station were absent. In *Homage to Catalonia* (1938), Orwell is at pains to note that everyone from general to private drew the same pay, but the essential point of the system was 'social equality between officers and men', Orwell explained, adding that that they 'ate the same food, wore the same clothes, and mingled on terms of complete equality' (Orwell 1997 [1938]: 26). Equality on the front, so understood, was realised because everyone could look their fellows in the eye without feeling fear or deference and because class differences were replaced by loyalty and affection of the sort that Orwell felt for the nameless Italian soldier that he immortalised. To utilise some philosophical terminology, Orwell's egalitarianism is *relational egalitarianism*, as distinct from *distributive egalitarianism*: the latter conceives of justice primarily in distributive terms and implies that morally valuable equality is achieved only when all persons have an equal share of something distributable, be it income, welfare, opportunities or whatever; the former does not conceive of justice primarily in distributive terms even if some redistribution is necessary to secure domination-free social relations.

The case for regarding Orwell as a relational egalitarian is powerful, partly because it explains why Orwell thinks that bringing about socialism and free speech requires a cultural transformation and not simply an economic one. But Orwell's various remarks about equality are not unequivocal, and he clearly struggled to work out what equality demanded in theory and practice. *Perverse Humanity* illuminates Orwell's struggle especially in Burgess's discussion of the 'manifesto', the product of an ultimately failed collaboration with Arthur Koestler and others to reanimate the old League of the Rights of Man. Burgess's account is especially detailed, one of my favourite parts of the book.

Burgess carefully records the events that led to the production of multiple drafts of the manifesto. One draft survives in the George Orwell Archive at University College London, another is housed among the Koestler Papers at Edinburgh University Library and was published by David Smith (Smith 2018: 230-234). But Burgess is clear that 'there were *at least* three drafts of a manifesto': Orwell's first draft (sent to Koestler on 2 January 1946); a revised draft that incorporated suggestions from Michael Foot (sent to Koestler on 27 February); and a final draft, the product of multiple persons (produced at some point between 14 March and 28 April) and later distributed (p. 210, italics in the original). Burgess is also clear that these drafts are *not* equivalent and differ in important ways. Notably, 'the later version of the manifesto weakens the insistence that economic inequality would necessarily make democracy and freedom impossible' (p. 211). If the earlier draft offered 'a more resounding defence of the importance of equality' (p. 215), the later draft 'immediately weakens the insistence of the earlier draft on the priority attached to equality' (p. 213). Burgess wonders which version is 'likely to be closer to Orwell's original draft?' (p. 209), but the nearly irresistible suggestion is that the earlier version, the one that places comparatively greater weight on equality, is likely closer to Orwell's original since it was more obviously the product of Orwell himself and not multiple other collaborators.

I find Burgess's discussion of the historical record of these matters to be thoroughly convincing, but it is also valuable insofar as it helps to purge some seeming inconsistencies in Orwell's remarks about equality. The various versions of the manifesto refer to 'economic inequality', 'equality of opportunity', 'equality of chance', 'equality of income' and variations of the same. These are not equivalent ways of cashing out what equality demands since they suggest different *currencies* to be distributed equally. As such, a reader could be confused for thinking that Orwell was a distributive egalitarian, albeit one who was seriously confused about what was supposed to be distributed equally. But this mixed bag of proposals is entirely predictable if later versions of the manifesto were the work of many hands, that is, not the product of Orwell himself, such that any seeming inconsistencies reflect disagreement at the level of the collective authorship and not confusion on Orwell's part. It may follow from all this that the published version of the manifesto, while significant, does not accurately represent Orwell's own understanding of what equality demands and is, to that extent, less interesting to those of us trying to understand the normative dimensions of Orwell's thought. But that is why philosophers, like me, count on historians like Burgess.

There is much more in *Perverse Humanity* that I commend: I found Burgess's destruction of the myths of Orwell's supposed Tory anarchism earlier in his life convincing, for example. But I also find a tension in his interpretation of Orwell, one that highlights just how difficult it will be for Orwell, or any faithful liberal, to bring about justice, liberty and equality as Orwell understood them.

Recall what we know about perverse humanity. Perverse humans are not gramophones: like Orwell, they are nonconformist, plain-spoken, direct, fearless, eccentric and inclined to speak truth as they see it. None of these traits ensure that perverse humans will not be seriously toxic nor anti-social. If Orwell lived his perversity, so did Salvador Dali and Gandhi, both of whom Orwell chided for their anti-humanism, as did Oswald Mosley who should remind us that that plain-spokenness and a proclivity for direct speech are not moral virtues since they can be used for corrupt ends. Perverse humanity is no guarantor of whatever is necessary to live together as equals or even peacefully. But then what do we do with those perverse humans who are not merely crankish but threaten the liberal order? Can we compel them to become more social? Can we refuse to tolerate the intolerant? Can we deny them the strong protections of free speech that the rest of us enjoy?

To answer these familiar questions, Burgess finds utility in appealing to 'that iconic figure of liberal thinking' (p. 31), Mill, to illustrate and augment Orwell's answers. I think appealing to Mill is useful in bringing out the tension I allude to above. One concern is that Mill and his defence of free speech are avowedly utilitarian – early in *On Liberty*, Mill explains that 'I forego any advantage which could be derived to my argument from the idea of abstract right as a thing independent of utility' and that 'I regard utility as the ultimate appeal on all ethical questions' (Mill 1977 [1859]: 11) – while Orwell is not usually read as a utilitarian. Still, there is something to the suggestion that Orwell 'defended a position very similar to that of John Stuart Mill', namely, that speech and expression 'was to be limited only when it risked doing what Mill called "harm"' (p. 175). Burgess explains that, in Orwell, we find 'a strong presumption in favour of tolerating opinions and theories, however extreme, however unpalatable' and that it was 'only when those ideas threatened to do real harm, that is they ceased to be just theories or opinions, that some level of restraint is needed' (p. 190). It is worth recalling Orwell's various apt remarks from 'Freedom of the press', including his suggestion that:

> [W]hen one demands liberty of speech and of the press, one is not demanding absolute liberty. There always must be, or at any rate there always will be, some degree of censorship, so long as organized societies endure (Orwell 1987 [1943]): 104).

And that:

> If the intellectual liberty which without a doubt has been one of the distinguishing marks of western civilization means anything at all, it means that everyone shall have the right to say and to print what he believes to be the truth, provided only that it does not harm the rest of the community in some quite unmistakable way (ibid: 104-105).

All this does have the consequence that Orwell, like Mill, is committed to censoring some speech such that his commitment to free speech 'was, if not absolute, then *maximalist*' (p. 256). Burgess summarises Orwell's 'view in microcosm' here: 'even evil views should receive a hearing; even evil views could be well enough expressed to deserve a literary award – but evil they remained and no one should be deterred from unmasking or denouncing the evil' (p. 180).

But now the tension I allude to above is palpable. Evil views deserve a hearing and their proponents must be allowed to express them: that is a demand of free speech. No one should be deterred from unmasking and denouncing evil views and their opponents must be allowed to critique them; that too is a demand of free speech. But denouncing and unmasking evil views, especially in concert with one's fellows, is bound to take the form of that moral coercion of public opinion that Mill, and Orwell, regarded as anathema to free speech. Burgess's reading of Orwell seems to require both that the faithful liberal tolerate and oppose a significant range of speech and expression and puts the faithful liberal in an impossible dilemma: we will not have free speech unless the moral coercion of public opinion is curtailed but if we curtail the moral coercion of public opinion we will not have free speech. Perhaps the hope is that active and vigorous criticism of evil views need not morph into the moral coercion of public opinion. But how? Does recent experience lend much cause for optimism?

Things are actually worse. Burgess seems to understand Orwell as thinking that we have a responsibility to respond, unmask and denounce, say, when he suggests that much of his writing 'was a reminder of the importance of holding people accountable to the truth' and so long as they lived 'in a society in which others could point out their mistake, all would be well' (p. 6). The problem with thinking, as Burgess suggests Orwell thought, that 'the greatest thing about the idea of free speech was that accountability was built in' (ibid) is that accountability is *not* built in: we are held accountable for what we say only if someone holds us accountable, and whether our speech is met with robust criticism or utter silence is really up to our audience. But possession of a gramophone mind is not the only reason why a person might remain silent: people may have their own reasons for declining to enter the marketplace of ideas. Silence on a large scale could be unavoidable unless we somehow *compel* speech in response to mistakes and untruths, another way of violating familiar liberal rights. Burgess's reading of Orwell seems to leave us with conflicting obligations: we must both refrain from informal or extra-legal censorship, and we must engage in it. Can it be both?

The tensions I find in Burgess's reading of Orwell are not the result of any confusion on Burgess's part: they may be endemic to a liberal society that both prizes individual rights and recognises that a certain kind of moral psychology is necessary for just and peaceful social relations. If so, the prospect of irresolvable conflict probably calls for a sceptical take when it comes time to assess Orwell's success in safeguarding the world for the perverse among us, or at least a more sceptical take than I detect in *Perverse Humanity*. But it is a

BOOK REVIEW

merit of Burgess's book that we are again encouraged to think hard about what we owe to the cranks among us and why protecting them matters morally.

REFERENCES

Mill, John Stuart (1977[1859]) *On Liberty*, Robinson, J. (ed.) *The Collected Works of John Stuart Mill*, Toronto: University of Toronto Press

Orwell, George (1997 [1937]) *The Road to Wigan Pier*, Davison, Peter (ed.) *The Complete Works of George Orwell, Vol. V*, London: Secker & Warburg

Orwell, George (1997 [1938]) *Homage to Catalonia*, Davison, Peter (ed.) *The Complete Works of George Orwell, Vol. VI*, London: Secker & Warburg

Orwell, George (1987 [1943]) Freedom of the press, Davison, Peter (ed.) *The Complete Works of George Orwell, Vol. VI*, London, Secker & Warburg

Orwell, George (1998 [1945]) Books and the people: A New Year message, Davison, Peter (ed.) *The Complete Works of George Orwell, Vol. XVII*, London: Secker & Warburg pp 7-12

Smith, David (2018) *George Orwell Illustrated*, illustrated by Mike Mosher, Chicago: Haymarket Books

Peter Brian Barry,
Saginaw Valley State University

In Praise of Failure: Four Lessons in Humility
Costica Bradatan

Harvard University Press, Cambridge, Massachusetts, 2023

ISBN: 9780674970472

This is a strange text. Reflections on humility and failure lie at its heart (and here George Orwell has a somewhat problematic walk-on part). A wide range of important, challenging issues are explored including death, democracy, Gnosticism, meaning, nihilism, nothingness, power, revolution, self-assertion, storytelling and transhumanism. But *In Praise of Failure* somehow manages to be a mix of profound insight, superficial generalisation, New Age gobbledygook, self-help guide, deliberate provocation and rapid historical overview.

The Japanese writer, Yukio Mishima, is one of the failures considered, alongside the Stoic Seneca, the French mystic Simone Weil, the Romanian-born French intellectual, Emil Cioran and Leo Tolstoy. Mishima's suicide by *hara-kiri* ends up a terribly botched affair. His assistant, Morita, 'cut into Mishima's shoulder and then into his neck, without actually beheading him, thus prolonging rather than reducing his agony: Hiroyasu Koga had to step in to clean up the mess and give Mishima the decisive blow, before doing the same thing for Morita. Mishima's ending thus became an unsightly site of butchery and clumsiness' (p. 230).

But when Bradatan earlier discusses Mishima's *Confessions of a Mask* and his detailed description of his first ejaculation, he offers this fascinating psychological insight:

> The self we eventually weave is not just the sum total of what we have done, but also of a long series of *absences*: all that we've longed for but never got, the love that was not reciprocated, the unkept promises, the missed opportunities, the unfulfilled desires, all that we have only imagined or fantasized about or have not even dared to dream. The missing parts may be more important than the real ones (p. 190, italics in the original).

In his Epilogue, he comments, provocatively: 'Human beings are fundamentally narrative-driven creatures. Our lives take the shape of the stories we tell: they move this way or that as we change the plot. ... These stories we tell about our life are sometimes more important than life itself' (pp 236-237).

In contrast, some of the historical sections are full of oversimplifications. Take for instance Bradatan's comments on the emergence of capitalism (covered in a few pages): its most important principle, he argues, may not be 'the free market' or 'private initiative' or 'the freedom to conduct a business' but 'something much humbler: ranking' (p. 164). After dubbing as failures the Bolshevik Revolution in Russia, Mao's Cultural Revolution in China and the Khmer Rouge regime in Cambodia, Bradatan concludes: 'In all of these cases, a high price was paid for a rather banal lesson: there is more to humanity than mere reason' (p. 87). Later, he describes the 1917 Russian Revolution as 'a pretty lame affair': 'The work of small-time arsonists who set their homes on fire to collect the insurance money. But the bodies piled up all the same' (p. 110).

Bradatan is clearly not an admirer of Mahatma Gandhi (another of his failures) and his promotion of what he calls 'fakirism'. 'For someone who managed with so little eating, Gandhi's obsession with food is puzzling. Food is everywhere in Gandhi: in his published texts and his correspondence, in his sermons and private chats. His *Autobiography* is to a large extent a book about food' (p. 96). Moving on to discuss Gandhi's ideas about dress and his 'lifelong striptease project', Bradatan says: 'Non-dressing was no less important for Gandhi than non-eating' (p. 97). Moreover, for someone who was not supposed to have many needs, 'the size of his army of aides, assistants, disciples, and private secretaries was remarkable' (p. 99).

He quotes approvingly the poetess Sarojini Naidu: 'It cost a great deal of money to keep the Mahatma living in poverty' (ibid).

On the 'death of God' and the decline of the 'traditional frame of reference', Bradatan's comments are somewhat clichéd: many of us are 'left swinging endlessly between self-worship, compulsive consumerism, social manipulation, and political demagoguery – anything that might give our lives an illusion of meaning' (p. 78). One is left wondering if Bradatan counts himself amongst this group…

He goes on to ponder the 'proliferation of conspiracies', using Umberto Eco's *Foucault's Pendulum* as the starting point. They reflect a 'desperate need for meaning that secularization can't satisfy'. This all leads to a generalisation about (unnamed) populist politicians: 'a charismatic leader, even of dubious morality and no civic credentials comes to embody a promise of meaningfulness for a spiritually starved community because he tells them the stories they need to satisfy their hunger for meaning' (p. 79). Bradatan fails to acknowledge the relevance of 'conspiracy theory' in an age in which secret states (waging secret wars and keeping watch on populations with massive surveillance operations) dominate across the globe. Thus, while some 'conspiracy theories' are clearly nonsense, others can offer important insights.

How does Orwell fit into all of this? Well, Bradatan devotes a few pages to his 'investigative tramping' with the down-and-outs as an example of humility in action. Paradoxes lie at the core of this text. For instance, while discussing the French Revolution, he writes: 'Before the Revolution, what distinguished Robespierre was that there was nothing distinctive about him. … Since the failure of the Revolution was not an option, any means were justified, in his view, as long as they contributed to its success. Which, ironically, is always a recipe for failure' (p. 92). On Orwell, he writes: 'There is something odd about poverty, Orwell discovers as soon as he starts tramping: it's mostly the concern of those who are not genuinely poor. You typically obsess over poverty when you are on the bright side of the divide' (pp 144-145). Under the sub-heading 'The dead cat', Bradatan concludes that from his tramping experiments Orwell learned that 'ultimately, regardless of their wealth, people are fundamentally the same' (p. 152).

The words 'humble' and 'humility' actually rarely appear in Orwell's work. Indeed, his tramping expeditions are best seen as ways in which Orwell expiated the guilt he felt having worked for five years serving the 'evil despotism' of British imperialism as a policeman in Burma (1922-1927). As he writes in the second, idiosyncratic, highly personal section of *The Road to Wigan Pier*: 'I felt that I had got to escape not merely from imperialism but from every form of man's dominion over man. I wanted to submerge myself, to get right down among the oppressed, to be one of them and on their side against the tyrants.'

Out of Orwell's millions of written words, Bradatan appears to have read only *Down and Out in Paris and London* (1933), his part fiction/part memoir of his time tramping and working alongside the hop pickers in Kent, and no secondary sources. Had he explored further afield he would have found, in fact, that Orwell was obsessed not so much with humility but failure. D. J. Taylor had a whole section of his 2003 biography devoted to it (pp 318-321). Of his time at St Cyprian's prep school, recounted in his essay 'Such, such were the joys' (again part fiction/part memoir) and published only after his death, Orwell concludes: 'Failure, failure, failure – failure behind me, failure ahead of me – that was by far the deepest conviction that I carried away.' He certainly had a low opinion of all his novels. On *Burmese Days* (1933), he wrote in a letter to his friend Eleanor Jaques: 'I am disgusted with all save a few parts of it.' On *A Clergyman's Daughter* (1935), he complained in a letter to another friend, Brenda Salkeld, that it made him spew. He refused to have his next novel, *Keep the Aspidistra Flying* (1936) reprinted during his lifetime; he described his time as a producer on the Eastern Service of the BBC (1941-1943) as 'two wasted years', and he was even critical of his dystopian masterpiece, *Nineteen Eighty-Four* (1949), telling his American colleague Dwight Macdonald: 'I mucked it up really, partly because I was ill almost throughout the time of writing.'

His novels in many ways are also studies of failures. Flory in *Burmese Days* ends up disgraced and committing suicide. Dorothy, the anti-heroine of *A Clergyman's Daughter*, escapes from her dreary life of toil only to find herself back in the soul-destroying routine from which she thought she had freed herself. George Bowling, in *Coming Up For Air* (1939), takes a trip down memory lane only to find the pond where he had spent idyllic moments as a child built over and the site of a rubbish dump. *Nineteen Eighty-Four* has Winston Smith submitting to his torturer O'Brien with these grim words: 'He loved Big Brother.' Even *Down and Out* ends in a sort of failure, but Bradatan misses this. As Orwell writes: 'I should like to know people like Mario and Paddy and Bill the moocher, not from casual encounters, but intimately; I should like to understand what really goes on in the souls of the *plongeurs* and tramps and Embankment sleepers. At present I do not feel that I have seen more than the fringe of poverty.'

Bradatan adds on to his reflections on failure a sort of New Age self-help guide. Failure, he says, is 'the best starting point for any journey of self-realization' (p. 9). 'We absolutely need the

BOOK REVIEW

accumulative experience of disconnect, disruption, and discomfort if we are to come to terms with our next-to-nothingness. For it is only in the crucible of this experience that we can achieve humility, which gives us the chance to be healed of hubris and egocentrism, of self-illusion and self-deception, and of our poor adjustment to reality' (pp 9-10). Elsewhere, he writes: 'We can use the experience of failure to extricate ourselves from the entanglement of existence (physical, political, social, biological) with a view to gaining a better understanding of it, and in the hope of leading a more enlightened and wiser life' (p. 232).

While the play on paradox lies at the heart of this text, the writing of a work about failure (which comes much-praised judging by the various glowing endorsements on the cover) by a highly successful academic (Bradatan is Professor of Humanities in the Honors College at Texas Tech University and Honorary Research Professor at the University of Queensland), intriguingly, is one paradox that is not confronted.

Richard Lance Keeble,
University of Lincoln

AND FINALLY

A new, lively diary item to intrigue and entertain Orwellians.

What did George Orwell have against the Zoroastrians? Would he ever have recognised Freddie Mercury? Freddie's Indian co-religionists, called Parsees, do receive a mention in Orwell's work but Zoroastrians (now being persecuted in Iran) *nada*.

This thought was inspired by Ian Bloom's article in a June issue of the *Jewish Chronicle*, 'The ever-present antisemitism of George Orwell'.[1] Bloom, in turn, was following up on Comino Verlag's new selection from Orwell's *Complete Works*, *On Jews and Antisemitism* (edited by Paul Seeliger).

Orwell's paternal grandfather was an Anglican priest. It may explain but does it excuse every one of his references to Nonconformists (he usually refers to Nonconformists but occasionally and specifically names them as Baptists and Methodists, too) being negative? Given changing influences in the world, the one area of which Orwell showed least awareness was the political potential of Islam – one's fingers and toes are enough to count those mentions.

***

With credit to Orwell's time in Spain, the Citizen Collective of Huesca and The Orwell Society are promoting the funding of a public sculpture to Orwell in the city of Huesca. There is an online donation site at https://www.gofundme.com/f/escultura-publica-orwell-toma-cafe-en-huesca.

***

Animal Farm, an opera composed by Alexander Raskatov with a libretto by Ian Burton and Raskatov, had its first night in Amsterdam on 3 March 2023. It was due to go on to Vienna, Palermo and Helsinki. Meanwhile, Lorin Maazel's opera *1984* had its German première at the *Theater am Bismarckplatz*, in Regensburg, Bavaria, in June to good reviews.

***

'Do it to Julia! Do it to Julia! Not me! Julia I don't care what you do to her. Tear her face off, strip her to the bones. Not me! Julia! Not me!' When Winston Smith cracked and named his lover as the alternative victim he did not hold back. One in eight words was the name of his preferred target. Winston was naming someone he loved to someone he knew was a torturer. He could hardly have been more explicit.

The bent of this autumn's feminist re-visioning of *Nineteen Eighty-Four* (Anna Funder's *Wifedom* is the second after Katherine Bradley's *The Sisterhood*) seems to have started with the absence of Eileen Blair's name from *Homage to Catalonia*. Would Orwell, though, have wanted to identify his wife to the NKVD? Particularly as wives and relatives in the Soviet Union had been taken in the political terror? How early Orwell became aware of the level to which the secret police would go is unclear but he mentions the Gestapo's literary examinations in his *Tribune* 'As I Please' column of 16 February 1945: 'The Gestapo is said to have teams of literary critics whose job is to determine, by means of stylistic comparison, the authorship of anonymous pamphlets. I have always thought that, if only it were in a better cause, this is exactly the job I would like to have.' Whether fear of kidnapping or invasion was the reason, during World War Two Orwell and his wife adopted separate identities: he was George Orwell, she was Emily Blair. In 1947, Nell Heaton dedicated her door-stopping *Complete Cook*, which must have taken most of Faber & Faber's paper ration, 'to George Orwell and Emily Blair to whose sympathy and encouragement I owe so much'. Sonia Brownell took Orwell's name; Eileen O'Shaughnessy made her own.

***

Congratulations to David Pearson. In March 2023, he was awarded the Academy of British Cover Design (ABCD) 'winner of all winners' award for his redacted Penguin Classics design of George Orwell's *Nineteen Eighty-Four* – the one where the title disappears over time.

NOTE

[1] Online at https://www.thejc.com/lets-talk/all/the-ever-present-antisemitism-of-george-orwell-5122MDndMJNOyUr2sd9eon. A recent analysis of antisemitism and George Orwell was (by *GOS* co-editor Tim Crook) in his Afterword, 'Antisemitism: Moving beyond upbringing and preconceptions' to Richard Lance Keeble's collection *Orwell's Moustache* (Abramis, 2021)

George Orwell Studies

Subscription information
Each volume contains two issues, published half-yearly.

Annual Subscription (including postage)

Personal Subscription

UK	£45
Europe	£50
RoW	£55

Institutional Subscription

UK	£100
Europe	£115
RoW	£120

Single Issue copies can be purchased (subject to availability)

Enquiries regarding subscriptions and orders should be sent to:

Journals Fulfilment Department
Abramis Academic
ASK House
Northgate Avenue
Bury St Edmunds
Suffolk, IP32 6BB
UK

Tel: +44(0)1284 717884
Email: info@abramis.co.uk

www.ingramcontent.com/pod-product-compliance
Lightning Source LLC
Chambersburg PA
CBHW080732300426
44114CB00019B/2568